DISCARDED

W9-BWY-353

Brooks - Cork Library

P.O. 73588

12-7-00

Brooks - Cork Library
Shelton State
Community College

Southern Churches in Crisis Revisited

RELIGION AND AMERICAN CULTURE

Series Editors
David Edwin Harrell
Wayne Flynt
Edith L. Blumhofer

Southern
Churches
in Crisis
Revisited

Samuel S. Hill

THE UNIVERSITY OF ALABAMA PRESS
Tuscaloosa and London

Copyright © 1999
The University of Alabama Press
Tuscaloosa, Alabama 35487-0380
All rights reserved
Manufactured in the United States of America

New edition 1999. Originally published 1966 by Henry Holt and Company.
1 2 3 4 5 6 7 8 9 • 07 06 05 04 03 02 01 00 99

Cover design by Shari DeGraw

∞
The paper on which this book is printed meets the minimum requirements of
American National Standard for Information Science–Permanence of Paper for
Printed Library Materials, ANSI Z39.48-1984.

Library of Congress Cataloging-in-Publication Data

Hill, Samuel S.
  Southern churches in crisis revisited / Samuel S. Hill. — New ed.
    p. cm. — (Religion and American culture)
  Rev. ed. of: Southern churches in crisis. 1st ed. 1966.
  Includes bibliographical references and index.
  ISBN 0-8173-0979-9 (cloth : alk. paper)
  1. Protestant churches — Southern States. 2. Southern
States — Church history. I. Hill, Samuel S. Southern churches in
crisis. II. Title. III. Series: Religion and American culture
(Tuscaloosa, Ala.)
  BR535 .H5 1999
  280' .4'0975—dc21   98-58067

British Library Cataloguing-in-Publication Data available

To the memory of my father

Samuel Smythe Hill

*who, in his integrity, openness of mind,
and magnanimity of spirit, embodied the
finest qualities of the southern church
in his generation.*

Contents

Acknowledgments

Grateful acknowledgment is made to the following publishers for the explicit use of their publications:

Abingdon Press, Nashville, Tennessee, for Emory S. Bucke, ed., *The History of American Methodism*, copyright © 1964, and for Colin W. Williams, *John Wesley's Theology Today*, copyright © 1960.

Belknap Press, Cambridge, Massachusetts, for Perry Miller, *Errand into the Wilderness*, copyright © 1956.

Doubleday and Company, Garden City, New York, for Gerhard Lenski, *The Religious Factor*, copyright © 1961, for Franklin H. Littell, *From State Church to Pluralism*, copyright © 1962, and for Ross Phares, *Bible in Pocket, Gun in Hand*, copyright © 1964.

Funk and Wagnalls, New York, for James McBride Dabbs, *Who Speaks for the South?*, copyright © 1964.

Harper & Row, New York, for Kenneth K. Bailey, *Southern White Protestantism in the Twentieth Century*, copyright © 1964, for Clement Eaton, *The Growth of Southern Civilization*, copyright © 1961, for Langdon Gilkey, *How the Church Can Minister to the World Without Losing Itself*, copyright © 1963, for H. Richard Niebuhr, *The Kingdom of God in America*, copyright 1937, and for H. Richard Niebuhr and Daniel D. Williams, eds., *The Ministry in Historical Perspectives*, copyright © 1956.

Alfred A. Knopf, New York, for W. J. Cash, *The Mind of the South*, copyright 1941, and for Francis B. Simkins, *A History of the South*, copyright 1953.

John Knox Press, Richmond, Virginia, for Ernest Trice Thompson, *Presbyterians in the South*, copyright © 1963.

Longwood College Press, Farmville, Virginia, for Francis B. Simkins, *The South in Perspective*, copyright © 1959.

Louisiana State University Press, Baton Rouge, for Walter B. Posey, *Religious Strife on the Southern Frontier*, copyright © 1965, for Francis B. Simkins, *The Everlasting South*, copyright © 1963, and for C. Van Woodward, *Origins of the New South*, copyright 1951.

The Macmillan Company, New York, for John Samuel Ezell, *The South Since 1865*, copyright © 1963, and for Howard W. Odum, *The Way of the South*, copyright 1947.

Oxford University Press, New York, for Albert C. Outler, ed., *John Wesley*, copyright ©
1964, and for James F. White, *Protestant Worship and Church Architecture*, copyright © 1964.

Princeton University Press, Princeton, New Jersey, for James Ward Smith and A. Leland
Jamison, eds., *The Shaping of American Religion*, copyright © 1961.

Random House, New York, for Robert Penn Warren, *Segregation: The Inner Conflict of
the South*, copyright © 1956.

Charles Scribner's Sons, New York, for Albert Henry Newman, *A History of the Baptist
Churches in the United States*, copyright 1915, and for Thomas Jefferson Wertenbaker, *The
Old South*, copyright 1942.

University of Chicago Press, Chicago, for Winthrop S. Hudson, *American Protestantism*, copyright © 1963.

University of Kentucky Press, Lexington, for Walter B. Posey, *The Baptist Church in the
Lower Mississippi Valley, 1776–1845*, copyright © 1957.

University of North Carolina Press, Chapel Hill, for W. T. Couch, ed., *Culture in the
South*, copyright 1935, and for Hugh Talmage Lefler and Albert Ray Newsome, *North Carolina: The History of a Southern State*, copyright 1954.

Westminster Press, Philadelphia, for Victor Obenhaus, *The Church and Faith in Mid-
America*, copyright © 1963, and for George Huntston Williams, *The Radical Reformation*,
copyright © 1962.

Yale University Press, New Haven, Connecticut, for C. C. Goen, *Revivalism and Separatism in New England, 1740–1800*, copyright © 1962, and for L. C. Rudolph, *Hoosier Zion*,
copyright © 1963.

The original edition carried an expression of my thanks to many who
contributed to the conception and completion of the book. By now I have
acquired other creditors who have done much to place in public this "revisited" version. I am especially grateful to The University of Alabama
Press for venturing to reissue a book that was written in and for the era of
the 1960s.

The times have changed! But, one hopes, so has its author, toward
growth in knowledge and capacity for discrimination in valuing and understanding. To the degree that this has occurred, I have a great many
people to thank: students at Chapel Hill and Florida, as well as hearers
who have engaged me after public lectures; and just as much, readers of
the 1966 book and that large company of fellow scholars now collaborat-
ing with some of us "accidental pioneers" who gave the study of religion
in the South an early impetus.

My gratitude to them all is warranted and offered genuinely.

Samuel S. Hill
Gainesville, Florida

Southern Churches in Crisis Revisited

Rarely does an author have the chance to revisit a study he or she wrote two or three decades earlier, but I have been given just such an opportunity in preparing for this reissue of my 1966 book, *Southern Churches in Crisis*. That opportunity is due in part to the continuing life of the original book, a condition that surprises me as much as it gratifies. When one composes a study, he or she generally just does it, not giving much thought to whether the result will be regarded as useful. Somehow this particular book continues to be read, quoted, and cited—despite its having been out of print for nearly a quarter century.

A second justification for this reprint edition has to do with the dramatic changes that have occurred in southern religious life since 1966. We may put it this way: Whatever the crisis may have been during the 1960s, it is hardly that now. In fact we even have to confront the question of whether today's condition constitutes a crisis at all.

A third reason applies most directly to those of us who analyze the region, in particular its religious history and the changes overtaking this storied section of the United States. Succinctly, the study of the religious history and ongoing life of the South is a burgeoning enterprise. Long neglected, it has evolved into a virtual cottage industry. Books, articles, dissertations, and scholarly papers examining southern religion appear regularly from scholars, fledgling and veteran, all over the country.

Two features of the present state of these studies assure their continued growth. One is the launching of a journal devoted to this field, the *Journal of Southern Religion*, in January 1998. Its being an on-line publication seems to add just the right touch to its recent emergence, a thoroughly modern enterprise! The other is the quietly dramatic fact that scholarly study of religious life in the South is now simply taken for granted. Teachers, researchers, authors, and publishing houses engage in it with enthusiasm.

In this new introduction and the essay "Thirty Years Later," which follows, the first and second of the incentives just mentioned receive considerable airing. The third prompts the inclusion of a representative listing of articles, essays, and books on the subject written in the 1990s. That list appears at the end of this introduction.

With regard to why this book has some continuing life, a fairly brief response should suffice. It sought to address the social crisis that engulfed the American South (and the rest of the nation) from c. 1954 to the early 1970s. Moral to its core, the crusade to eradicate racial segregation was the compelling issue facing the South for that entire period. What could be more precisely an ethical triumph than achieving basic human, constitutionally guaranteed rights and opportunities through building a just society that looked askance at isolating any sector of the population for special treatment?

To speak of morality and ethics in the setting of the American South is to draw attention to its churches. This most visibly religious region of the country looked to its ubiquitous churches and their pervasive evangelical Christian worldview for directives on how to practice godly living. Thus a book that sought to delineate the popular religion of the people, and that made some effort to relate that powerful animus to the racial revolution that was occurring on domestic soil, was "relevant" (to use the buzzword of those times).

Recently a fellow longtime student of the South's religious tradition observed with reference to my book and its durability that it took a theologically trained person to write it. Although not a point that I would have seen myself, the insight is probably valid. I am suggesting that the blending of those two strands has contributed to such usefulness as the book has had. Reflecting my training and concomitant concern, *Southern Churches in Crisis* was a theological treatise from beginning to end, perhaps more so than almost all other studies of that era.

Although no one seems to have characterized the book as an instance of undue advocacy, the passions of the author are not difficult to sense. I knew this at the time of composing and can readily see now that I did not check my personal investment in the subject at the door of my study. Those were critical times, and I was a man of the church who cared considerably about how things were to turn out. I had to write the book; doing so was an existential necessity. Perhaps all books *have* to be written, in some sense, or they would not be produced. But this one was an unmistakably personal venture. And there is some manifest anger; there are traces of spilled blood on the pages. I have not forgotten, for example, the reaction of a trusted friend who did me the favor of reading portions of the manuscript in early draft. He was disappointed, he said, thinking and hoping that this was going to be a lovers' quarrel. I hope that there is some of that in it, but there is undeniably pain, passion, and anger.

The crisis of those years provoked the study. But sooner or later this southerner and man of the church had to work through the particular form of the Christian faith that his culture had suggested to him and that he had willingly given himself to. Thus *Southern Churches in Crisis* is in part an autobiographical reflection, with special reference to the contours of the faith that was so much a part of me. Circumstances were providing me fresh perspectives. Having interregional experience, a year of study in a British university, and then membership (from 1960) on the faculty of a state university, I had abundant occasion to see the southern popular theology in a comparative light. Understanding that tradition, penetrating its distinctive shape and dynamic that were my heritage, became a burning necessity. So, besides being a tract for the times, the book was a confessional manifesto resulting from personal pilgrimage. It turned out that the act of writing the book was therapeutic, a major step toward displacement of regional orthodoxy in favor of something more satisfying (because more classical, I intended).

The second reason for reprinting this book is to answer the demand for greater consideration of dramatic changes that have occurred in southern life, notably its religious dimensions, since the heat of the civil rights revolution cooled down. I have chosen to approach that examination by asking what I did in the 1966 study that has been proven accurate and by marking the blind spots and misinterpretations that informed that venture. These are tasks that one can relish only when given a chance to revisit. More salient is how the earlier study presaged what has taken place in the subsequent years, or failed to do so, either by being quite misguided or by falling victim to the unpredictable turns that the religious story lines have taken. In other words, where did we go wrong, and what did we see that was really there?

The book's most widely used feature seems to have lain in its attempt to define the contours of evangelical Protestantism. In preference to listing and explaining the doctrines that the southern popular churches taught, I chose to draft a kind of pictorial metaphor to capture the operating system of convictions that informed the hearts and minds of the faithful. Centrally, what does the shape of reality look like? Who and what are present in the most rudimentary sketch of human nature and responsibility? I concluded that reality boiled down to two personal beings, the holy God of the Bible and each individual human creature. Much else "exists," of course—other people, society and culture, and the vast physical universe—but the holy God of the Bible takes greatest joy in having created the individual person; what each such being is and must do became the essence of the churches' message and mission.

The southern evangelical tradition distilled "all reality" to a shorter list and simpler complex than do other, more traditional, evangelical heritages. In this historical setting the sinfulness of the archetypal human being and the requirements of God drew the design of what is really important and therefore of the focus of the churches' preaching and ministering. Personal forgiveness, the salvation of the soul, was evaluated as basic, fundamental, an imperative condition. Without the experience of conversion each individual was hopelessly guilty and eternally condemned. Mercifully the all-demanding but all-loving God gave his son to the world; Jesus lived, and was raised from the dead, but most significantly he was crucified. His death provided the benefit of an atonement. Each and every person by rights should have had to pay the consequences of their sins against God. Instead, a gracious Lord offered his own, in a sense, himself, as the sacrificial lamb to be the atonement. By accepting this Christ as savior and the forgiveness thereby effected, the individual bridges the unbridgeable gulf between God and humanity.

When "all reality" is so depicted, nothing else much matters but that message, that act of sacrifice, and each person's availing him- or herself of it. The churches that so envisaged the shape of things were being altogether faithful when they concentrated their functioning in this way. Evangelism is their mission par excellence. And this message became "what every schoolboy knows" about what Christianity stands for (hardly a figure I would employ now).

That manner of describing the operating theology of "popular southern religion," although bordering on simplism and therefore being somewhat misleading, has the merit of shedding some light on how those good people, possessed of sensitive consciences, could miss the ethical demands of their black southern neighbors and of the region's historic opportunity to set right what had been so oppressive to so many for so long. More is involved in their behavior than that, but seeing this helps us understand how their theology did little to challenge their view of what their society should be doing.

I believe this is an accurate and fair portrayal of the particular ethical vision that guided their decisions to act and not to act. But, to borrow a common authorial phrase, I was wrong where I was right. This analysis applied in some cases, especially among the Southern Baptists and the others who subscribed to the revivalistic variant of Evangelicalism. Many Presbyterians ended with the same ethical decision, expressing their ethical theory about public social involvement in this way, but did so out of the theological heritage of that body, a position they termed the "spirituality of the church." These Presbyterians, although not called to save souls according to revivalism's prescriptions, lived by the commandment to practice church through preaching and believing faithfully. God was not calling them to become involved in social causes but rather to nurture the spiritual life of the church.

This reference to the practice of many traditional Presbyterians illustrates a major flaw in the earlier book. I offered a too-general, undifferentiated account of the prevailing popular theology. Lumping together Baptists, Methodists, and Presbyterians and classifying them all as evangelical was particularly misleading for the case of the last. Although many Presbyterians abstained from participation in the region's defining ethical activity of that era, they did so out of a distinctive formulation. Also I gave too little attention to those Christians of many denominations who did participate, some in quite visible ways, some more subtly, many with great courage. Most of all I regret failing to note that some Baptists and some Presbyterians reached conclusions different from the majority position among their fellows and acted directly in the struggle. On this subject as on others, generalizations are not adequate. Even so, the prevailing popular theology seems to have functioned in some such way as I sought to present and to have stood as the most widespread position in southern Protestant ranks.

It is important to point out here, as I did not do earlier, that people of the church often transcend the popular interpretations of its teachings or, alternatively, that they reconfigure the standard elements within what is, after all, a several-part body of teaching. From the standpoint of the regular (the "normal") procedure, such actions and the people who practice them may be branded as too liberal, as "out of line," even as heretical. Yet on inquiry these people may turn out to be quite regular in subscribing to the teachings. What marks off their positioning may be a judgment that the whole is greater than the parts or that a dialectical, not serial, manner of treating the many correlated teachings is more authentic. Or still again, they may demonstrate an ironic view of truth and truths; in doing so they affirm that truth, notably truth that is not "of this world," is fraught with mystery, that divine revelation has many surprising twists and turns, that it is greater than our logic, and that it may be expressible only as paradox. As one nurtured in this regional popular tradition, I have observed many occasions on which the faithful saw quite beyond what they had been taught and heard (even that they did not hold to what they had been taught). A quiet sophistication abounds among the southern faithful, a sensitivity that reveals 20/20 penetration of the message. Such processes of distillation were among the propulsions, surely, that enabled courageous disciples to venture forth to address the social injustices all around them during those troublous times.

Acknowledging these shortcomings of the original study sometimes amounts less to "wherein we were wrong," as such, than to what I could not see. One does grow, one hopes, developing wider peripheral vision and greater depth as time passes. A major instance of "wherein we were wrong" had to do with something we all could see but were ill-equipped to recognize, or perhaps we were so morally insensitive that we did not recognize what we saw, namely, African Americans, the black churches, the other unit in the southern biracial society. The "invisible man" indeed.

Like other southerners endeavoring to understand the home society, I wanted to want to evaluate African Americans as fellow citizens, as full human beings, and as deserving of the redressing of centuries of injustice. Especially as I began to develop friendships with black fellow citizens and churchmen and -women, I longed to share life with them unimpeded by customs and laws as compounded by my latent racism. In particular the assignment to write a book that dealt with the southern church in the 1960s occasioned the need to know more about African American churches.

My own limited vision and undersized heart, I believe, were not the only major factors in confining the inquiry to the white population. The research had not been done, the data were not available, the historical records had not been examined. To be sure, resources were there that had not been tapped, but it is simply the case that the work awaited our doing it. Once we had begun, we uncovered much more than we had suspected of a culture with high rates of illiteracy, one more given to oral expression than to written.

But when I explained in the introduction to *Southern Churches in Crisis* that I was limiting my analysis to the religious life of whites, I meant to be acting more nearly from a sense of responsibility than from a governing prejudice. What I regret most keenly is how little we knew—in part how little we knew as to how much we really did have access to—and how partial the story I sought to tell was destined to be because the full story of southern religion, present as well as past, could not be examined.

One of the most exciting moments in my decades of addressing this subject came when I read Donald Mathews's observation that "black people made southern religion what it was." Leaving aside the qualifications that Mathews's statement requires, we know now that his insight is central to divining the dynamic and genius of southern culture and religion.

Mathews was the first to show me that southern church preaching, singing, and praying result from the joint presence of whites and blacks in biracial congregations that existed during the long period of African American slavery. Singing and praying surely are the most profoundly constitutive elements in any group's public worship. With relatively little effort one can imagine oneself in a Baptist or Methodist gathering in the 1840s, say, and hear the commingling of vocal and instrumental musical sounds. The songs and hymns were composed and chosen by the ruling white portion, but the cadence, pace, and vitality were ineluctably affected by the people of African descent, no matter their proportion among the worshipers. In praying, too, black groaning and rejoicing infused the sound and spirit of the occasion for all present. And the preaching: responding, Amen-ing, and shouting, if the preacher was getting it right, that is, determined the fervor, even the length, of the sermon. There can be little challenging the conclusion that white church services developed their character partly as an outgrowth of this interaction. More than evangelical piety, more than evangelistic urgency brought about the styles that characterize white church gatherings for public worship.

The great percentage of the early studies in "religion in the South" limited themselves to the white population. One thinks of the work of Kenneth Bailey, John Boles, and Brooks Holifield, among others (including myself), who simply focused on the white churches and their place in southern culture. (Later, Boles would become the principal reporter of the biracial makeup of many churches in the old Southwest, and Holifield would direct a dissertation that did for the elite of the black clergy what his *Gentlemen Theologians* had done for the elite white clergy.)

Two landmark studies appeared in the late 1970s: Donald Mathews's *Religion in the Old South* (just referred to) and Albert Raboteau's *Slave Religion*. Mathews's book dealt more directly with the evangelical faith of whites, but in the very process of telling that story he could not, and did not, overlook the presence of slaves and free blacks. His acknowledging their constant interaction with their owners and masters represented a breakthrough in the field. Still, we learn little directly about the church life and religious faith of that sector of the South's population.

The task of filling this gap in the research fell to Raboteau, who took on the huge burden of recounting the African religious heritage of the South's black population. Little work had been done on that historical record before Raboteau, and not enough has been done since. Given the scarcity of materials available, however, Raboteau's amounted to a large contribution. Then in the last two-thirds of the book he turned to the religion practiced by the slaves and provided for our grasp of that field a framework that still persists twenty years later. He showed us that three forms of Christianity enjoyed a promi nent place among blacks: biracial churches, independent black con- gregations, and the "invisible religion" of the plantation quarters. Raboteau's work was groundbreaking, although in its focus on the South's black population, it excluded whites in the same way that whites-based studies had excluded blacks. Only Mathews had be- gun—begun— to work on the intractable fact of interaction.

The pattern of focusing on one or the other, blacks or whites, per sisted, with limited exceptions, right through the decade of the eighties. Then, under Leon Litwack's direction at Berkeley, Paul Harvey gen- erated a dissertation, *Redeeming the South*, that would become the first book of the third generation of scholarship in the study of reli- gion in the South. Its subtitle suggested its novelty and its secret: *Religious Cultures and Racial Identities Among Southern Baptists, 1865– 1925.* The plurals *cultures* and *identities* suggest a new approach for a single study, but the larger clue is found in the harmless phrase "south- ern Baptists." Harvey refers to both major parties of Baptists who lived in the South—black and white—not to just the Southern Bap- tist Convention. By the period of Harvey's research many more docu- ments concerning black history had become available, much more material culture acknowledged. Doubtless, Litwack's guidance helped, but Harvey deserves the credit for seeing what was there and for be- ing willing to take it on. Then, too, the accumulation of the work of many scholars in this still young field contributed. The time had ar- rived for trying out a new paradigm.

Looking back, I wish that I had at least acknowledged how inter- active the two racial religious formations had been, how mutually implicating they were. Myopia took its toll, however, and that is a real weakness within *Southern Churches in Crisis*.

No comparable explaining will suffice for another oversight or omission or act of neglect, whatever precisely it was. I refer to the lack of attention I gave to the role of women in southern churches. One does not have to desire to be politically correct to recognize the importance of making some sort of distinction between the roles men and women played in the formation and evolution of church life in the region. Mathews cites chapter and verse of the magnitude of female membership; beyond doing that he reports on the leadership provided by women in education, philanthropy, and humane activities on behalf of slaves.

Because, however, women could not be ordained as pastors or serve as deacons, stewards, or chairs of organized efforts, most of us failed to acknowledge their participation. Anne Firor Scott in 1970 and Jean E. Friedman in 1985 began to redress this oversight, and by the 1990s no one could justify excluding women from studies of southern religion. *Southern Churches in Crisis,* however, does not manage even to raise the issue of gender roles and respective involvements.

On a quite different topic, I wish now that I had not forced so much to rest on the denominational structure of the South's church life. Denominations did provide an organizing framework. Moreover denominational life, distinctions, statistics, and emphases were and are one legitimate way of conducting the study of religious history. Yet proceeding that way is apt to shortchange the independent congregations common among Fundamentalists and in the Appalachian forms of Protestantism. Also, this approach invites the mistake, already mentioned, of overgeneralization. This applies to the makeup of particular denominational bodies. In addition, it treats all Baptists, for example, as Baptists, when there is this, that, and the other sort of Baptist.

We whose lot was to work in the early years within this field of study did begin to accumulate what has expanded so greatly by now. As "accidental pioneers," we appreciate no words of commendation more than "you showed us the way." A host of younger scholars are now finding their own way, so often noting and compensating for our omissions and jaded procedures.

Perhaps the most arresting recent piece that I have read in our field is the product of research and acute reflection by Beth Barton Schweiger, in her unpublished essay "The Captivity of Southern Religious History." (The larger study will appear in *The Gospel Working Up: Progress and the Pulpit in Nineteenth-Century Virginia*.) Schweiger offers the challenge that the field of southern religious history is "in captivity." In what respects and to whom? we must ask. To us, the "accidental pioneers" who generalized too much, answers the second part of this question. To answer the first part, Schweiger constructs a compelling revisionist argument that targets the claims, assumptions, categories, and emphases that have become received tradition in southern religious studies.

Schweiger summarizes her concerns by contesting the standard scholarship's preoccupation with "establishing the South's uniqueness." This perception of the South, she contends, "exists by virtue of (1) the homogeneity of religious practice in the region; (2) the similarity of doctrinal positions among Protestants who are dominated by . . . 'the Baptist-Methodist hegemony'; and (3) the dominance of revivalism and fundamentalism among southern congregations." I am singled out, correctly I suspect, as the "most self-conscious formulator of this position." Further tightening the hold of the old standard interpretation is the sharing of these general assumptions by a good many historians (including C. Vann Woodward) who, not having made religion an integral part of their research, may not be especially well informed about the work being done in this quite new field.

Schweiger underscores the issue that we have examined earlier in this new introduction: that there has been too much generalizing about religion practices and an indefensible argument made that these practices cut across denominations, social classes, and subsections of the region. Any careful surveying of the regional scene as far back as the mid-eighteenth century does reveal a good bit of diversity. To start with, there have been several different strains of Baptists and Methodists. (This historic diversity is a topic I addressed in my 1996 book, *One Name but Several Faces*.)

Around 1800 a new indigenous impetus appeared, the Restoration Movement, which has always aimed to recover original Christianity, what its devotees have called "New Testament Christianity." Declaring such a recovery, a repristination, to be both possible and obligatory, the faithful of this school of thought might have been expected to be united, not disposed to nor tolerant of schism. But even here in the Stone-Campbell tradition divergences have been common, some more nearly following Stone, others Campbell. Also such an ideal view ignores the debating, judging, and strife within a movement devoted to simplicity and purity.

As stated, there have been various sorts of Baptists. Within the company of white Baptists there have been Primitives, Landmarkists, revivalistic and nonrevivalistic, and so on. Black Baptists from their earliest years of sponsoring their own congregations and organizations after Emancipation have experienced division and instances of charges and countercharges.

Schweiger is right, and now far from alone, in insisting that we pay attention to diversity even within the same denominational family. Where we are most indebted to her, however, is in her recognition that these generalizations have resulted in the more sweeping claim that Christianity and Christians have commonly knuckled under to the regional culture. Thus her work tells us not only that the field of scholarship has been held in captivity by certain assumptions and main themes but also that this scholarship has been confident that when given the choice, "Christ or culture," loyalty to the ethics of Christianity or loyalty to the South, southerners have opted for the latter.

This contention—that in effect southern Christians were more southern than Christian—is persuasive only insofar as it can be shown to be consistent with the evidence. Enter Schweiger's research into nineteenth-century Virginia church life. The tack that the evidence leads her to take requires challenging an assumption underlying the standard line of scholarship, namely, the claim that the history of churches in the South is marked by consensus and continuity.

Convinced that on the issue of modernity the churches of that time and place were neither premodern nor antimodern, as the standard line would have it, Schweiger proposes that serious discontinuity erupted. The churches organized along the lines of modern business, encouraged their ministers to pursue theological education, and adapted the rural styles of church life to suit the new and growing urban population. So much, to repeat, for taking as the definitive description of southern church life the fact of an identifiable and persis-

tent continuity in manner and structure from the colonial era to recent times. When the times changed, as they were doing by the last
two thirds of the nineteenth century (hardly for the first time), the
churches changed with them. Adopting the values and processes of
modern business and social forms in the interest of adapting to new
surroundings and cultural conventions, they broke with the past. Also
we must not miss the subtler point that not all did so, meaning that
consensus fell when the old forms and practices underwent serious
revision. But I do want to say that Schweiger offers an insufficient
recognition of the persistence of what she labels premodern or
postmodern.

Schweiger has flung down the gauntlet. She offers us much to dis-
cuss, although undertaking such discussion is not integral to this introductory essay. What is highly germane is that in her work, as in
Paul Harvey's on southern Baptists (black and white studied together),
we are witnessing the maturation of a field of study. The work of
revision, expansion, and further critical reflection goes on, and these
fresh surges to its power suggest a promising future.

I take a moment to suggest two areas of inquiry that no one has
undertaken and that I regard as fundamental to a fully elaborated
field. (Doing this is by way of sampling tasks needing our attention in
the immediate future.) Two facts of life in the southern evangelical
setting seem to reflect strange and, perhaps, indefensible lacunae in
the practice of the Christian life. One is the relative absence of "disciplined spirituality" in the church life of the region. The other is the
paucity of instances of radical Christianity and radical communities
of faith. We have to be surprised that, in terms of historical development, such a high-intensity form of faith has not bred a keener interest in cultivating personal piety, at least with regard to so-called spiritual formation and some variant of mysticism. Of radical communities there are few, indicating that little challenging of social conventions has dotted this landscape. Knowing how devout the people are
encouraged to be, and so often are, we have to express surprise at how
comfortably at home they are in the world. Making this point takes
us well beyond the matter of their being at home in the culture of the
region to wondering why there have not been more withdrawals from
a world in which there is abundant evil and no forms that approximate the kingdom of God. Doubtless my list of two is no more than

a start on conceiving where we are now with regard to what asks for our involvement.

As pledged, I present here at the end of this introductory piece a representative list of studies on "religion in the South" that have appeared since 1990. Readers are reminded of two seminal bibliographic essays. The earlier was written by Rosemary M. Magee and reviewed the field to about 1980; its design was to offer a critical review of eight book-length studies, from 1964 to 1978, and to comment on the state of this area of inquiry. It appeared in *Religious Studies Review*. The more recent is the contribution of John B. Boles, "The Discovery of Southern Religious History," in *Interpreting Southern History: Historiographical Essays in Honor of Sanford W. Higginbotham* (Louisiana State University Press, 1987). (Note that he judges the work that began in the 1960s to be a "discovery" and not a "recovery.") Here four books are reviewed at length and the whole field is canvassed, from the "protofounders" (my ascription) of the 1950s until the season of his writing. By reading those two essays and perusing this list, one gains a reasonable grasp of this still young but quite vibrant field of study.

Studies since 1990
A Representative List

Alvis, Joel L., Jr. *Religion and Race: Southern Presbyterians, 1946–1983*. Tuscaloosa: University of Alabama Press, 1994.

Ammerman, Nancy Tatom. *Baptist Battles: Social Change and Religious Conflict in the Southern Baptist Convention*. New Brunswick, N.J.: Rutgers University Press, 1990.

————, ed. *Southern Baptists Observed: Multiple Perspectives on a Changing Denomination*. Knoxville: University of Tennessee Press, 1993.

Anderson, Jon W., and William B. Friend, eds. *The Culture of Bible Belt Catholics*. New York: Paulist Press, 1995.

Ayers, Edward L. *The Promise of the New South: Life After Reconstruction*. New York: Oxford University Press, 1992.

Bloom, Harold. *The American Religion: The Emergence of the Post-Christian Nation*. New York: Simon and Schuster, 1990.

Boles, John B. *The Irony of Southern Religion*. New York: Peter Lang, 1994.

Brasher, J. Lawrence. *The Sanctified South: John Lakin Brasher and the Holiness Movement*. Urbana: University of Illinois Press, 1994.

Clarke, Erskine. *Our Southern Zion: A History of Calvinism in the South Carolina Low Country, 1690–1990.* Tuscaloosa: University of Alabama Press, 1996.

Crews, Mickey. *The Church of God: A Social History.* Knoxville: University of Tennessee Press, 1990.

Dalhouse, Mark Taylor. *An Island in the Lake of Fire: Bob Jones University, Fundamentalism, and the Separatist Movement.* Athens: University of Georgia Press, 1996.

Dorgan, Howard. *The Airwaves of Zion: Religion and Radio in Appalachia.* Knoxville: University of Tennessee Press, 1993.

————. *In the Hands of a Happy God: The "No-Hellers" of Central Appalachia.* Knoxville: University of Tennessee Press, 1997.

Flynt, Wayne. "'A Special Feeling of Closeness': Mt. Hebron Baptist Church, Leeds, Alabama." In *American Congregations,* ed. James P. Wind and James N. Lewis. Chicago: University of Chicago Press, 1995.

Georgia Historical Quarterly 75 (Summer 1991). Articles by Andrew S. Chancey, Samuel S. Hill, E. Brooks Holifield, Timothy Huebner, Martin E. Marty, Christopher Owen, and others.

Grammich, Clifford A. *Local Baptists, Local Politics: Churches and Communities in the Middle and Uplands South.* Knoxville: University of Tennessee Press, 1999.

Hankins, Barry. *God's Rascal: J. Frank Norris and the Beginnings of Southern Fundamentalism.* Lexington: University of Kentucky Press, 1996.

Harper, Keith. *The Quality of Mercy: Southern Baptists and Social Christianity, 1890–1920.* Tuscaloosa: University of Alabama Press, 1996.

Harvey, Paul W. *Redeeming the South: Religious Cultures and Racial Identities among Southern Baptists, 1865–1925.* Chapel Hill: University of North Carolina Press, 1997.

Heriot, M. Jean. *Blessed Assurance: Assessing Religious Beliefs through Actions in a Carolina Baptist Church.* Knoxville: University of Tennessee Press, 1994.

Heyrman, Christine Leigh. *Southern Cross: The Beginnings of the Bible Belt.* New York: Alfred A. Knopf, 1997.

Hill, Samuel S. *One Name but Several Faces: Varieties of Popular Denominations in Southern History.* Athens: University of Georgia Press, 1996.

Huff, Peter A. *Allen Tate and the Catholic Revival: Trace of the Fugitive Gods.* New York: Paulist Press, 1996.

Hughes, Richard T. *Reviving the Ancient Faith: A History of Churches of Christ in America.* Grand Rapids, Mich.: Wm. B. Eerdmans, 1996.

Ketchin, Susan. *The Christ-Haunted Landscape: Faith and Doubt in Southern Fiction.* Jackson: University Press of Mississippi, 1994.

K'Meyer, Tracy Elaine. *Interracialism and Christian Community in the Postwar South: The Story of Koinonia Farm.* Charlottesville: University of Virginia Press, 1997.

Leonard, Bill J., and Mary Lee Daugherty, eds. *Christianity in Appalachia.* Knoxville: University of Tennessee Press, 1998.

Martin, Robert F. *Howard Kester and the Struggle for Social Justice in the South, 1904–1977.* Charlottesville: University of Virginia Press, 1991.

Mathews, Donald G. "'Christianizing the South'—Sketching a Synthesis." In *New Directions in American History,* ed. Harry S. Stout and D. G. Hart. New York: Oxford University Press, 1998.

McCauley, Deborah Vansau. *Appalachian Mountain Religion: A History.* Urbana: University of Illinois Press, 1995.

Miller, Randall, Harry S. Stout, and Charles Reagan Wilson, eds. *Religion and the American Civil War.* New York: Oxford University Press, 1998.

Minnix, Kathleen. *Hammerin' the Brethren: The Life of Sam P. Jones.* Athens: University of Georgia Press, 1994.

Montgomery, William E. *Under Their Own Vine and Fig Tree: The African-American Church in the South, 1865–1900.* Baton Rouge: Louisiana State University Press, 1993.

Morgan, David T. *The New Crusades, The New Holy Land: Conflict in the Southern Baptist Convention, 1969–1991.* Tuscaloosa: University of Alabama Press, 1996.

Owen, Christopher H. *Sacred Flame of Love: The Story of Methodists in Georgia, 1790–1900.* Athens: University of Georgia Press, 1998.

Ownby, Ted G. *Subduing Satan: Religion, Recreation, and Manhood in the Rural South.* Chapel Hill: University of North Carolina Press, 1990.

Pitts, Walter F., Jr. *Old Ship of Zion: The Afro-Baptist Ritual in the African Diaspora.* New York: Oxford University Press, 1993.

Queen, Edward L., II. *In the South the Baptists Are the Center of Gravity: Southern Baptists and Social Change, 1930–1980.* Chicago Studies in the History of American Religion series. Brooklyn, N.Y.: Carlson, 1991.

Quist, John W. *Restless Visionaries: The Roots of Antebellum Reform in Alabama and Michigan.* Baton Rouge: Louisiana State University Press, 1998.

Rankin, Richard. *Ambivalent Churchmen and Evangelical Churchwomen: The Religion of the Episcopal Elite in North Carolina, 1800–1860.* Columbia: University of South Carolina Press, 1993.

Religion and American Culture: A Journal of Interpretation 8, no. 2 (Summer 1998). "Forum: Southern Religion," several articles.

Richey, Russell. *Early American Methodism.* Bloomington: Indiana University Press, 1991.

Schweiger, Beth Barton. "The Captivity of Southern Religious History." Paper presented to the Southern Intellectual History Circle, February 1997.

———. *The Gospel Working Up: Progress and the Pulpit in Nineteenth-Century Virginia.* New York, N.Y.: Oxford University Press, in press.

Sensbach, Jon F. *A Separate Canaan: The Making of an Afro-Moravian World in North Carolina, 1763–1840.* Chapel Hill: University of North Carolina Press, 1998.

Shibley, Mark A. *Resurgent Evangelicalism in the United States: Mapping Cultural Change since 1970.* Columbia: University of South Carolina Press, 1996.

Sparks, Randy J. O. *Jordan's Stormy Banks: Evangelicalism in Mississippi, 1773–1877.* Athens: University of Georgia Press, 1994.

Stowell, Daniel W. *Rebuilding Zion: Religious Reconstruction in the South, 1863–1877.* New York: Oxford University Press, 1998.

Turner, Elizabeth Hayes. *Women, Culture, and Community: Religion and Reform in Galveston, 1880–1920.* New York: Oxford University Press, 1997.

Wills, Gregory A. *Democratic Religion: Freedom, Authority, and Church Discipline in the Baptist South, 1785–1900.* New York: Oxford University Press, 1998.

Wilson, Charles Reagan. *Judgment and Grace in Dixie: Southern Faiths from Faulkner to Elvis.* Athens: University of Georgia Press, 1996.

Thirty Years Later

An Interpretive Essay

Were the southern churches in crisis in the mid 1960s as the title of my book averred? If so, what was the nature of that crisis? Did it come to an end? Are they now in crisis? A crisis, if at all, in what respects? Has the South always been in crisis? The last question arises rather readily, and its validity at least seems arguable. *Crisis* and *South* seem to fit together rather comfortably.

It is telling that the title was not of my own formulating. That fact reveals more than my inexperience in publishing, meaning that a Holt, Rinehart & Winston editor had to take on the task of assessing what the book was really all about and creating an arresting title (as we both hoped). What it really shows is that an involved insider lacked perspective on the situation he wanted to describe. I could hardly have missed knowing that a critical era had dawned, but I was focused more on the immediate scene than on the place of this crisis in the South's historic development, notwithstanding the study's grounding in regional history.

In this new reflection I want to look again at the period during which I wrote and about which I was writing. I acknowledge that the social upset was broader and deeper than I could grasp then. My emphasis on the onrush of alternative lifestyles and worldviews, actual conditions of the time that my study examined and that I viewed as a central part of my task, would prove to be less dramatic than the displacement of a way of life, of living, and of understanding.

The Crisis of the 1990s

Contrasting the crisis of the 1960s with that of the 1990s reveals that the former was not perpetrated by any social group in cultural power, whereas the latter demonstrates one cultural elite's passion to create a crisis in order to rectify a condition intolerable to them because it is abominable in the eyes of their God. Simply stated, the wrenching events of the sixties did not arise from the initiative of the ruling classes in the society, but those of the nineties came about precisely because one sector of those with know-how and power judged that things had gone awry.

To put another way, what happened with the sixties generation had to do with often-unplanned cultural change. Civil rights reformers mounted a determined effort to bring the South's biracial society in line with the American Constitution, the biblical call to justice, and the prevailing codes of ethics in the Western world. Although more than a few in the churches supported the changes being insisted upon, most did not; furthermore, the (white) church organizations did not provide the impetus for the changes. What was occurring was the invasion of modern secular (though moral) and religiously diverse forces into a formerly more isolated and homogeneous culture.

During the 1960s, conditions and forces arose that the churches mostly did not initiate but were forced to respond to. A new social/cultural situation, which was not of their own making, overtook them in spite of the enormous influence the churches wielded in that society and culture.

By sharp contrast, the recent religious upheaval is just that, a religious one—initiated by the churches and having to do with parochial matters, quite pointedly their doctrinal orthodoxy. A large and growing number of leaders throughout the churches, especially in the Baptist and Presbyterian bodies, asserted that theological teachings and ethical values had drifted off course into heresy, relativism, and liberalism (functionally synonymous terms), all spelling faithlessness. A crisis of promulgation was occurring. This situation necessitated a forceful strategy for turning from erroneous ways to paths of truth. Clearly this is a different order of social perturbation than the one that I sought to address in the 1966 tract.

In this new analysis we need to examine each putative crisis, compare the religious upheavals of the two decades, and ask what bearing (if any) the earlier had on the later. Throughout we must recall that the former upheaval was broadly cultural while the latter is, at the obvious level, a matter internal to the churches. Churches are, after all, only one institution in southern society. Yet we must consider whether these changes in that single institution were limited in their impact to that one element in southern society, having only peripheral influence on the culture at large.

The Very Real 1960s Crisis

Societies have been known to dramatize turbulent conditions, rating their capacity to upset the status quo as possessing more significance than the facts warrant. Not so the American South in those dynamic years following the Supreme Court's ruling against segregation in 1954. Real, profoundly real, is an accurate description of those goings-on.

The traditionalist southern response was altogether consistent with the actual gravity of the situation: from Governor Wallace's "stand in the schoolhouse door," to Bull Connor's turning firehoses on the demonstrators to scatter them, to white churches' closing their doors to black people attempting to enter for worship services, to a thousand undramatic events in hundreds of local communities. Nor were the Freedom Riders' ventures into the Deep South an excessive reaction to the state of change being portended by events. Real, indeed.

What made these events so compelling was the inevitability of the outcome, strange as that depiction may sound. There was simply no possibility of maintaining the long-standing racial arrangements of the region. All that conservatives could hope for was to slow down the change, but even the prospect of deferring the rearrangement of the racial order was doubtful. At some level everyone knew that the change was inevitable and not deferrable.

The outcome was revolutionary: Every person, community, and institution was in process of being permanently altered. So many aspects of life were affected: the economic, the moral, education, the family, the political, the religious, and the rest. Such conditions as those disclose the entrenchment of racial and interracial customs and laws in the history and ongoing life of the regional society and culture.

Few white churches were liberal—composed of men and women who believed that the entire population had to be liberated from a wrong and destructive pattern of social relations. Rather, most of the white churches were divided between those whose members practiced the doctrine of "the spirituality of the church," certain that they were called to avoid public matters in favor of authentic (churchly) priorities, and those who actively opposed the forces for change that were at work. But few people were without opinion, even conviction, on what was taking place. Curiously, all parties knew this to be a moral issue, something their God had an investment in.

Of course the black churches too were in a critical phase. This was their chance to see through to effectual completion the crossing of the Red Sea to the land their God had promised to all his people. Looking back we may glibly say that history was on their side and that their cause could not lose. True as that is, the leadership knew that no delay could be brooked, no chances taken that yet again rights and opportunities could be denied. Like all who want freedom, black people wanted it now. Their visions and efforts betrayed a messianic impatience. They preached and performed as a people possessed, as if there was no tomorrow. "Mine eyes have seen . . ." expressed a sentiment shared by most if enunciated only by their spokespersons. They were indeed bound to win this struggle, but the air of crisis was their sustenance as much as it was the Problematik of the dominant white culture.

Yet those who defended the laws and mores being overturned experienced the upheaval far more directly and with great pain. A way of life and of doing society's business, myriad patterns simply taken for granted, were in danger of dissolution. Returning to our "looking back" perspective, we are justified in saying that their alarm and fright were defensible. Schools would never be the same, communities would be altered, political life would be transformed, and even churches would not escape the effects of the projected resolution of the crisis. These threats to convention were made all the worse by the congregational polity of many of the popular churches. If you cannot have your way in the churches governed by the will of their members, what freedoms are left to you?

The Crisis More Sociological than Ethical

In *Southern Churches in Crisis* I addressed that racial situation, of course. Nobody could have denied its centrality. And I made clear my conviction that the churches had been disobedient and indifferent in failing to seek justice for the region's black citizens—that desegregation and more, such as strides toward reconciliation and true community, were required by the biblical tradition.

Racial matters were not an issue touched on lightly. But what I made of them had to do more directly with that policy's tarring the churches' reputation, pointing to them as morally shallow, as ignoring a grievous condition that cried out for redemption. To shirk so imperative a Christian command as racial justice would drive off sensitive progressive younger generations, I argued, and do great damage to the churches' standing in the society. Also that cadre of leaders would be persuaded that the Christian faith was inherently amoral or immoral, far from worthy of their embracing it. I forecast the very real possibility of a high-minded secular morality displacing the churches as providing the soul of the society. The oncoming generations of leaders would be disaffected with the church, judging it insufficiently soulful to attract them.

Thus the emphasis of the book was on the churches' abdication of their role in and responsibility for the life of the South. While the racial-justice theme was certainly not ignored, the central thrust of the study was more sociological than ethical. I deplored an unfaithfulness that rendered Christianity irrelevant to the real world, devoted instead to a self-serving otherworldliness; also being preoccupied with the churches' institutional life.

Expressing that concern was hardly frivolous, but what has actually transpired does not bear out my prediction. I can go on to say that I wish it did—for reasons unrelated to any personal desire to be vindicated and that have something to do with the faith I affirm as a man of the church. Yet it occurs to me now that some of those outside the churches might have found them less inviting if the churches had staunchly stood for the radical Christian racial ethic. In other words "relevance to the real world" is neither a univocal nor an inherently persuasive category.

But the subject of relevance, overworked and treated naively so often in the 1960s and 1970s, had some pertinence then and has considerable now. The white churches genuinely yearned to provide existential resources. Their theology may have been otherworldly in some basic ways, but it also sought to address lives and life—to be relevant. The addressing of lives had largely to do with personal salvation. Hence heavy priority was accorded to evangelism, the mission to convert each person. Bringing people to faith in Christ outranked all other concerns. Typically, religious conversion was seen as occurring in and through a conscious and memorable experience, usually with real, sometimes vivid, emotional responses. But the point to be made here is that the church maintained the conviction that much, even most, of what was wrong with individual lives and society would be rectified by conversion. If everyone experienced this new life in Christ, then what was required for the well-being of the individual would have been accomplished; furthermore, what was necessary for the creation of a good and just society would also be guaranteed. Also those churches continued to provide a vital pastoral ministry that sought to care for people in all their joys and adversities.

Moreover there was a place for ethical ministries. The churches devoted money, time, and strategy to the cleansing of society from designated odious evils. Chief among them was the liquor industry—the manufacture, sale, and consumption of alcoholic beverages. Gambling, the sex industry, wasteful and harmful activities, and other personal sins were attacked, often through highly organized efforts. Thus, in part, their ministry engaged the powers of an evil world in direct fashion. This augmented the churches' confidence in the personal transformation and the practice of godliness. We must note that the class of sins they singled out was personal and interpersonal, not social. The stress was on social concern and social ministry rather than social action. Changing the human environment was less the focus than changing individuals and directly solving specific problems.

A New Ethical Agenda

Regarding the subject of purity, the principal energy of the past decade or so, I mention some important changes that have been occurring in the area of ethical ministries. The evils of drinking, gambling, and sexual perversion have been overshadowed by a new agenda. "Sexual perversion" remains high on the list, but from the standpoint of these ethical ministries, its most abominable expression nowadays is homosexuality. This attitude toward homosexuality is old but has acquired a new force, no doubt in part because of the appearance of the virus that leads to AIDS. In the first wave of the attack on AIDS, these morally ardent Christians judged that there was a direct link between homosexual practice and the contraction of the new illness. Lately we are hearing much less from them about this cause-effect transpiration, surely because that linkage has been shown to account for a small percentage of cases of the outbreak. According to this religious group, homosexuality persists as a particularly odious violation of biblical commandments.

Commanding even more concern has been abortion. On the subject of sexual ethics, this campaign has consumed a huge amount of the energy expended. To all appearances, abortion has taken over the public-sin-number-one ranking, replacing the use of alcoholic beverages in the most castigated category. That abortion is a serious moral (and psychological) matter is readily apparent to all. That it should vault to top ranking among southern church people is something of a historical and theological curiosity. At least it never has ranked so high before. The practice has been widespread in the region for a long time, and not alone to deal with miscegenous relationships. Of late, opposition to it has become strident and relentless. The timing and intensity of this crusade is notable and, to this interpreter, somewhat puzzling. Perhaps the reasons for it are complex.

Just as puzzling is the adoption of natural law ethical theory as basis for this moral crusade. The region's popular forms of theology have had to do primarily with the dynamics of personal relationships and with obedience to biblical injunctions. One would have thought that the traditional Protestant existentialist ethical understanding would have continued as the ground for viewing abortion. Instead a more essentialist perspective has taken over. In the newer interpretation, the fetus *is* the person. The age of the fetus is no issue, the state of the liaison has no bearing, and the health of the mother is not of decisive consequence. To my knowledge this acceptance of an essentialist, a kind of natural-law, basis for judging abortion, is new in the South's religious-ethical history. Some practical instances of deist or quasi-deist thinking have functioned before. By and large, however, the dynamic of the person's relation to a personal God has held sway. Perhaps this puzzlement refers to something as simple as a turning to a pertinent and well-established theory when the issue of abortion first acquired prominence and required resolution in the setting of the South's public life.

So while the use of alcohol is still frowned on, the seriousness of that transgression of a life of holiness has receded sharply. In its place have surfaced the sex and gender related acts of homosexuality and abortion. Whether as cause or effect, or for some other reason, a hitherto unused or little-used theory has been conscripted for making the case. While hardly revolutionary, this does amount to an important change (not exactly the first; for not long ago, the paramount issue was slavery and later segregation, that is, the social ethic of maintaining the South's social structure, with white people in their place and black people in theirs).

The South as Part of National Movements

In both cases, the era when drinking stood as the sin most denounced, and now when sex and gender related matters have replaced it there, the South has been part of wider ethical developments. The crusade against alcohol did not originate in the region; its impetus arose in several northern states, Maine and Kansas among them. In fact southern ministers and laymen enjoyed consuming spirituous liquids quite openly until a decade or so after the Civil War. Nevertheless, once the "temperance" movement invaded the South, it quickly became a formidable force. Such national organizations as the Anti-Saloon League and the Women's Christian Temperance Union were widely adopted in the South, and it made no difference to the southern population that the organizations originated in the North and were led mostly by northerners. Thus, while the regional organizations of national religious families were steadfastly unwilling to heal sectional breaches, and as they criticized the northern churches for embracing the new liberal theologies, national crusades against wickedness were accepted and leadership was given to northern churches by southern Christians.

Related developments have marked the recent campaigns against gender and sexual moral calumnies. "Related" refers to the fact that southern denominations have not led the way in the warfare against homosexuality and abortion, rather some of the various groups composing the "Christian Right" have southern sources, leaders, and support. The Moral Majority and the Pat Robertson-led ministries have carried a distinctly regional flavor, to be sure; yet they are not denominationally affiliated, nor is their constituency predominantly southern.

Historically considered, the religious life of southerners has not exported very well; it has been regional in formation and in following. No longer can that be said with regard to its influence on the nation's moral and political life. The Moral Majority, now defunct as a specific organization, was highly influential in the early days of this national crusade. Robertson's leadership stands near the top of the national effort. Thus, while the South-specific bodies have not much infiltrated the national scene, some of the region's conservative causes and the impetus they have provided have made a large national difference. The interpretation that southern religious forms and styles have "not exported very well," accordingly, now must be revised. This of course is of a piece with the ever greater interaction of the region's people and institutions with the country at large. Regional ways are now less parochial and less anomalous. Both in the act of originating and in the process of contributing, regional religious life has emerged as a vital part of the public scene. It has not always been so.

So one can observe that *southern* churches, in any singular sense, are not in crisis now, but maybe the churches of this nation *are* in crisis, or *the* Church, the Body of Christ, is (that is a "whole 'nother" issue). If such a crisis exists, the churches identified with all the regions of the USA face a trying situation. Even so, I want to begin to point to some peculiarities and critical aspects of the life of the southern regional Christian heritage that pose vexing problems for that heritage—and for the health of the society south of Mason-Dixon.

Doctrinal Purity as Today's Central Theme

Purity, I suggest, is the new driving force of the southern religious community. In the setting of the ethical discussion just offered, that may be taken to mean, purity in practical living. Specifically, heaviest weight is assigned to monogamous marriage, to the sole legitimacy of heterosexual relationships, to personal integrity, and of course to the right of the fetus to live.

These ethical references are a valid use of purity. But there is something new and distinctive about the recent accentuation of purity: its preeminence in the rational arena—purity understood as absolute insistence on absolute devotion to absolute truth. If any dispose to respond by asking such questions as, according to whom, on what basis, or isn't that an interpretation, one can only reply that the questioner does not understand the rationalism that is now so powerful a force in the southern churches. Reiterating, this is purity in the form of absolute devotion to the truth.

Purity is a familiar entry in the southern evangelical glossary (as it should be, surely, for all Christians). But its primary reference point, for all Christians, has indeed been morality. That passionate concern has now been applied to beliefs, to the rational dimension, to propositional precision. On today's terms, this action calls for more than propriety, more than faithfulness, more than clarity, because "propriety" and "faithfulness" fall under the heading of purity. This fresh way of evaluating a group's or a person's orthodoxy (straight-thinking) has far-reaching implications. I do judge the enforcement of rational purity to be new, though not an unheard of consideration, for the large, popular, "mainstream" southern perspective.

In ways that will be examined, this amounts to a form of Fundamentalism, and Fundamentalism has not been standard fare for the South's conservative Protestants. Such an understanding of truth and suitable doctrinal propriety has been alien to the southern mainstream. Indeed being called a fundamentalist has usually been taken as an insult to the leaders and followers in those conservative traditions.

When people so identified have turned up in southern churches, they have been castigated as "trouble-makers" (or worse) and thought of as a veritable leprosy on the body religious. To be sure, there have been fundamentalists around, but they have been independents, wanting no part in the denominations that were practicing apostasy, and treated with condescension (at best) by the organized bodies. These traditions have been conservative but generically evangelical and not fundamentalist (even if the popular view of the press and of many observers elsewhere in the country has not differentiated between them).

The prevailing wind of recent storms within the religious bodies has been rationalistic. For a long time before this recent development, each person's religious experience has taken precedence over belief and behavior. "Twice-born religious experience" has stood closer to entitling the region's textbook, so to speak, than has "the idea of the holy." With the introduction of the Separate Baptists and the evangelical Anglicans (most of them to become Methodists) into the southern scene in the mid-eighteenth century, knowing God in one's heart and experiencing Christ's presence deep within one's being became the hallmarks of the churches' dynamic. Some rationalism, and much insistence on orthodox teaching, has been present, to be sure, a story not requiring our attention here. Within the past two decades or so, however, the dominant sensibility has become the rational, grasping and promulgating the authoritative or even infallible truth of God—actually, the truths of God.

For the long season from 1760 or so to about 1975, there were specified criteria that defined worthiness for church membership and authentic discipleship. That may be presumed for a high-intensity religious setting such as the traditional South's; this was not the land of an Established Church or congenital spirituality. What distinguished this regional version of high-intensity was its defining the faith and personal faith in devotional or experiential terms. Each person was expected to verify that a personal experience of grace and forgiveness had overtaken his or her life, transforming it from godless to God-directed. Ethical behavior must accompany such a claim, of course. Moreover, correct belief inheres in a life so redirected. Nevertheless, a great deal of stock was placed in the individual's testimony of saving grace. It has not been common to challenge the integrity of personal testimony, certainly not in the modern era since the rigors of church discipline were relaxed. That one was aiming to follow biblical commandments for righteous living and holding to sound doctrine has been more the subject for encouragement and teaching than a topic to be scrutinized.

A clue to the relation of experience to belief is provided by the ordinary use of "confession" among evangelical Protestants in the South. That word has referred almost exclusively to a person's experience, and in particular to confessing that one is a sinner and in need of saving grace. Historically and today in the Protestant world generally, "confession" refers to "confessions of faith," the doctrinal corpus that sets off one theological school of thought from others. Thus there is a Lutheran Confession and a Calvinist Confession, as there was the "confessing church" during the National Socialist era in Germany. (In contemporary United Methodism a renewal group calls itself the "confessing movement.") The frame of reference in these standard usages is totally doctrinal—broadly rationalist. Recent studies of the evangelical family of Protestant churches in the United States have drawn the distinction between confessional and conversionist types of evangelical Protestantism. The southern region accounts for much of the need to make such a distinction, since most of the manifestations that fit the second description have been located there. It comes as no surprise then that the intellectual firepower, so to speak, of American evangelical life has come from beyond the South's borders. (In fact most of it has come from one confessional heritage, the Calvinist.)

Christian rationalism has largely been the property and a distinguishing mark of Christian communities in the North. Now that northern dimension and concomitant sensibility have risen to prominence, often to dominance, in southern church life. Purity is our theme, let us be reminded, with that characteristic and aim, having acquired a new primary meaning. Purity of belief, of affirmation, of doctrinal preaching and teaching, comprise the norms by which faithfulness, soundness, authenticity, are evaluated. If earlier the test of legitimacy had to do with the claim of having God's presence and forgiveness known with certainty to be in one's life, the evaluation now pertains to a claim of orthodoxy. Cleansing the seminaries of the heretical has been the agenda of the Southern Baptist thrust in recent years. It matters less, though still much, that the teachers of future ministers embody purity of heart and of action. Those qualities are necessary, but they are not sufficient qualifications for that calling. Ascertaining the orthodoxy of faculty members has become the template issue, a concern of great urgency.

In entrusting the training of ministers to the doctrinally-correct, the Baptist seminaries (some more than others) are searching quite beyond denominational boundaries for teachers to be hired. What a fascinating development this is! In the first place, it reveals that the talent pool within the denomination is limited, a datum that seems to corroborate their conclusion that the churches (led by the graduates of their own seminaries), have veered from the straight line of biblical teaching. We have here a full circle. The former teachers have had to leave, under pressure or by realizing that they were no longer at home in the home institution. And the pastors who have been catalysts in the vocational decision to go to seminary have misled those young men.

Time for a transformation! Moreover, many of their own graduates are not suitable to train the next generations, because they have ingested heresy. Whether or not this is the preferred way of indicating to the public what is happening, this is where those theological institutions find themselves. (One wonders what will be the alumni response to the drastic changes in process. How loyal will these loyalty inclined clergymen be?)

Continuing around that circle, we note also that the seminaries, historically so denomination-conscious, so disinclined to appoint faculty members even from other branches of the Baptist family, are becoming quite ecumenical, that is, within the Baptist fold. So far, there seems to be no disposition to identify non-Baptists. But what may not be apparent to observers is seeing how much variation there is within that Protestant communion.

Against the backdrop of Southern Baptist history, it is all but revolutionary to infuse those seminaries' life with northern conservatism, some of it a step removed from a culture-hostile Fundamentalism. Or, more commonly, to appoint men hailing from pietist Baptist communions. What makes the latter action innovative is the paucity of "disciplined spirituality" within Southern Baptist ranks. It may turn out that such persons will contribute to toning down the traditional preoccupation with evangelism, the datable and memorable experience of conversion under revivalistic circumstances (perhaps even the rationalism so stressed today).

One has to wonder if an additional shift may occur, in addition to the new "ecumenism"; namely, the emergence of some tendency to embrace "multiple imperatives." Revivalistic Evangelicalism and Fundamentalism are characterized by a penchant for being single-minded in message and practice, almost as if there were only one mandate in the Bible. Respectively, they have latched on to the conversion of the lost and a preoccupation with authority—the Bible's as expressed in select doctrines. Perhaps the infusion of new schools of thought will over time generate a kind of comprehensiveness of understanding and mission. Were that to happen, these Baptists might take on some of the hues of classic Evangelicalism, which has been committed to a multiple imperatives approach; within classic Evangelicalism these imperatives have not functioned so much as multiple as they have several teachings correlated comprehensively.

This part of the story is complex because of the variety from one seminary to the next and owing to the diversity of styles of piety and evangelism, but there can be little doubt that these changes will bring about some new conditions. A hint of possible things to come may be reflected in the ruminations of Paige Patterson, a major leader of the Southern Baptist Convention fundamentalist forces, now a seminary president, as quoted by David T. Morgan in *The New Crusades, The New Holy Land.* Patterson disowns any sympathy whatsoever with bibliolatry. He grants that many noninerrantists are among the saved and insists that inerrantist convictions do not guarantee or even bespeak personal salvation. Such convictions are necessary but not sufficient.

Just as intended by the rescuers of a body that had lost its way toward the wasteland of liberalism, change in the form of a radical rejection of the Convention's traditional leadership is the order of the era, but the severity and manner of the change are yet to be revealed. Perhaps the preoccupation with revivalistic evangelism will be softened, as suggested. Perhaps the more systematic approach to comprehensive Christian meaning found in Calvinism will alter the serial approach with which the Southern Baptist theology—and Fundamentalism—has functioned. Also, the more systematic approach might enlarge the prevailing vision of Christian responsibility. Perhaps, just maybe, a significant portion of the takeover (or takeback) reflects institutional disruptions more than an ideological revolution. To suggest any such possible eventuality, however, does not diminish the totalistic nature of the fundamentalist party's hold on accountability, responsibility, power, and control within the institutional life of the Southern Baptist Convention. The party of the moderates has been effectively disenfranchised.

This very regional body may evolve toward becoming less regional and more a participant in international evangelical circles. Perhaps cleaning house at home, so to speak, will extend the size of the household (which is what the word *ecumenical* means). There are many ironies and much uncertainty as to how all these changes will come out, but for the Southern Baptists it is a whole new ball game. The traditional regionalism will, perforce, undergo some shifting. (We still do not know what will be the responses of the laity to all these mostly professionally led crusades.) It is in that sense that I have offered in print the hypothesis that the "fundamentalist takeover" of the Southern Baptist convention may contribute to a greater change in the southern religious situation than the civil rights revolution has done.

To mention the civil rights revolution introduces a different part of this story. Not all the seminaries and congregations are reconstituting themselves in this ecumenical way. Some are carrying out their commitment to purity otherwise, by insisting that their leadership be both of the regional denomination and fundamentalist. Theirs is a more strident voice, a more exclusivist spirit. Instead of casting about broadly to find new teachers or pastors, instead of having some intercourse with "northern" or international Evangelicalism, they grow their own, or find them close at hand.

They thus continue the tradition that extends back to the early twentieth century of keeping the circle unbroken, of limiting their significant contacts with members of their own cultural guild. Perhaps they act this way because their contacts are limited to their own circle. Or it may be that they choose deliberately to retain purity of contact. Whatever the reasons, they identify those in their ranks who are pure. We should not be surprised that there is a body of Baptists who share the fundamentalist spirit of exclusion and who are censorious of all other points of view and holders thereof, given the wide range of conservatism among them. People of this persuasion have been emboldened by recent developments and have moved from being marginal to certified players in the new arrangement. Whether they will find or acknowledge like-minded spirits is something we cannot predict. But in the near term they will exhibit a regional provincialism. *Purity* is more than watchword; it is a way of life and the sole manner of practicing faithfulness. Radically rationalist, they are ill-disposed toward social-cultural involvements and they eschew all forms of dialogue. They stand fast: there is truth—which differs from declaring that one form of truth is right, all others pernicious. Interpretation is a disallowed category, for the simple reason that the truth is what it is, not an interpretation of anything.

To sum up, then, purity is the aim of the new ruling party among the Southern Baptist leadership, some Presbyterians, and a good many others. Purity refers to doctrine; it is a rationalist category in their current usage. Variety is apparent, but the goal of steadfastly defending the faith is widely shared. There is more agreement on the commitment to there being absolute truth than to the exact forms it takes. One eventuation to look for is whether this commitment leads to a reaching outward to fellow rationalist purists, some of them grounded in historic Calvinism or merely to home versions of positioning. Thus less regionalism will appear, perhaps, or maybe more.

A final topic requires treatment here, the role of women in this new configuration. Of the greatest importance is the close correlation between the new perspectives on ethical purity and the revitalized insistence on doctrinal purity.

The most visible manifestation of the newly emphasized role of women is the strict denial of ordaining them to the ministry. In Southern Baptist ranks, the number of ordained clergywomen has never been large, and few have served as primary or senior pastors to congregations. Moreover this situation has occurred principally in limited areas, usually the upper seaboard South, and not much on a general scale. Perhaps the infrequency of female ordinations has contributed to its escaping the limelight. Whatever may have been the case, the relentless attention given to this issue within the past decade reveals its gravity to the party now in power. No minor matter, this has emerged as a virtual test of orthodox faith.

The intended and stated reason for the firm stand now required is biblical teaching. Put simply, it is as disobedient to ordain women to the pastoral ministry as it would be for churches to baptize infants or to shift to an episcopal polity. New Testament passages make it amply clear that men only are called to this service. So strongly held is this injunction that churches and individuals are disfellowshiped when they are in violation. More difficult to monitor but just as vigorously heralded is the really quite novel definition of the Christian marriage and family as characterized by the wife being submissive to the husband.

There is no question that a link exists between the two "purities," ethical and doctrinal, when judging the ordination of women to the ordained ministry to be a serious breach of biblical teaching. In today's climate, let us recall, ethical purity identifies sex and gender related issues as the most pressing. Although it is not readily possible or even fair to associate opposition to homosexual practices and abortion with the strong stand against female ordination and the wife's "equality," it can hardly be gainsaid that these stances are derived from common and fundamental concerns. Other implications of ethical and doctrinal purity exist, but none is so striking as the roles of women in church and home.

Developments in Other Denominations

The immediate reference point of much of the preceding analysis is the Southern Baptists. That, I believe, is a warranted focus, considering that body's size and influence in the regional culture, as well as the decisive and dramatic changes wrought in it by the fundamentalist takeover or takeback. This denomination does pay a price for being so visible, so influential. Its lot leads so naturally to the necessity of being responsive to whatever big is occurring in the society. There is a sense in which it is "damned if it does and damned if it doesn't." In this regard nothing has altered the condition I wrote about in 1966, that an inherently sect-like tradition has acquired a church-like responsibility.

Because I want to avoid repeating the fallacy of misplaced concreteness that weakened the 1966 study, however, I acknowledge that the South's "mainstream" is enlarged, now including independent churches and many standing in the Holiness and Pentecostal traditions, one or both. In the independent movements, the concern has always been with the rationalist issues: correct belief, doctrinal purity. Indeed, they exist in order to provide the true way in a society that has ample opportunity to pursue deviant ways—including those of the Southern Baptists, the Churches of Christ, and other fundamentalisms. One wonders what changes to expect from and in them, their numbers and availability, in view of the rightward drift of the older and very large evangelical bodies. Perhaps not much since some social class and society-perspectival divergences come between them and those communions. Little likelihood exists that the larger bodies will swallow them up.

As for the Presbyterian family, for a long time its largest company has been oriented toward biblical meaning and theology authenticity. Yet it has stopped short of extending that disposition to a thoroughgoing rationalism. Spirit as well as Word in the Calvinist diad of "Word and Spirit" has helped diffuse any strict allegiance it might have paid to rationalism. So its preaching and teaching have manifested mystery and irony; moreover it has been more energetic with its own preaching and practice than given to exposing the fallacies of others.

The historic regional body, known so long as the southern Presbyterian church, has lived with considerable tension. Then in 1973 that tension erupted into conflict, resulting in a painful separation and the official formation of a new body, the Presbyterian Church in America (PCA). More factors than sound doctrine precipitated this crisis; most notably the proposed merger between the southern church and the more liberal northern body, a merger that occurred in 1983. Offering that explanation does not contest the PCA's defining commitment to rationalism, however.

Dissimilar as they are, the Southern Baptists, the PCA Presbyterians, and the independent movements all embrace rationalism. That for many, especially the Baptists and the "mainline" Presbyterians, spells a major transformation. Their internal life is not the same; their place in the society has been rendered a less-comfortable fit.

The "Southern Religious Situation"

Regarding the southern "religious situation": one cannot speak of it with a very confident univocality in the late 1990s. This observer may have done so a bit too robustly in 1966. Yet the temptation was present then where none invites now. And, if so permitted, I offer the view that much about that analysis was valid. An old regional tradition and condition were ending; perhaps it took the transformation to make visible what had been so long the South's religious-cultural way. That ending has come; the 1980s and 1990s have ushered in a new day.

Even those who have not doubted that the South is a distinct regional culture, contending that there really is "a South," have to grant that a small semblance of normative patterns now exists. Some real distinctiveness persists, I believe, mostly as function of the region's history, but the declaration of "a southern" anything misses the mark of reality. (Or even a few southern anythings.)

The old ascription does not work very well any longer. The primary cause of today's condition is that rationalism has replaced experientialism, as we have been noting, within the religious communities on their own terms. Of course many "external" factors have contributed to this change, even down to the shapes that rationalism has taken. We will have to wait to see what this seismic shift does to the category of religious experience, and most tellingly to the coexistence of the thinking and feeling religious person. It is worth noting that in the past the South has not negotiated gracefully the presence of two or more imperatives or sensibilities, inclining more readily to serial thinking and a single imperative.

The New Political Ethic

Further complicating (and also clarifying) this revolution is the ethical picture we have glanced at earlier. That is, southern religious conservatism has joined forces with kin national movements to set aside the old "finger sins" line, a list of do's and don'ts incumbent on the pious person, with "no alcohol" at the head of the list, all of this in favor of family, gender, and sexuality related issues. The question of which is more salient, the new list or the fact of joining forces with broader causes and movements, is unanswerable. The same must be said of determining which came first, the national concern to address these issues or the act of making a bond with "outside" movements. Obviously, this development is connected to the nation's political life.

The political shift in the South's public life is one of the top stories of the last two quarters of twentieth-century America. The shift is now so complete—a huge percentage of southern white people are registered Republicans—and of such duration—a third of a century—that we may take too lightly the conversion from one kind of solid South to its opposite. Overwhelmingly committed to the Democratic Party from Reconstruction to the 1960s, the *white* South is now the single most solid region within the national Republican Party. What has caused this is far less straightforward than the effect it has wrought. Deeply pertinent, however, is what characterizes the attraction and affiliation. Part of it is conservative economic orientation, a preference for state and local management of public affairs over federal, centralized policy formation. The South's "political culture" is a major factor. Probably more so in the South than elsewhere in the nation, politics follows the contours of the culture. That culture sets limits on what is acceptable. History thus contributes to this powerful force, but its effect must not be allowed to diminish the impact of the moral vision established by the churches.

Directly related to the issues being raised in this essay is the palpable moral passion and agenda that has its home base in the GOP. Addressing and arresting the nation's moral decay is their preeminent calling. Atop that crusade are sex and gender related issues. Now it is time to examine the context of vigorous, zealous opposition to abortion, homosexual practice (especially social approval of it), sexual promiscuity, and the wholesale breakup of families. Beneath these concrete sinful practices lies the philosophy of relativism; that is the real enemy.

"Addressing and arresting the nation's moral decay" summarizes the agenda for which there is such zeal and determination. Since it is the national Republican Party that takes up this agenda, that party provides a hospitable environment. (The Democratic Party does not: its preoccupations are with freedom, provision of resources for the disadvantaged, and human rights, that is, more with civil matters than with items of personal morality or with economic issues.) How central these concerns would have been on the national party's agenda without southerners' participation and leadership makes for an intriguing question. The region's seeing hopes in the GOP and enrolling there has gone very far to make the party what it is; that much is indisputable. Alongside the famous southern political roster of Gingrich, Lott, Armey, Helms, and others is the region's ethical vanguard of Pat Robertson, Jerry Falwell, Gary Bauer, Ralph Reed, and more. The Republican Party looked inviting, so to say, and the southerners who entered its door have done much to bring about the realization of these ethical goals.

I continue to be struck by the South's apparent attraction to what we might call political "totalism," with such a high percentage of its white population earlier in one party and lately in the other. This curious phenomenon is not the result of the deliberate pursuit of an agenda that includes keeping all white Southerners allied to the same party; the matter is not so rational as that! Still it is perplexing that "all" were Democratic for a century, then "all" became Republican so rapidly. Could it be that there really still is "a South," this political datum the living proof of it? Just how different was the old southern Democratic perspective from that of the GOP of the recent South? Many analyses of this phenomenon have noted that the Republican Party's ascendancy in the region was concurrent with the racial revolution that altered traditional southern ways; historical observation teases us toward that conclusion. But it is quite unfair to charge the GOP with crassly exploiting the dominant issue of that era, also to branding it a racist party.

Over the ninety or so years of the Democratic Party's being home for the region's (white) people, both personal and social moral issues were recessive as matters of public political concern. This national affiliation did not function in such a way as to draw out the moral instincts of that population. Even if it had offered incubation for any such occurrence, sons and daughters of Dixie probably would not have participated. Their notion of what morality is and what political responsibility entails did not feature a focused, intense interest in "legislating morality" and using laws to root out sources of moral decay. Southern morality concerned itself with local matters, with personal and interpersonal issues far more than with public and social ethics. Electing "good people" to office exemplified the dominant view of what Christians should do to express their faith in action.

By the 1960s everything was changing. The party of moral conservatism had become the primary agent of social ethics. (It is fascinating to see that the Social Gospel of the early twentieth century had arisen from liberal ranks, by contrast with today's social-ethics cause that locates the root of evil within individuals and not, as with the liberal tradition, in various social constructions.) We cannot be sure how deeply and for how long this ethical crusade will register heavy impact on the society at large. But there is no questioning several things about the South's influence on the Republican Party, and even more significantly, that the whole sense of Christian public responsibility has acquired a new countenance in the southern region. Electing "good people" to office persists as an aim, but the term no longer carries a passive meaning. From its former meaning of "honest, godfearing, considerate of the constituency," it has come to refer to active, aggressive, issue-focused, ideological, uncompromising zealousness. Purity is, here also, the characteristic quality.

This is further borne out by recent political studies showing that a much larger percentage of clergy in the South are actively involved in politics and public moral causes than historically has been the case; and they are far likelier to preach on these topics and encourage their parishioners to take sides in elections. For a long time their public postures were generally apolitical, perhaps reflecting the tradition of "church-state separation," so strong in the Baptist tradition especially.

Purity and Other Virtues

In two different arenas, in two distinctive forms, *purity* has become watchword, battle cry, and operative criterion for the conservative movement within southern Christian life. Its rationalist application governs the arena of belief, doctrine, preaching and teaching. In the ethical sphere, its delineation clarifies the behavior that defines the society so badly in need of redemption from the grip of moral decay. The quality of purity is upheld as the surpassing Christian spirit and goal; even though a specified list of evils, and not all human transgressions, demand attention. To state the matter that way is to highlight the strengths and potential pitfalls of choosing that, or any single, ethical style as the one road on which Christians are called to walk, never to detour.

Purity is not the sole Christian virtue; it is not even incontestably the highest virtue or ambition. For the Christian mode of living also entails *risk*. The pursuit of purity makes it difficult to envision involvement with other persons, and it forces action—as premium Christian virtues—resulting in the life of risk. Perhaps we can state the matter this way: while you are safeguarding purity, what are you not doing? Purity is predicated on selection, acknowledging that some courses of behavior are totalistic in their claims upon you. Presumably there are other worthy interests; they must be set aside because they stand outside the circle of purity. One must select out all that other in the interest of sole, intense devotion to what is supremely, seemingly exclusively, important. Rightly so, from the perspective of purity. Limitation of concern and energy to what is indispensably important follows from the very nature of the commitment to purity.

In the setting of the recent southern religious revolution, this limitation of concern and energy has concrete implications. In the ethical sphere it means that Christians are careful about whom they associate with. One does not get involved with people who are misguided or flagrantly evil in their ethical practices. If one does consort with "pro-choice" people on the issue of abortion, for example, it is to convince them of their errant ways. If you do interact with homosexual men and women, you do so to show them how transgressive their ways are. Such ways of relating to the disobedient preempt any notion of unconditional love. The righteous have nothing to learn from the transgressors on any score, nothing to give to them except redemption from the particular wrong attribute that is taken to define just who they are. They are indeed defined by one aspect of their complex beings, whatever other qualities they may possess.

Here we are witnessing an expression of another moral law, the "truth over persons" philosophy; that is, treating the tenacious commitment to the truth as more constitutive of Christian character than unconditional love of all persons. Absolute adherence to truth, in this case, ethical propriety, supersedes acknowledging their worth as the persons they are in and of themselves. Risking giving to them and learning from them is not a defensible option. In these moral cases at least, how people behave is what defines them; there is nothing to talk about except their perversity on paramount ethical issues. Nor is this point gainsaid by the well-meant maxim, "love the sinner and hate the sin," commonly heard in sermons.

A comparable pattern exists in the rationalist arena. People whose positions are manifestly in error are to be shunned, or condemned, or converted. To engage in dialogue would be a compromise, and nothing besmirches the purity of the truth like compromise. Indeed when purity is the goal and commitment, the ultimate sin is compromise. Again, the pure in thought have nothing to learn from the impure, nothing to give except rectification of perverse positions and the people who hold them. As with the ethical application of purity, risk has no merit at all.

Both uses of purity concede nothing, never grant any possibility of error. All positions are nonnegotiable. Furthermore, irony is an inadmissible category. Perfect correspondence links the truth and the purist's reception. This is because the God who "thinks" the absolute truth and true virtue deals in rational categories. His ways with his human creations are apodictic, rather than personal, dramatic, and historical. No wonder biblical revelation may be trusted in the same way, as definitively rational, rather than personal, dramatic, and historical by nature. The Bible is treated as a virtual extension of divinity, as "pure" as the God revealed in it.

Orthodox doctrine then is the distillation of a perfect rationalism into pure, unexceptionable units of truth. Also, then, we are not surprised by the conclusion drawn that interpretation amounts to human tampering with self-evident and self-justifying revelation. Expressions like the following ones capture the intent of this approach. "Just take the Bible for what it says." "Let it disclose its own message." "Our great God would not leave us to wallow in such uncertainty as human interpretation." "There is no need to equivocate when God has spoken univocally."

Recapitulation of 1960s and 1990s Analyses

Now let us step back from this excursus into today's prevailing pattern of thinking to gain fresh perspective on what we are doing in an essay meant to bring up to date major forces and changes in the church life of the South. The 1966 book *Southern Churches in Crisis* offered the view that the churches were indeed in crisis, in large measure because their message, the governing popular theology, was an inadequate and uncompelling presentation of the Christian message. What I identified as its myopia or its misdirection had to do with some assumptions that missed the power and authenticity of the classic Christian tradition, of historic orthodoxy.

I concluded that the heart of that misdirection lay in the nature of

revivalistic Evangelicalism. This popular theology had become so intent on the personal redemption of all that it misrepresented the full,
grand, many-splendored Christian message by exalting one part of
the message and making it the whole. Bringing every person to a conversion experience had become the preoccupation of that theology.
Much else was left out of that comprehensive message or subordi-
nated in importance, with the result that the wide range of Christian
meaning and responsibility was compromised. The particularly serious consequence of that perspective in the 1960s, of course, was lack
of commitment to the ethic of racial justice.

A major aim of that tract for those times was to delineate the theology of the conversion experience as practiced by the southern
churches, the anatomy of revivalistic Evangelicalism. Succinctly stated,
it pictured reality as the relation between the one God and each individual. All other dimensions of reality were tangential to that single
one-to-one relation. The person was defined by his or her sinfulness
against the righteous and demanding God. Until the matter of straight-
ening out that relation by making it into a relationship was accomplished, the person was lost, condemned, and lacking what every person was created for, to know and love this demanding but pardoning
God. I sought to make it clear that ethics was secondary in importance, as was the affirmation of and care for the physical universe and
all other aspects of life in the cosmos. Once conversion happened, the
saved one was expected to practice a devout life, to be sure. But the
churches' central task was to bring about the conversion experience. A
single concern and goal had become the central message and the dominant feature in the agenda.

The situation in the 1990s is significantly different. We have noted
that the crisis of this era is a crisis within the churches; that is, what
the churches are riveted upon has to do directly with their own integrity, their own performance of their responsibilities under their God,
with cleaning themselves up by means of reclaiming purity in belief
and message. They are hardly unmindful of the surrounding society
and believe devoutly that righting themselves will afford major and
redemptive guidance to a world that has gone astray. Nevertheless,
their direct, explicit, urgent work is internal, returning to the orthodox teachings that are revealed in the infallible Bible.

So intent are they on achieving that goal that they disown many who have been their fellow members but who refuse to repent their erroneous beliefs and teachings and come around to subscribing to truth. They are obligated to check credentials at the door. Anyone not foursquare in matters of doctrine is excluded, unless and until, of course, they see the light and reassert faithfulness in proper believing. No other qualities suffice, not even a manifest spirit of love for God, neighbor, and the church. One test must be and is imposed upon all.

The society within which these rational-truth-minded believers live does not recognize that this mission has anything to do with the world outside the church enclaves. These churches' efforts are seen as truly parochial, even as narcissistic. Accordingly, the people who are outside their ranks, including many other Christian worshipers, are increasingly alienated from them, dismiss them, and see no reason to regard what they are and stand for as magnet to personal involvement with them or resource for social concerns. That is an inevitable byproduct of commitment to purity; devotion to this quality makes a group self-reflexive. Not running risks, it renders itself invulnerable. Outsiders are not accepted for what they are or for what they might have to give, but for their concurrence, or not, in what the dominant group prescribes. Purity, thus, cuts a deep divide between those who are pure and all others. It is one thing to be snubbed or found unwelcome, quite another to be defined by your errors and required to rectify.

Comparing the attitudes and behavior of the churches in the 1960s and the 1990s is instructive. In part to present this entails only a summary of interpretations just presented. But there is an important more, soon to be considered. To summarize, first: In the tumultuous years of the civil rights struggle, the churches were reaching out, involving themselves in the lives of people outside their membership. Their overtures were to individuals, men and women in need of hearing the Christian message of personal salvation. Thus they were stepping outside their own ranks, totally committed to winning the world for Christ. Any group that enlarges its community of course takes a chance of altering itself through newness, of persons, ideas, and behavior. At the same time, those churches were not much involved in social ethical matters, most notably the cause of racial justice, not even in organized measures to oppose the changes being brought about. But their perspective on the world did transcend their own rolls.

The major agenda of recent years has been different in both substance and implications. It has been rationalist, insisting on absolute adherence to absolute truth. The traditional concern to convert individuals to faith in Christ remains important, but the movement's primary energy has gone elsewhere. Purity of belief is not only the movement's driving force but, being more certifiable, is also what it is known for. Taking chances, running risks, is not its style. The consequence is that if you are alien to the perspective demanded, you are alienated from the message and those who deliver it. Thus the southern Christian movement is less known for its participation in the life of the society in general and more often thought of as a self-contained community.

Continuity between the 1960s and the 1990s

We return now to the "important more" mentioned above, a feature that may startle us into realizing how little things have changed while they were changing very much. Despite the divergences between the two concerns, a remarkable continuity binds the revivalistic Evangelicalism of the earlier period with the doctrinal rationalism of recent developments: the conviction that everything about the churches' message and mission is supernatural. No human logic, no commonsense reasoning, no amount of perceptive observation serves as the means by which God is known or, it follows, his truth and his salvation are received. The theology that informs these claims has no time for flirtation with naturalistic philosophies. An unyielding dualistic cosmology underlies this worldview. In one way or another worshipers hear it made clear that "nothing that is possible can save us," nothing can rival or suffice for the revelation of God's truth.

Such a radical and consistent supernaturalistic worldview has become less and less common among other branches of the Christian community in the post-Enlightenment era. That contrasts sharply with the explicitness with which this conviction is held and asserted in the South.

Surely the intention of the Lutheran denomination and the Calvinist (Presbyterian and Reformed) bodies has always been to affirm exactly this same conviction. Yet the practical ways in which this is done diverge. Among the southern popular churches, notably the

Southern Baptists, the force of supernatural revelation makes for a different response; single-mindedness and explicitness are its hallmarks. When the revivalist strain is operative, the uncompromising message is that every person is lost, in absolute need of redemption, and that no amount of human achievement or effort is sufficient. Only through the miracle of conversion is there any relationship with the Almighty. One is either lost or saved. In the rationalist case, there is to be no questioning of the truth of doctrines, no challenging of the infallible authority of the inerrant Bible. "Miracle" applies here too, referring to the fact and nature of the divine revelation of the truth.

The distinguishing "practical consequences" produce identifiable expectations and motivations. They make for a degree of certainty that means that the truth is complete, in fullness and accuracy, and that the experience of conversion is the defining moment of a person's life, standing as a kind of microcosmic B.C. and A.D. It is the highly explicit presentation of these conditions and the assurance that they are genuine that sets off this way of thinking from apparently related positions such as those held by Lutherans and Calvinists. With those two communions there is a certain modesty of pronouncement, a greater confidence in the need to be faithful in so speaking and acting than in certainty that the resultant ends have been fully realized. Such Christians believe and proclaim the message without calling attention to how adequately they have presented it. Similarly they trust that they are forgiven and embraced by the Lord without dwelling on their personal conversion.

Stated simply, such Christians as the Lutherans and the Calvinists *trust* for sure, whereas the southern Christians described here *know* for sure. In a different vein, those classical Protestant communions honor the irony of a radical particularity that does not result in an exclusivist theology or spirit.

Still another consequence arises from such "knowing for sure," one that in some respects is altogether admirable. Namely, the kind of urgency demonstrated by those so conditioned. If you believe for sure in the full veracity of a text, then you declare its veracity with vigor and zeal. If you are certain of the necessity and reality of conversion, then you live with an urgency toward being instrumental in the conversion of all. It is this kind of intensity expressed so explicitly that catches people off guard, including many fellow Christians; and this kind of intensity is the reason that many people consider the South a truly distinctive religious region. Incidentally, this same quality is often manifested in the sacrificial life-style of southern deeply devout Christians.

Equitable thinking does not permit presenting these Evangelicals as more orthodox than classical Protestants, or as more trustful of the divine grace and forgiveness than Luther, Calvin, Karl Barth, Richard Niebuhr, and other stalwarts of the faith. But from the outside it is tempting to view them that way, to assess their explicitness as indicative of a whole region of "born-again Christians." The absence of a critical spirit also contributes to this perception. Niebuhr's theme of the "Protestant principle" sheds some light on how these Evangelicals differ: nothing in our history can be absolute; an uncritical outlook always tempts toward idolatry. Purity, in this sense, is a perilous goal, even when the motives are the highest.

Thus, ironically, "absolute" is not a univocal or pure term, nor is authority, or trust or commitment to the sovereign God of love. To grasp the nature of the kind(s) of purity sought for and claimed by these southern movements, we understand better through comparing their positions with classic Protestant orthodoxy than by contrasting them with modernism and liberalism.

This description of the popular form of revivalistic Evangelicalism that I offered in 1966 and have reiterated here does not pertain to everyone in the revivalism-oriented denominations—a truism that almost goes without saying, in view of the size and diversity of that family, especially the Southern Baptists. I mention two sectors of that company that pursue a quite different course. One is those ministers and laypeople whose theology is guided by a sense of God's presence in their lives and in the world, but who do so without being fixed on the issue of who is saved and who is not. They are better classified as spirituality-oriented or service-minded than as conversionist. A different agenda beckons them to faithfulness. In the eyes of the evangelistic and fundamentalist parties these colleagues are heretical; "liberal" is the epithet attached to them. It is true that by and large these church men and women do not measure authenticity by either of the two standards in widespread use in the churches, a person's conversion experience, or absolute devotion to sound doctrine. This sector is most often found in the upper seaboard South, as is the other, for that matter.

That smaller fellowship stands closer to classical Protestantism, inasmuch as it builds its message around the "scandal of particularity." Although they do not use "liberal" to characterize the dominant conversionist and rationalist parties, that term comes close to capturing their digression from historical orthodoxy. This is held to be especially true in their fastening onto one or two teachings (personal salvation or correct belief) to the diminution of a correlative and comprehensive honoring of the revealed faith as a many-splendored reality.

The powerful and pervasive changes that we have been describing make for a different religious setting than I sought to examine in the 1960s; with, of course, the exception of the continuance of a straightforward and uncritical supernaturalism. The hold of that conviction has not weakened at all; the only decisive change has come with its shift in emphasis from the experiential to the rational. Notwithstanding this continuity, the lineaments of the southern religious scene look sharply different today.

The Discontinuities

Curiously, one major change is implied in the shift in emphasis from the experiential to the rational; namely, that proper belief has to be insisted upon, virtually enforced. For so long there was such little deviation from the orthodox line that only minor brush fires had to be dealt with. A small number of liberals were around, as well as a handful of ethical radicals. But these people all but isolated themselves by appearing so strange and out of line alongside a remarkable unanimity of belief. And what has happened in the past twenty or so years does not bespeak much growth in the ranks of either liberals or radicals. There is little more "liberalism" represented by the seminary faculties; critical study of the Bible and of theology has marked the work of those teachers for many decades.

The new departure seems to arise from three factors. The first is the churches' loss of unrivaled, taken-for-granted dominance in regional life. Secularism and diversity of peoples and positions have become commonplace; the old evangelistic message is not any longer "what every schoolboy knows." The rise of truly urban centers and the in-migration of nonsoutherners have helped to take care of that.

The second factor that has generated the crusade to preserve or recover the old alliance between the culture and the religion that was one major part of the culture is the dissipation of homogeneity. Ironically, the upsetters of that stable condition of things often turn out to be fellow Christians, indeed fellow conservatives. In other words, the old "big three," or the "Baptist-Methodist hegemony"—include the Presbyterians in the first reference—are no longer dominant. Still very strong, still found everywhere, they now share influence with the Pentecostal denominations, northern (or more classic) evangelical forms of Protestant life, and other "sects" like the Churches of Christ, all of which have long been present but lacked cultural power. In fact it is the loss of that power and influence that has altered the context that was "owned" by the Baptists, Methodists, and Presbyterians for so long. The South, which the dominant evangelical churches knew and helped shape, is no more. Doing deference to the churches and their message is not a near-universal condition as it used to be.

I judge the crusade to recover and preserve orthodoxy to be impelled more by the churches' diminished hold on the culture than by the rise of liberal beliefs. After all, the strengthening of orthodoxy is largely a result of the desire to guarantee that future ministers will be "in line" or "all right," as it is sometimes expressed in the South. The missions to excise heresy have little to with the culture, except indirectly, and mostly to do with the restoration of the authenticity of the denominations. They are losing some ground in the battle for people's loyalty and primary self-identification. And it is eminently clear that the uncontested hold of the evangelical churches and that perspective on the regional culture has been broken. The South is neither theirs by right, as it were, nor for the taking any longer.

Incidentally, concerning the Southern Baptist warfare, I personally take the view that ideology was what was at stake; it was not at root a power struggle within the body itself. The true enemy is the changing world all around them. The denominational fundamentalists' way of defeating it is to reinstate the straight line of believing and behaving that once nurtured a godly society so healthfully. Thus, the restoring of orthodoxy, paralleled by combating liberalism, is itself a way of practicing a social ethic. Perhaps the worst potential outcome of these decades of contest would be that the culture proved to be unrecoverable. (If that were to happen, at least the churches would not be open to the charge of selling their souls to secularism and liberalism.)

I surmise that the new Fundamentalism in the South amounts, in part, to a cry of the heart for the loss of the bond that for so long linked evangelical Christianity to the culture. The South has had to surrender many of its accustomed ways in the past half century. Many of them needed removing, most citizens would now agree. But acknowledging that condition does not make change any easier. Moreover, the excision of some of the traditional ways and forms is lamentable, to say the least. Religion and the culture need each other as much as ever. A campaign to restore their coexistence is worthy of endless efforts.

The churches have become concerned that the integrity of the faith is severely threatened. Holding the line against such incursions is a God-called duty. Subversions that have crept into the culture present the necessity of a battle as if to the death. The churches may find themselves pushed to a more sect-like stance, that is, set over against the culture; that would be a novel occurrence (at least since the early days of Evangelicalism in the first years of the nineteenth century). I∏n any event, the former "cultural fit" is being challenged. What will replace it is something only time will tell.

Responses to the Changes

Responses to the religious battles of recent decades vary from great relief and joy for some to profoundly saddened hearts for others. Southern people are hardly strangers to civil strife. Yet these denominational and theological wars have left permanent scars on southern Baptists and Presbyterians, and many thousands of others share the pain. Feelings run high, sensitivity is acute.

Recent conversations with ministers have offered me some insight into this poignant condition by illuminating how different the religious frontline concerns are now from when I was trying to penetrate the situation in another pain-wracked era, the 1960s. Then the progressives who were in distress yearned for liberation toward fresh forms of worship, more critical and applicable styles of reading Scripture and doing theology, an enlarged sphere for conducting the godly life, racial issues and more, and less denominational and regional self-consciousness.

Standing on the cutting edge now means something quite different: resisting alien forces, holding more firmly to the ancient faith, and mounting crusades against indulgent living and relativistic standards. Listening to the leaders who sought to address what was wrong in that earlier critical period, and observing those who are doing the same now under greatly altered circumstances, touches the heart. This is true despite the two visions of the churches' urgent calling having much in common; both are reformist; each has been "relevant" and "progressive."

Another dimension to the poignant response of the earlier leaders who find themselves out of step, their counsel sought infrequently, the bearers of good news that seems to have so few takers today, is the direction in which denomination-switchers and church-changers are now moving; it is from left or center to right (whether near or far). They are apt to be responsive to more authority-minded contexts, or to more high-intensity and expressive Spirit movements. What they seek is not "liberation" but "groundedness," certainty of truth and/or certainty of the Lord's nearness and inspiration. Not at all necessarily reactive, they affirm the sturdy, the sure, the defined, the focused; and/or the sure and palpable presence of God intimately known. Theirs is a generation that reckons that the culture, the everyday surroundings and even the "oldline churches," do not provide the true message or nourish the life of faith. They are drawn to the right-thinking and expressively devout congregations where the reality and truth of God are demonstratively presented.

I mention one other source of sadness and bewilderment affecting those still ministering, whose halcyon days of ethical dedication existed a short quarter of a century ago. It is their seeming abandonment by the black leaders with whom they developed such strong bonds and alongside whom they worked so courageously. Still possessing shared memories, the black church clergy and laity of the fifties and sixties are preoccupied with their own religious and social agendas, and the white leaders have to be satisfied with their diminished roles. "Abandonment" is not what is intended, and gratitude across color lines persists. But the scenes of action are different, and those once wed in a common cause are apt to see very little of each other. My, but times have changed; the excitement of public involvement has been replaced by distinctive spheres and tamer causes.

To be sure, far from all who are seeking personal faith and a church setting are described along these lines. But this is the arena that is so dynamic, the locus of so much activist spirit—"where it's at." Moreover such yearning to find the "real thing" may occasion changing congregations and not denominations. For example, a number of Methodist and Episcopal churches, even some in the Churches of Christ brotherhood, bear similarity to the dynamic and high-intensity denominations referred to. Thus a person or family may simply turn to another unit in the home tradition for tapping into greater certainty or expressiveness. There may be as much congregation-switching today as there is denomination-switching.

Rapprochement?

Whether there is any genuine chance that these two frameworks, the evangelical and the liberal (neither term is quite suitable), can progress toward each other is, in human and Christian terms, an insistent question facing both groups today. That issue joins the much older matter of black southerners and white southerners progressing toward each other. The South may not always be in crisis but bringing all its people together in reconciliation, justice, and mutual concern perdures as a mandate for the well-being of each person and the entire society. The recent overt strife may be more religious-cultural than racial-cultural, but strife is still a feature of regional life.

Some of us have been remarking for many years that the study of religion in the American South is endlessly fascinating. Nothing has happened to alter that assessment or to diminish the significance of the interaction of religion and culture in that storied region. Human and cultural well-being are at stake, therefore the stakes are very high.

Introduction

The South today is in crisis. For a surprisingly long time it was able to retain its accustomed ways, while the world about it underwent radical change; now it finds itself beset by ideas, social forces, and human groups which cannot be prevented from altering regional folkways. This will doubtless be true of every aspect, feature, and dimension of life in the South, for the whole culture is experiencing the dynamic impact of the revolution in progress.

Inevitably, the southern churches are caught up in the modifications now taking their toll of entrenched attitudes and practices. Long noted for the intensity of their religious concern, the southern people are facing novel conditions and challenges which threaten to play havoc with their traditional religious modes. Whatever happens to particular individuals and groups—

no doubt some will follow a reactionary course, while others reject Christianity outright because of the way it has been represented to them—the health of the society is intimately tied to developments in its religious life. Indeed, it is unlikely that developments in any other phase of southern experience will have more telling effects upon the stability and creativity of the nascent culture.

Since the nation's well-being is significantly influenced by its southern section, what goes on in southern churches during this turbulent era is of the greatest importance to the United States as a whole. One of the two major purposes of this book is to examine the quality and potential of "popular southern religion"—a peculiar variety of evangelical Protestantism which has not flourished anywhere else in Christendom over a long period—with an eye for ascertaining its effect upon the South during transition and beyond. Because religion's role is so basic in southern society, the entire region's maturation will be closely related to the prevailing state of religious affairs. Whether the burden of studying the religious factor falls upon "secular" or ecclesiastical agents, the task must be undertaken for the sake of that maturation.

The second and more explicit of the book's two major purposes is an analysis of the southern religious situation in the interest of the churches themselves, predicated on the observation that a grave crisis is upon them. A diagnosis of their illness is clearly a precondition of Christianity's regaining its relevance for those to whom it seeks to minister. Through the use of historical and sociological tools, this study endeavors to provide the church with a richer and more authentic vision of itself and its mission.

As a first step toward fulfilling these purposes, an overview of the relation between southern religious history and the social revolution currently under way is presented. Here it is suggested that regional faith and culture have long been harmonious, with each adapting to and influencing the other, but that a formidable wedge is being driven between the two in the present era. As a consequence of this disruption, the validity of the old religious formulations and approaches is being called into question. The future may well seem ominous to a conservative and culturally pampered institution as it confronts a new social order and climate of opinion.

Next, an effort is made to account for the unique character of southern religious patterns. Analysts and participants alike have noted the divergence of the region's religious ways from those common to other sectors of Christendom, including other sections of America. Part I tries to isolate the standard form of regional religion with reference to what it regards as ultimately important and what traits mark it as a distinctive religious subculture. The terms "fundamentalism" and "revivalism"—not one but an intriguing medley of the two—are cited as most fully descriptive of popular regional religion—the latter "softening" and controlling the former toward the all-consuming goal of evangelizing the "lost" without compromising its doctrinal selectivity and rigidity.

The religious history of the Colonial period is scanned and found to be surprisingly unimpressive, until, that is, the eruption of the southern phase of the Great Awakening among the Presbyterians in the 1740's, followed by conflagrations of Baptist and Methodist zeal in the decades before the Revolution. The spectacular growth in membership and influence of evangelical Protestantism is traced, and the central formative influences in the creation of a distinctively regional religious syndrome—the frontier situation, a rural style of life, and cultural insulation are examined.

In Part II, the determining principles and attitudes of popular southern religion are reviewed and classified as resembling evangelical Protestantism on both its theological and ethical sides. The central theme of the regional churches is found to be the mandate to convert the lost from a state of guilt before God the Righteous Judge in a datable experience of salvation. The message disseminated to all who will hear is that forensic pardon from guilt and its consequences after death is granted to those who trust Christ, and the hearers are assured that the knowledge of sins forgiven is direct and sure, this doctrine of assurance being the touchstone of southern Evangelicalism.

Accordingly, all programs and value-preferences are seen to be oriented to the evangelistic objective and its ethical corollary, purity of private morality. Such a position has obvious effects on such matters as scripture study, modes of worship, the emphasis on personal testimonies of conversion, and the low priority assigned to theological education.

The apparent indifference of regional religious groups toward the current civil rights struggle in the South is found to be consistent with the general evangelical stance, which simply does not view responsibility toward God or man in the light of a social ethic. The white Christian's duty toward the Negro, as seen by the southern church, is to convert him and befriend him (in a paternal framework), not to consider altering the social traditions and arrangements which govern his (and everyone else's) life to so significant a degree.

Part III, entitled "Classification of Popular Southern Protestantism," treats the object of our study from the perspective of historical Christian developments and the church-sect typology in sociological theory. These kinds of analysis are necessary if sense is to be made of the peculiar course regional religion has followed against the backdrop of historic Christian developments, especially for those nurtured in Christian things by the southern church and culture.

Historically, southern Protestantism is an interesting compound of medieval theological concerns and Reformation "solutions." Doctrinally, southern religion is revealed as consistently left wing, or radical, in terms of the historical Christian spectrum. This is true of such important considerations as the nature of the church and the proper form of church government, its position on the relation between the divine sovereignty and human free will, its attitude toward change, and its conviction that it approximates the New Testament church in doctrine and practice.

Although it is widely agreed that the church-sect typology has very limited value as applied to the American religious scene at large, this device has continuing usefulness for perceiving the role of religion in the South. For there is a revealing contradiction between the long-held sectarian intentions which led the major southern bodies to dissociate themselves from a secular culture deemed impure and their growing acceptance of that culture and, by now, their nearly complete identification with it. As a result, over the past several decades a significant tension has existed between role-intention and role-expectation, a feature which tells a great deal about the religious situation in the South.

Part IV attempts to interpret the confrontation between traditional religious patterns and the region's new social-cultural ethos. Owing to its prominence in the common life of the people, religion has served many functions, some very commendable, others less so, by Christian standards. On the positive side, church and faith have sustained, inspired, guided, and liberated. Millions have derived hope and direction from Christian ministry more than from any other source, and many have been encouraged vocationally and educationally by concerned church people.

After two centuries of being regarded as an integral and constructive element in southern life, however, popular religion today faces serious challenges. The religious leadership to date appears both ill equipped to cope with the challenges attendant upon social change, and impervious to the necessity of fundamental modifications. Increasing numbers of younger people are defecting from the church altogether, while others are leaving the popular churches in search of enriched Christian meaning in Episcopal and Presbyterian congregations. Educated, cosmopolitan, sensitive people find it hard to accept the simplism which prevails throughout the life of the popular churches—in biblical interpretation, in worship, in ethical theory and practice —both because they insist on a comprehensive truth-system and because they have intuited that the Christian faith is richer than it has been represented. Moreover, the church's message and ministry are discredited in their eyes by being so closely identified with such reactionary interests and values as the economic status quo, racial segregation, the prohibitionist cause, and rigidity of spirit vis-à-vis the separation of church and state.

The concluding chapter puts forward the far more serious charge that the southern church is failing grievously to undertake its divinely commissioned task. Although originally imbued with sectarian impulses, the southern churches have by their vast success earned for themselves the responsibility to be and do *all* that a dominant (church-type) religious body should in executing a comprehensive Christian ministry. In light of this responsibility, although they have done certain tasks well, they have left many others entirely unattended. Finally, an effort is made to pinpoint the realms of failure and suggest some avenues by which a subresponsible performance in the present can be exchanged for full-orbed, faithful, and relevant service.

The book is inevitably unbalanced because of one monumental omission: Negro Protestantism in the South is nowhere treated in depth. Grievous—or inexcusable—as this omission may seem, it is consistent with the religious state of things in Dixie. Although it would appear that "popular southern religion" includes the faith-life of southern Negroes—especially since a huge majority of them belong to the same two denominations that dominate the white culture—this is simply not the case. Negro and white religion *are* different, resisting meaningful comparison under the same categories. Competence in dealing with the religion of the white society does not insure facility in treating what Joseph Washington calls "black religion." The definitive work on the southern Negro church has not been written, and one suspects that only a southern Negro could produce it.

It is also regrettable that the Roman Catholic people and influence in the South have been excluded from consideration. A study of them and their role needs to be undertaken as well, but it will require special data and skills of interpretation, both falling outside the range of the present effort. For one thing, as more and more families move into the South from outside the region, Catholic growth undoubtedly can be expected—not to mention the increase resulting from magnetic witness and effective service. Already there are centers of Catholic strength, some of great duration, in the South. At present, however, the Catholic segment hardly deserves inclusion in a book on "popular southern religion."

Mention of these omissions leads us to conjecture that no single feature of the southern religious picture is more revealing than the absence of pluralism and diversity from the popular denominations—and to a large extent from the other white Protestant bodies also. It is the homogeneity of that picture which marks southern religious history as distinctive, and invites the critical stage in which the southern churches find themselves today.

Part i
The Distinctiveness
of the Southern
Religious Picture

1

The Changing South
and Regional Religion
An Overview

For a very long time now, the American South has been seeing certain of its basic folkways overturned and pressured into abrupt change, usually at the primary instigation of forces based outside the region. The dramatic uprooting of slavery, the region's "peculiar institution," is the ranking illustration of this point. It is intriguing to contemplate just when southern society might have gotten around to abolishing slavery had it been left to its own devices. Plausible arguments have been advanced that because the southern people had breathed in so much of the air of liberty, and because the tide of modern history was rising toward democracy, in time the South would have discarded this traditionally central economic and social dimension of its life.[1] The point is that when a *coup de grâce* was administered larger national forces were its agents.

Much the same can be said for other features of the accustomed regional way of life. For example, the introduction of economic industrialism after the Civil War, with its attendant social consequences, began to dislodge the older agrarian ways. Viewed from one angle, the social history of the South from the 1830's to the 1950's was a struggle between the kind of life desired by certain groups of Southerners and mounting national and global pressures to adjust regional ways to wider human patterns. As recently as 1930, twelve prominent intellectuals issued *I'll Take My Stand,* a forthright manifesto championing the retention of the South's traditional agrarianism in the face of industrialist incursions.

In history's long view, the most important development of the 1950's and 1960's may be that they relocated the sources fomenting change from outside the region to its own people. After being granted a decisive assist from the Supreme Court in 1954, southern Negro leaders, with help from some southern whites and northern-based civil rights organizations, set in motion the forces which are surely, and now not so deliberately, restructuring southern society.

Still in the embryo stage is the regional revolution in religion. Despite its limited visibility, its reality cannot be doubted by those in touch with the ferment on southern campuses today. Unlike the racial revolution, however, religious change is not being brought about by professional leadership in organizational high places, a fact that tells a good deal about the character of the movement. It belongs to the people, in part to a growing minority of younger ministers who have not (yet, at least) risen to key political positions in denominational life. But the greater impact is likely to come from the expanding proportion of lay membership which is becoming aware of the feasibility of alternative belief-systems. Thanks to the improved quality of public and higher education in the region, and to Southerners' more influential contacts with the wider world, a new generation is arising, the first ever to have anything of an ideological orientation. This has already meant the decline of sentiment and tradition as the norms of religion, and the demand for a comprehensive and coherent presentation of Christianity has intensified. Southern Protestantism, having restricted its concerns largely to the conversion of individuals, the cultivation of piety, and institutional expansion, is beginning to find itself painfully unprepared.

But in addition to problems in the realm of belief, social concerns now possess the "new breed." Southern eyes are being opened to the stark reality that issues bear directly upon the well-being of individuals and the society at large. Many are learning that life is solidaristic, that individuality and the social structures are intimately correlated in an interdependent society. Regional traditions, being rural, are seen to have less meaning in a society becoming urbanized, and laissez-faire theories of self-righting metaphysical powers are no longer self-evident. The church is being asked to come forward as healer and spokesman in the service of modulating explosive problems into constructive energies, but it is ill equipped for this role, because of its history and its reigning values.

This encounter with ideological and social revolution is something quite new for the church in the South. Until the 1960's, it has been part and parcel of the region's cultural horizon, indistinguishable in its personality from the other facets of southern life. Popular religion has been borne along on cultural tides, driven to few exacting self-evaluations concerning the character of its ministry to the people. Now suddenly, a vague sense that it is irrelevant, even irresponsible, threatens to undermine the church's good name and its key role in regional society.

In finding itself embroiled in crisis, the southern church mirrors the general regional situation in the 1960's. Change—dramatic, basic, overarching change—is today's ranking fact. Everywhere old moorings are breaking loose, deeply entrenched attitudes are being shaken, traditional patterns of social life are gradually giving way and being replaced by new.[2] Industrialization uproots people from farms and small towns and removes them to urban communities. The farms themselves become industries rather than family occupations, larger in size and more demanding in skill than ever before. Urbanization furthers competition and enthrones economic as against humanistic interests, thus modifying the manner of personal life, in some instances overwhelming men with loneliness and despair. Education stretches perspectives and calls into question cherished customs, beliefs, and ideals. Mobility brings "outsiders" into Dixie and paves highways for outmigration, resulting in a heightened awareness of other national subcultures.[3] Federal Government activities throw into closer contact on an increasingly level plane the white and Negro subcommunities which have been separated and graduated for so long. The catalog of disruptions is virtually endless.

So obvious is the massiveness of social change in the contemporary South that some interpreters are being duped into pronouncing the region's death. This pronouncement is not only premature, it is misguided. We may expect a continuation of many Old South customs and value-preferences.[4] It is scarcely imaginable that so distinct a regional identity could ever vanish entirely. Nor is it likely that American society has no place for distinctive subcultures within the total social framework.[5]

Nevertheless, the South cannot turn back. A beleaguered Mississippi cannot even consider secession. The adamant lawyer-governor of a "sovereign" commonwealth cannot block the law of the land as interpreted by a Supreme Court in substantial disagreement with his own canons. Desegregation of public facilities proceeds apace, symbolizing the demise of southern history's "central theme."

The central significance of the present upheaval is that the South is continually drawing closer to the national mainstream. More and more it identifies itself as one part of the national whole. Detachment is no longer a live option. Two very different currents in regional life demonstrate how true this is, the more dramatically because they amount to a coincidence of opposites. One is the way in which ever greater numbers of leaders devote themselves to hastening the process of reintegration and to making provision for a salutary transition. The other is the tenacity and furor surrounding the lingering resistance of some to social change, a pretty sure sign that its reality is already pressing in upon them. The matter is as simple as James McBride Dabbs's statement of it: the Southerner "daily . . . becomes more American." [6]

One result is that the South will be in a better position to make its distinctive contribution to the richness of national life. As historian C. Vann Woodward—and the Agrarians themselves in their own way—have argued convincingly, certain of the experiences and values ingredient to southern life can enrich national society.[7] On the other hand, southern mores will be tempered by the confrontation with other American subcultures. At many points the regional style of life will experience significant modification under the impact of these external cultural influences, some of which are almost as alien to the South's heritage as if they were imports from distant nations.

For the analysis of popular southern religion, the nature of the present study, a third consequence is the most important: southern traditions and institutions may now be viewed in the light of alternative positions, which implies, of course, that alternative positions possess intrinsic merit. As everyone knows, the southern region was isolated from the national mainstream to an important degree, from about 1830 until an astonishingly short while ago. During this century and a quarter, men of Dixie had little opportunity or incentive to compare their way of life with that of the rest of America. In the decades before the Civil War, for example, "thousands of Southern youths" attended northern colleges and medical schools, but did not "seem to have become more national minded or more liberal on the slavery question as a result of their Northern experience." [8] Even in the later years those merchants, students, and vacationers who did travel into the North apparently returned home without having been transformed themselves, or having developed a disposition to challenge the entrenched patterns of southern culture.

If self-understanding and the gift of self-transcendence are of the essence of social maturity, the South has only very recently come of age. Regional life has not wanted for scrutiny; it has been said that the American South is the most studied *region* in the world. Moreover, some of the nation's finest scholars have been sons of the region whose lifetime tasks have focused on elucidating this or that dimension of its heritage. The fruits of their labors, however, have been marshaled infrequently toward the goals of seeing the South, first, as one among many world cultures, second, in the light of norms which transcend any given empirical society, and, third, as the product of a multiplicity of socioeconomic factors. Generally, what reflecting on itself the society has done has been in terms of its own values, traditions, and norms. Scholars, novelists, and common people alike have tended to bring to their assessments of the homeland a poetic, as distinct from an analytic, turn of mind.[9] Partly because the poetic mode has been predominant, the South has described itself better than it has examined itself.[10] Neither well-educated regional residents nor their less cultivated fellows have possessed the habit of mind which prompts men to compare their heritage with that of others or to evaluate their own heritage's outlook and customs.

In other words, for the most part Southerners have viewed personal and social reality in line with the accepted outlook, attitudes and values deeply imbedded in the regional personality. A number have been able to describe the prevalent culture with sensitivity, but few have looked at it through bifocal lenses. Many more have known what the southern attitude to life is than have had perspective on where it came from, how it has survived, how it compares with others, and how well it is suited to serve a society already plunged into a new era.

Now, however, it is unmistakably clear that the South is coming of age. Charles G. Sellers can with integrity entitle his 1960 volume *The Southerner as American* and have reference to the present and future as well as pre-1830 history. Increasingly, regional life is marked by significant diversity—diversity of peoples, of means of livelihood, of priorities and social customs, of world views. Nothing delineates "the changing South" so graphically as the introduction of this all-permeating diversity. The South being born is distinguished from the Old South by its decisive interrelation with non-South America at such crucial points as self-understanding, basic social structures, and hetero-geneity.

The southern churches have sensed the cultural revolution and have done some changing of their own. Over the past 50 to 75 years, astonishing transformations have taken place in the appearance of church buildings, the structure of church organiza-tions, and the style of churchgoers. Most conspicuously, the operating methods of churches and denominations reflect acquaintance with up-to-date organizational techniques. On the surface there is much to suggest that the region's religious life is caught up in the same progressive movement which dominates regional life as a whole.

But what is this change from and toward what is it going? Essentially the break is with a past which has seen the South cut off from the rest of the American development. That a distinctive subculture should take shape in the South was dictated in part by the temper and motive of its beginnings, as contrasted with the origins of New England. Long before Eli Whitney's fateful invention of the cotton gin in 1793, and the emergent "nationalism" which began three decades or so before the Civil War, a South was coming into being. Greater depend-ence on Old World social traditions, a rural culture, an individ-ualistic and emotional style of life, the absence of a strong intellectual tradition, the lack of a large and influential middle class, the separation of religion into a level of life generally unrelated to the life of society in the large—these and still other factors helped to turn the South into a region apart.

Nevertheless, it was the controversy over slavery which afforded the first impetus to the crystallization of a vigorously self-contained and self-conscious sectional society. Before 1830 the South had its own patterns of life and its peculiar flavor, to be sure, but not at the expense of its being a part of America. The Southerner's primary identity was as American—that is, to the degree that he was aware of needing or having identity on a scale larger than that of family or immediate neighborhood. The contest over slavery changed all that decisively. Had the states south of the Potomac been willing to negotiate the future of the "peculiar institution," the sectional rupture might have been avoided. Instead, they developed an intransigence of spirit, marked both by an unflagging loyalty to a way of life (which was in many ways attractive), and by a mounting, near-pathological defensiveness.

From approximately 1830 forward, the Southerner knew full well who he was. The creation of a quasi-national entity, the Confederate States of America, only consummated the hardening process begun a third of a century previously. With defeat in The War and the ensuing period of Reconstruction, for the first time a self-conscious southern society was turned in upon itself. It did not champion any active cause, not even that of its own survival, contenting itself with such defensive objectives as the preservation and justification of its own heritage. Nor did it take pains to test the congruity between what it praised as a glorious past and the bald empirical facts of that past. A fictional southern sociology, asserting the superiority of the South, superseded responsible regional self-understanding.

The post-Civil War South stood as a culture unto itself, a way of life, a state of mind, a self-attitude. The slavery controversy had erected an almost insurmountable barrier between the old Confederate States plus two or three others, and America at large. Readmitted to the union, the South retained its alien identity. With remarkable tenacity and consistency, that identity transcended state boundaries and characterized an entire region. The new phrase "the Solid South" served as an apt description of a society bound most obviously by common political affiliation, but more tellingly by a shared memory and something of a mass personality.

Before the tragic War, the ostensible predication for drawing the boundaries of southern territory was slaveholding. Those states which permitted the practice were by that fact associated with the South. It is well known that much of mid-nineteenth century American history hinged about the conflict over expanding slaveholding territory, which, seen in one light, meant the expansion of southern culture. This fact is ironic inasmuch as less than one-third of southern whites actually owned slaves, most owning fewer than five; the vast majority were either non-slaveholding yeoman farmers or the radically dispossessed. To focus on the marrow of the issue: though the slavery question did set formally the boundaries of the South, the slaveholders' outlook was not really pervasive of the general society. Other values, practices, and outlooks were at least as characteristic of the pre-War southern society as slavery. And what was true in the ante-bellum period comprehended the South of the later 1800's and on into the current century.

Basic as the slavery factor was, together with its later corollaries and numerous implications, many other elements entered into the formation of the insulated South. Plainly, the political unity, which bordered on uniformity, flavored the southern personality. Similarly, the "agrarian style of life," a catch-all phrase encompassing the economy, family and community patterns, and a particular conception of civilization, penetrated regional life.

Many who have sought to understand the South have over-looked, or taken rather too lightly, the religious factor in its shaping and preservation. As stated earlier, southern society has been examined almost exhaustively from the standpoint of general history, politics, economics, sociology, and literature. Yet with few exceptions, neither scholars nor religious leaders have given the religious element the rigorous attention it deserves.[11]

Perceptively, Edwin McNeill Poteat, after calling attention to the "curious way" that religion has for "affecting nearly every-thing in life though much of its impact is unique and disguised," notes the solidarity of the southern religious picture in contrast to the fluidity found in the North and the West. The upshot of this, in Poteat's judgment, is that the term "Solid South" has as important reference, intrinsically, to religious homogeneity as to political.[12] Similarly, Francis B. Simkins, in listing the various factors within southern life which make for ease and difficulty of transition in the 1960's, writes:

> Faith in the Biblical heritage is a factor second only to
> White Supremacy as a means of conserving the ways of the

South. The historians often say revolutionary changes that enveloped the European continent in the last few centuries stopped with the Pyrenees. Historians of the United States say with equal reason that revolutionary changes in this country stop with the Potomac. Spain and the South have remained conservative because of the unrelenting piety of Spanish and Southern peoples.

The hold of orthodox Protestantism upon Southerners of the twentieth century is a likely explanation of why the section, in the face of earth-shaking changes in industry, transportation, and education, has kept its identity as the most conservative portion of the United States.[13]

In this interpretation, the religious element ranks second among the shaping forces in the southern mentality and personality.

Strange as it may seem in the face of this assertion, the pervasiveness of religion is a comparatively new fact of southern life. A religious solidarity did not emerge until approximately 1830, and then only in principle. Not until the period of Reconstruction did the churches' near-complete conquest of the population get under way. Religious statistics climbed steadily thereafter, culminating in a formidable statistical total in the 1950's.

But we do not mean to intimate that 1830 was some minor turning-point. For it was about this time that left-wing, Low Church, Protestant orthodoxy outdistanced any and all rivals in the race for the allegiance of the people. Prior to this time, several ideological claimants labored in the field, without clear indication that any, much less any particular one, would sweep the masses of people into God's Kingdom. In fact, the southern populace for the greater part of the Colonial period was unreligious (not to say, irreligious). Following the first flush of religious incentive during Virginia's infantile years, that colony settled into an essentially commercial existence. The Church of England, formally established, did serve to carry Old World traditions as well as to render spiritual comfort and challenge to a minority. But everything considered, after 1625 lethargy and indifference characterized Virginia's religious life. Elsewhere in the southern colonies, Anglicanism fared no better, sometimes worse. In its broad contours the American South was still Christendom; nevertheless, few persons were seriously religious and the spiritual state of the colonies was low.

The tide did not begin to turn earlier than the 1740's when New Light (pro-revival) Presbyterian sentiment erupted in the rural areas near Richmond, whence it spread, mainly north and west, and into the Appalachian valleys being overrun by new Scotch-Irish arrivals from the Old World by way of the Middle Colonies. Flamboyant as their successes were in contrast with the Establishment, they were soon outdone by Baptist revivalism which took root in the late 1750's and the far-flung Methodist efforts dating from around 1770.

One of these three denominations, numerically the first in the South to advertise revivalism, that new American improvisation, gradually lost its front-running position. For while Presbyterianism managed to keep and win numbers of Southerners, its victories diminished in frequency. Meanwhile its two fellow Protestant bodies surged dramatically ahead, enabling revivalistic Protestantism to carry the day. So effective were the Baptists and Methodists that their preachers and churches began to blanket the sprawling territory. Once the movement had scaled the Appalachians, it hit upon the camp-meeting technique, which added to its luster and dynamism.

By this time, that is, about 1800, a general pattern of southern Protestant life had evolved. So appropriate was it to the southern personality, and so against the stream were the more traditional religious currents that in a short while all conservative approaches had been routed (never to gain a large following in the South again, at least up to the present). Episcopalianism, on the whole, continued to slumber. Presbyterianism pressed ahead, but increasingly its membership was confined to the better-educated, higher classes of society. After showing signs of life before and after the turn of the nineteenth century, deism came under strenuous attack from the clerics; its adherents were pressured out of key occupations and into more orthodox theological positions. By 1830, popular orthodoxy had the field virtually to itself.

The variety of Protestant Christianity which had climbed into the saddle (to remain there for the remainder of the South's history as a region apart) was of a readily specifiable sort. Among its several traits, the most dominant was voluntarism, stressing the central place of individual decision in all stages of the life of faith. Particular presentations of the Christian message seemed to strike fire with the populace almost in direct proportion to the prominence of the voluntaristic emphasis within them. Men were told that it was up to them to decide whether they would spend eternity in heaven or hell. The preachers' appeal was to men's emotions on the route to their will, precisely because this was the arena wherein, as they reckoned, destinies were determined. Accordingly, the Calvinist dimension of the classical Baptist heritage receded under the stress of the frontier preachments, as did the high Arminianism (some have thought it a crypto-Calvinism) of the Wesleyan tradition. Voluntaristic in the extreme, this variety of Christianity concentrated on exhorting individuals to act upon an irreducible brace of doctrines, man's sin and Christ's proffer of forgiveness, or else pay the eternal consequences. Nothing else greatly mattered. The sweep of the biblical revelation was represented as devolving upon God's one demand, that guilt-ridden men "get right" with God through salvation.

This conception of the religious life was of course far from the South's exclusive possession. First in New England, then on the early frontier in areas like western New York, finally on the frontier in the old Northwest Territory and beyond, emphases were comparable and aims identical. As the nineteenth century wore on, however, southern religious patterns departed from those of the national mainstream. Stated more accurately, the course of mainstream American religious life began to diverge from what had been common both to it and the South. Primarily the divergence consisted in the South's retaining, entrenching, and institutionalizing the frontier tradition of revivalism, during a time when Christianity in the North and West were being subjected to numerous modifying factors. That is to say, what was a transitional phase in the culture of the North remained the characteristic religious outlook of the South.[14]

Until mid-century, popular American religious life was more or less of a single piece, especially outside New England. By this time, liberal traditions of dissent, which had been gaining strength in the Northeast for a century, wrought some alterations in religious patterns in America, the South only excluded. More important, emergent social changes directed much northern concern toward such social problems as the abolition of slavery, the amelioration of urban living and working conditions, and other national moral problems. Moreover respect for learning and the appearance of new categories of thought in science, philosophy, sociology, history, and other disciplines could not be prevented indefinitely from influencing religious understanding. A leadership class which was in touch with major movements in Western civilization continually made its weight felt. The Protestant church in non-South America lived in the throes of a tension which forced reappraisals, modifications, and flux. Whether the shifts of posture were good or bad is not the issue before us now. What is significant is that the old Evangelicalism lost its hold and gave way to a new religious configuration of which it was a very minor part.

Southern religion before The War had been helped to acquire its peculiar shape by a leadership class which was notably unsophisticated and provincial. Especially among the Baptists, who steadily moved into the forefront of the regional religious picture, informed, circumspect leadership was wanting. All things considered, education ranked low on southern religion's list of priorities, being suspect, even anathema, in the eyes of many. It is true that almost everywhere the churches grew. But the products of this era of growth manifested a provincial appearance by virtue of being isolated from more widely based influences, and even from ordinary dialogue. The predisposition to conceive of Christianity in terms of an orthodox belief-structure which was later to be termed fundamentalism, and a particular means-ends syndrome, namely, revivalism, became almost ubiquitous among the southern populace, fastening its grip even upon many of the descendants of Calvin and Knox (though in a certain sense this conception of Christianity was equally foreign to Wesley and to the Baptist heritage).

The prologue and aftermath of the Civil War sealed the South's tendency toward introversion. What had been a predisposition and a partially accomplished fact of its religious life was transformed into a sacrosanct attitude and a finished fact. Although not everyone's name appeared on church rolls, scarcely anyone dissented from the old-time religion which reigned supreme everywhere. After a century of incubation, evangelical and revivalistic Protestantism established itself as the South's popular religion. Cutting across denominational lines, the evangelical theology gave rise to the sober news that each man must decide for Christ in the moment of salvation—or else.

Nor did subsequent movements usurp the reign of this popular faith. During the 1840's and 1850's the three major denominations severed themselves from their respective kinsmen in America at large by creating separate and distinct southern organizations. Moreover the persistence of the tendency to feel (as against thinking) one's way through life shut doors which might have led southern religion into a deeper, wider, newly formulated understanding of itself and its mission. Again, resistance to, indeed unawareness of, world revolutions in thought prevented evaluation and adjustment. Finally, the need for religion or something like it, to cope with the novelty, the boredom, and the oppressiveness of life in mill villages and work in the factories springing up across the Cotton Kingdom, seemed only to reinforce religion's hold. In sum, a variety of religious life, toward which the southern masses were predisposed long before the rise of a cotton economy, took root under the cultivation of revivalism, flowered in the post-War South, and remained largely sheltered from serious challenges and obstacles until the present decade.

The only imaginable product of such a historical career—no matter how well-meaning and how valuable many of its contributions—is an immature institution. Victimized by its isolation and success, and in an ironic sense by its very devoutness, popular southern Protestantism has yet to learn the meaning of self-criticism. Also, it has yet to transcend its own presuppositions and preoccupations for any rich stock-taking of itself in terms of the biblical-theological norms it means so scrupulously to hold to—to say nothing of having any grasp of its relation to a society and world radically revised by revolutions of all sorts. In a word, the southern church typically ignores the setting in which its members and prospective members live, innocently concentrating on the inner life as though there were an "inner" disseverable from the "outer." It yearns for things to be as they once were—before the upsetting eruption of "sidetracking" ethical problems and "futile" theological controversies. It appeals to "historic" denominational witness, without a sense of the past, being infrequently aware that the specific features of church life in the past resulted from efforts to be relevant to given historical-cultural situations now long since disappeared, or that comparably new approaches are required by today's revolutionary times. Its history makes clear why it is often destiny-struck, defensive, and reactionary. The forces which inhabit the air that most human institutions breathe, calling for fresh evaluation, modification, updating, and renewal, have all been generally absent from the experience of the southern church, to its tragic harm.[15]

It is true that there have been changes in the *appearance* of southern church life. Regrettably, however, improvements on this level merely serve to deafen the ears of the leadership to sundry calls to *basic* renewal. The kind of self-study in which they have engaged aims at realigning existing patterns with a view to greater efficiency. It leaves untouched the operative presuppositions, objectives, and conceptualizations of the bodies in question —and in so doing misses the intent of the constructive criticisms forthcoming from so many quarters nowadays.

Many features of the southern way of life intrigue other Americans as well as citizens of foreign cultures. But what can be more intriguing than the virtual "establishment" of Baptist and Methodist denominations, heir-movements to seventeenth and eighteenth century English reactions against Establishment and the shortcomings historically associated with it? Ironically, many of those same shortcomings have cropped up in the South with correspondingly different faces, of course, owing to the different cultural and theological climate of the South. We will maintain—along lines and for reasons to be treated—that the "establishment" of a variety of Christianity inherently unsuited to Establishment in the long run is more threatening to the significance and survival of Christianity than the official Establishments have been. Nowhere else in Christianity's long history, not even in the American experiment, has a comparable form of Christianity played this role. The place held by the Baptist denomination in the South is singularly amazing, since everywhere else during its 350-year history, this tradition has occupied a decided minority position, often being a collection of despised and disdained outgroups. The flourishing of revivalism-fundamentalism in the American South is a cultural phenomenon unparalleled anywhere else. The steps by which this came about will claim much of the present study's attention.

The cultural-social complex in which revivalism-fundamentalism came to birth and flourished daily undergoes significant modification. The passing of the old culture spells the decline of this culture-religion spawned in it and so closely tied to it. As a result, the last four or five years have witnessed the first trends in scores of years toward the stabilizing of religious statistics. Although the denominations do not yet acknowledge it or grasp its significance, an unprecedented era, likely to be marked by flux and decline, is breaking upon them. The heart of the matter is that the ministry of the churches is ever more irrelevant to persons in the new society. Churchly ministrations smack of unrelatedness to the modern world, whether with reference to the thought-forms in which theological statements are presented, or to the concerns by means of which the church expresses its mission to mankind. If what the churches are doing does not relate the divine message, compassion, and power to men's real lives, their understanding, their needs, and their problems, the churches act irresponsibly. If the Lord of the Church calls his people to minister to *men* on whose behalf he became a servant, an irrelevant church is disobedient and unfaithful. When that is said of the church with any legitimacy whatsoever, it has been struck in its *solar plexus,* inasmuch as it has no other ultimate reason for existence than obedience and responsible service to its Lord. Effective refutation of the charge, radical renewal, reversion to a true sectarian position by withdrawal from the world, or culpable obstinacy are the only courses open to it. The task before us in this study is to point out the nature of the church's present irrelevance, how it came about, and how it might be overcome.

2

The Southern Accent
in Religion

The fact that the southern approach is distinct from world Christianity is clear to any sensitive observer. Any reflective southern churchman who has found himself in a discussion of religious topics with men who belong to other American subcultures (or world cultures) has discovered that he and they speak out of different orientations. Moreover, anyone who has attended a general gathering of American Methodists has discovered that although Midwesterners and Southerners come together in the fellowship at many points, their divergences are real. Even more dramatic is the deep estrangement between Baptists in South and North, as illustrated by a recent spokesman's poignant appeal to the two conventions to cease their civil war. It would be difficult to disprove the oft-heard dictum that greater similarity obtains among Baptist, Methodist, and

Presbyterian churches in the South than between an average southern regional church in any one of these denominations and its northern counterpart. The underrepresentation of southern church leaders in the councils of leadership which shape American religious positions, policies, and practices is also self-evident.

An examination of the chief institutional ways in which this distinctiveness manifests itself must now claim our attention, with the theological aspects awaiting dissection in Part II.

The Fact of a "Southern Church"

Although the South is in process of surrendering many of its traditional traits, no one can dispute that there has been *a South,* a distinctive American region with its peculiar subculture. Partly because the regional ethos has engendered in its sons an uncommonly spirited loyalty, but principally because there is *a South,* with an isolable culture, to a greater extent than there is *a* Northeast, or *a* Midwest, or *a* Far West, regional studies have abounded.[1] Needless to say, the South is no monolith. Variety prevails everywhere and on all levels. Consequently, generalizations describing the region and its people must be offered with some caution. At the same time, it can hardly be doubted that there is an essential southern homogeneity which more than justifies efforts to portray and classify it as a whole.

In the same way, it must be said, even after taking into consideration the obvious variety of denominations, doctrinal positions, and types of congregations, that *a regional church* exists. Southerners ranging beyond the boundaries of their home region and residents of other parts of America sojourning in the South alike have been struck by certain distinctive qualities which set off southern religious life as *sui generis.* This impression has been given convincing scientific documentation with the demonstration that seven distinct "religious regions" exist in the United States, each distinguished by the consistent prevalence, within a geographical area, of a common pattern of primary and secondary domination by specific religious bodies.[2] Thus the first rank or second rank of particular families of Christians marks off each territory as something of a whole, distinct from the religious regions which border it.

The South is declared a religious region, on the grounds that it is "readily identified as one in which Baptists are strongly dominant and Methodists form persistently large minorities," and is a territory where representative religion possesses a "uniformly British and native Protestant character." [3] Its boundaries on the north moving east to west are fixed roughly as follows: The Potomac River, the upper valley of Virginia, Highway 60 across West Virginia, the Ohio River, a line atop the southern quarter of Illinois, the northern tier of counties of Missouri, and the same in Oklahoma. The western and southern boundaries are eastern New Mexico, the Rio Grande Valley in Texas, and the Gulf of Mexico. In only four major subregions within the South is this pattern altered: the North Carolina piedmont, peninsular Florida, French Catholic southern Louisiana, and the German-settled area of east south-central Texas.[4] Geographically, there is a southern religious region, in a holistic though not uniform sense, with certain distinctive markings generally discernible across the 2,000-mile expanse from upper Tidewater Virginia to eastern New Mexico.

Taking these findings one level deeper, we contend that throughout this vast area, similarities in doctrinal belief and practical emphasis prevail among thousands of local churches of several denominational groupings, headed by the formidably conspicuous Baptist and Methodist bodies.[•] Outsiders are often unprepared for the high degree of similarity between the two largest groups, as well as between them and other such major families as the Presbyterian, the Disciples of Christ, the Churches of Christ, the Assemblies of God, and the Church of the Nazarene.[5] Simkins, sensing this, was prompted to write:

[•] In the light of Zelinsky's conclusion that "most denominational groups do tend, to a striking degree, to be national in distribution" (*loc. cit.*, p. 165), the contrast between the Baptist statistics in the South and the relative numerical inferiority of the denomination in other parts of the United States appears additionally strange. Though far from weak, northern Baptist concentration is spotty, limited largely to the coastal New England states, western New York, northeastern Ohio, scattered clusters of Baptist immigrants, and dispersed metropolitan centers.

"Superficially, the dissimilarity between Holy Rollers and upper-class churchmen was the difference between intense emotionalism and mannered restraint. Nevertheless, both groups were fundamentally Southern, both dominated by orthodoxy, natural piety, and hostility of rationalism and the spirit of free inquiry in biblical matters." [6] In terms of basic belief-structures and commonality of aim, the continuities are more conspicuous than the discontinuities. Among the sizable southern bodies, only the Episcopalians and the Lutherans resist inclusion in the large complex, and they more feebly, at least at the popular level, than might be expected. Somewhat surprisingly, Episcopal priests and Lutheran pastors report that they must labor diligently to convince their parishioners that the communion to which they belong is really distinct from the popular denominations.

Accordingly, we deem it legitimate to speak of a trans-denominational "southern church," embracing what may be called "popular southern Protestantism." Whereas only the Southern Baptist Convention stands as an institutional embodiment of it, its character permeates and constitutes the life of many other—in some sense, all—regionally prominent bodies. A basic set of assumptions about the nature and task of Christianity, which virtually ignores the formal demarcations between the subvarieties of Protestantism (without obliterating denominational self-consciousness), runs throughout southern religious life. This general tradition, "what every schoolboy knows," is the heart of the southern church's ideology. Catch almost any Southerner offguard, ask him what Christianity teaches, and he will produce the standard answer, a simple list of propositions to which the masses of churchmen almost unconsciously revert, irrespective of the fresh seeds some unconventional minister or theologically literate layman may have sought to sow. For the standard tradition has a powerful hold. It is a deeply embedded frame of reference.

As just implied, only a small number of regional residents, even among those systematically exposed to unconventional instruction, ever shake themselves loose from the hold of this popular theology, or transcend it enough to see what it really presupposes and stresses. One wonders if any people in the history of Christendom after the Middle Ages has been so thoroughly indoctrinated with a particular version of the Christian world view. Even graduate students in theology find themselves having to struggle manfully to extirpate the deep roots of the traditional categories of thought.

Different in nuance from the "southern church" is the "southern mainline," comprising the Baptist and Methodist groups supremely, but also the more rurally oriented segments of the Presbyterian Church throughout the South, as well as the Disciples of Christ, who are a conspicuous part of things in particular locales within the region. This is the sector of popular religious life which is both diffused throughout the territory and socially acceptable enough to stand at the center of regional power structures, secular as well as ecclesiastical.

The contrast between the southern mainline and "mainline Protestantism," a term familiar to those acquainted with American Protestant ecumenicity, serves to illuminate the southern church's distinctiveness. "Mainline Protestantism" is a coinage referring to all those denominations belonging to the National Council of Churches, ranging from Episcopalians and Lutherans on the right to American (northern) Baptists and Disciples on the left. Significantly, the chief criterion for distinguishing between the two "mainlines" is not their respective denominational compositions. For, all the denominations in the southern mainline, save the Baptist, belong to mainline Protestantism as well, by virtue of membership in the National Council of Churches. What separates them is the evangelical character of representative southern religion's theology and ethics, as against the more traditional orientation of mainline Protestantism. The nucleus of the divergence, historically conceived, is the lingering impact of revivalism and biblical conservatism in the South. But the weightiest consideration here is the way in which, at least until very recently, the denominations of the South which belong to both mainlines have had closer kinship with the regional mainline, as indicated by their distinctive identity in national ecclesiastical gatherings.

"Southern Religion"

Pending fuller treatment later, it is important now to ferret out those features of the southern church's life which are transparent to its deepest nature, its assumptions as to what is basic and most to be prized in the Christian vision. Through highlighting the dominant "personality traits," we may begin to isolate the southern accent within the larger rhetoric of Protestant Christianity.

The southern church is not identifiable as the sum of the denominations which comprise it, but is rather a complex of religious organizations which taken all together form a special variety of Protestantism (in sociological terms, an "ideal type"). This variety, "southern religion," preponderates in nearly all Baptist churches, across the sweep of the sects, in something more than a majority of Methodist churches, in a number of Presbyterian and Disciples congregations, and, irrespective of their church affiliation, is what the great mass of Southerners believe Christianity to be.

Southern religion is best delineated as a medley of revivalistic and fundamentalistic strains. On its revivalist side, it conceives of Christian faith in definitively inward terms. Faith is a reality to be experienced at the deepest level of one's inner life. Yet this is not classical Pietism, for revivalism places decisive stress on the memorable, usually emotional, moment of entrance into the Christian life. The remainder of one's life is in effect an appendix to the fact of entrance—or at least so much is made of the initial experience that hearers are likely to conclude that this is so. Consequently theology is relegated to the periphery, worship and evangelism are divorced, the importance of worship is minimized, and ethics, conceived in individualist rather than social terms, becomes a separate (if related) sphere. In short, revivalism focuses on the inauguration of the Christian life, conceived simplistically, with worship and ethics logically unrelated to conversion, and with preaching inclined toward the hortatory and persuasive, rarely toward the declarative and instructional.

On its fundamentalist side, southern religion calls for assent to certain doctrines—a relatively short catalog of them, actually—which are deemed to contain the kernel of Christian truth. The scope of the doctrines so honored is narrow, but intelligibly so, since only the truthfulness of the source of authority, the Bible, and the propositions which point to the cosmic transaction by which man's sinfulness is overcome and his salvation accomplished matter ultimately. This southern version of fundamentalism carefully sifts the biblical material and systematizes it into a series of truths around the central commission to save souls.[7] A systematic program of selection operates here in line with the southern church's evangelical aim.

The point is that the southern church's brand of revivalism is *also* a type of fundamentalism. The binding character of certain doctrinal statements is unquestioned. Churchmen are expected to subscribe to them. At the same time, southern fundamentalism is not classical Fundamentalism, in three principal respects. First, as noted, the southern church's dogmas are limited in number and reveal a highly selective process. The greater comprehension of classical Fundamentalism is absent from the southern version. Second, the keen apologetical interest of the standard tradition, mirroring its aim of seeking to make the Christian faith credible alongside competing belief-systems, is not matched in the southern variety, which has only rarely found itself in a circumstance where apologetical presentation was called for. Finally, the traditional version has not necessarily been tied to revivalism, and where it has been, its role as guardian of Christian truth has not been superseded by the concern to convert individuals, as is the case in the southern church. Inasmuch as it views truth and life uncritically, however, the southern church is fundamentalist in the popular sense of the term.

Although southern religion is best classified as revivalistic and fundamentalistic, some of its most representative traits—not necessarily implied by these classifications—are: the seriousness with which it takes its business; the subjective orientation of its life; its attitude toward change; its high self-estimate; and the peculiar relation which exists between the church and its culture.

One indication of the first characteristic, the seriousness with which the Christian responsibility is undertaken, is that in contrast to the meager knowledgeability of the masses of northern churchmen, a comparatively high proportion of the southern faithful are familiar with certain rudimentary propositions of the Christian faith and miscellaneous biblical data and quotations. Moreover, a reasonable percentage of them are aggressively articulate in bearing verbal witness to their faith. While it would be palpably false to intimate that religious knowledgeability or evangelical courage are universal in southern religious circles, a respectable incidence of literate and serious religiousness, in line with the norms of standard regional religion, does prevail.

For over a century, visitors to the South have commented on the expressive quality of personal faith there, rightly perceiving that churchmen are admonished to be anything but casual in pursuit of their religious commitment. There exists an impressive measure of acquaintance with the names of the biblical books, key texts, and the "plan of salvation," that selection of Pauline verses which are reckoned to set before the lost man the steps by which he may arrive at conversion. There is a corpus of information which "every schoolboy knows" concerning the Christian faith, and it includes theological as well as moral elements. Under conducive circumstances, many a Southerner could and would testify not only to his inner conversion experience and to what is morally right, but to certain affirmations, such as that "Christ died for our sins," as revealed in the Bible which is the "Word of God." The religious faith of the masses of southern people, within the limits of their understanding, is serious and relatively informed.

The orientation of this faith, however, must be termed subjective, inasmuch as the southern church's major stress falls on *man's response* to God, rather than on the objective Christian message itself. Its stated objectives, chosen techniques, and priority rankings all demonstrate a preoccupation with bringing about *man's decisions* to embrace and live out the Christian way. The real stewardship with which it considers itself entrusted is that of converting individuals and guiding them in righteous paths. Taking for granted its doctrinal basis, it proceeds to concentrate on declaring its direct message and urging men to act upon that message.

The absence of studious attention to the authentic quality of its message's content does not in any respect dilute the particularity of its doctrinal stance. The southern church certainly does not give credence to any or all dogmas; a hard core of biblical-doctrinal themes are known, treasured, and proclaimed.[8] Nevertheless, the primary energies are geared to convincing hearers and persuading them to receive the message.

Taking sociologist Charles Y. Glock's theory that religiosity has five different dimensions, the ideological, the ritualistic, the intellectual, the consequential (ethical), and the experiential, it is clear that southern religiousness has been virtually restricted to the fifth.[9] With a high degree of unanimity, Southerners have have made all the others secondary to the experiential. Their deliberate efforts have been directed almost entirely to engendering an awareness of the divine Spirit who seeks residence within each man. They do acknowledge a particular ideology, they do follow an approved ritual, and they do exhort religious men to exemplify appropriate behavior, but these do not really engage their direct efforts, owing to their confidence that the overflow from the experiential dimension will set the others in place.

As for the southern church's attitude toward change, it is apparent that much of what Southerners have stoutly defended as inviolable is in process of being snatched from them either by legal interpretations or by social, economic, and political pressures. A tradition-loving people is deeply hurt over seeing "institutions which they had thought were theirs . . . , relationships which they had thought secure . . . , begin to take on new shape and purpose."[10]

The church has not only been "their own" (subjectivist churchmen are far more likely than objectivists to think of it in this way), but in the eyes of its constituents it has also been the kind of institution which can be changed only at the expense of its integrity and supernatural reason for existence. According to this view, changelessness must be a basal feature of its policy. Moreover, while it is agreed that the church ought to look and function like an institution attuned to the 1960's in respect of its superstructure, in every other respect its commission is to conserve the unchanging truths of the faith. On the whole, the southern church has discharged its putative commission faithfully, because in fact the theology, emphases, objectives, and value-preferences with which it commenced during the formative period, 1740–1830, with modifications, remain the nucleus of its life.

Most southern religious leaders are gratified by the accusation which they sometimes hear from those hostile to religion, and even from many within the world church, to the effect that the southern church is "behind the times." The southern church is consciously committed to conservatism. It is wary of change, especially facile change, having no desire to respond to the pressure of every new wind that blows. From Methodist bishops and Baptist executives alike one hears repudiations of what is felt to be contemporary Christianity's excessive zeal for relevance. Down deep, the southern church's passion is for clinging fast to the simple, "timeless" theology long ago entrusted to its safekeeping. It construes the real substance and texture of Christian truth—in terms of form as well as content—to be unvarying. Accordingly, modifications have been restricted to the areas of technique and promotion. In this combination of change at the level of procedure and changelessness at the substantive levels, the southern church has achieved a high degree of success.

The fourth aspect of southern religion to be mentioned is its very special self-estimate, a feature which is not lost on "outsiders" and newcomers to the region. It aims at and believes itself to have attained measurably the simple faith and pure gospel of the New Testament. Its conscious objective is the rebirth of essential Christianity. Not infrequently, southern churches boast of their success in conforming to the New Testament ideal. In the case of the Southern Baptists, a whole denomination quite seriously entertains the notion that it is Christianity's purest expression since apostolic times. (Predictably, this body surges into the rest of the nation, as well as onto foreign mission fields, armed with the confidence that it is Christianity's best, or even last, hope.) But the Baptists are far from alone in the high rating they claim for the kind of Protestantism which permeates the southern scene. The notion that regional religion is less corrupted is commonly held by the masses of Southerners.[11] At the official denominational level, too, this attitude exists, as the continued separation of Baptists and Presbyterians from their northern kinsmen, whatever else it may demonstrate, attests. Similarly, the regionally self-conscious identity of southern Methodists in The Methodist Church cannot be explained simply in terms of racial attitudes, but also seems to point to a similar self-assessment. Surely this factor goes a long way toward accounting for the fact that religion stands as one of two or three areas in the compass of southern life which retain their isolation from the major changes now in process. As of now, there is clearer evidence of the break-up of the political and social "Solid South" than of any fundamental will to revise its religious aspect.

The fifth and final representative trait of southern religion derives from the peculiar relation which exists between the southern church and its surrounding culture. Tersely stated, it has been a long and happy union. The southern church is comfortable in its homeland, and the culture sits comfortably with its church. This situation is a product of the fact that alternative belief-systems have rarely penetrated the regional framework of thought, so that almost no one since 1830 has been prepared to deny the Christian truth-claims. Moreover, the dominant churches, owing in part to their subjective orientation and democratic polity, have cast the faith into a mold congenial to the popular mind. Both culture and church have manifested the classical rural value-preferences and tone. This rurality has come to the fore in many aspects, most clearly in the centrality of the "folksy" fellowship practiced by many congregations, town and city parishes as well as rural ones, no doubt because the members of urban churches are still a people with essentially rural attitudes and values. This is, of course, entirely predictable in light of prevailing conditions as recently as 1930, when between one-third and one-half of the South's urban population had been born in rural areas. A substantial shift in this pattern is now occurring, but southern cities traditionally have been notably uncitylike.[12]

All the popular bodies, their somewhat different penchants for emphasizing the subjective notwithstanding, have attained a close alliance with the chief features of southern culture. Despite the historical disinclination of all southern churches to make peace with their finite surroundings, they have blended in increasingly well with the general culture, imperceptibly espousing regional attitudes and beliefs which had little or no direct relation to the objective message which they hailed as their standard. This trend was continually being enhanced by the churches' driving compulsion to convert the entire society, a goal which encouraged a willingness to appeal to all the cultural thought-forms which might bring any individual over the line separating the unconverted from the saved.

The Remarkable Homogeneity

During a painful period of social unrest in the early 1930's, a distinguished southern journalist wrote concerning southern Methodism and Baptism that the members of these two groups "so dominate the region below the Mason-Dixon line that they are responsible almost wholly for its behavior." [13] This judgment is unexceptionable, and the situation to which it points has hardly changed in the intervening years. Indeed, if anything, lately the power of these two denominations has escalated as a result of the religious boom of the 1950's. Perusal of the raw statistical data concerning formal religious affiliation in the region goes far toward sealing this point—though there are other equally telling indices for it.

Returning to the work of the historical geographers of American religion, we find that although a high percentage of the individual counties in the fifty states is dominated by a single communion, in few instances is there a strong territorial leader. For example, the Midwest is a veritable hodgepodge of religious groups; likewise the Middle Atlantic States.[14] The Methodist Church, comparatively strong everywhere, is a kind of inverse illustration of the point in that it does not exercise geographical "control" over any region at large, and over only two states, Delaware and Maryland. The case of Nebraska is illuminating, inasmuch as eight different religious groups dominate at least one county. In state after state, several families have conspicuous contingents of adherents.

Outside the South, three bodies wield strong territorial leadership: the Roman Catholic Church in the industrial Northeast, French Louisiana, the Spanish Southwest, many places in the Mississippi Valley, and California; Lutheranism in the West North Central States, principally Minnesota and the Dakotas; and the Mormons, whose hold on Utah and contiguous sections of adjacent states is virtually uncontested. It is worth repeating that America's most representative Protestant family, Methodism, with churches and members across the length and breadth of the American landscape, cannot claim large areas of the nation as its own. Heterogeneity and diffusion are the rule, with surprisingly few exceptions.

A corollary of this fact of heterogeneity is no less important for the purposes of this study: where a single religious body dominates a region (exclusive of the Mormon domain), a great many countercurrents and challenges are in evidence. By way of example, Lutherans in the West North Central States and Roman Catholics in New England emphatically do not live to themselves. In the nature of the case, individuals within those communions "rub shoulders" with persons of other faiths. Generally speaking, religious institutions throughout the nation continually interact with other religious positions and attitudes, certain rural areas populated by homogeneous ethnic groups being exceptions. These regionally powerful institutions, whatever the degree of their theological dogmatism, engage regularly in the staccato of a challenge-and-response motif. In almost every instance the surrounding culture simply will not permit the luxury of a life unaffected by other groups in a religiously pluralist society.

Furthermore, no simple and tight unity of general culture and the dominant religious body exists in any of these regions. Thus, even though Scandinavian and German Lutherans are populous in Minnesota, the culture of that state cannot be described adequately as a Northern European Lutheran culture. Too many factors play in the maze of regional life for any such reductionism to comply with the facts.

By contrast, two features of southern society startle the observer of the region's religious patterns: first, the way in which the Baptist-Methodist syndrome dramatically overshadows all other religious families in the size and breadth of its numerical strength; second, the palpably intimate alliance between the Baptist-Methodist syndrome and regional life. Obviously, these two are by no means the only religious bodies enjoying prominence throughout the region. But they are huge and influential, virtually ruling out the possibility that any other groups should provide representative southern religion.

The dominance of the Baptists and Methodists is demonstrated along lines far more significant than mere statistical preponderance. Southerners customarily turn for services to these denominations rather automatically, without rating them as inherently superior to other Protestant churches. Baptist and Methodist churches are landmarks, "landmarks for seeking Southerners," it might be said. The second line, on which we touched earlier, is that other denominations both consciously and unconsciously vary from their historic practices in order to meld themselves into the pattern of religious life so successfully devised by the "big two." Capitalizing on their sensitivity to the categories in which the masses of men think and to the levels on which effective appeal can be pitched, the Baptist-Methodist complex has won the reputation for setting the tone for regional religious life generally.[15] Consequently, it would seem that the pacesetting Baptist-Methodist approach has had some bearing on the Congregational churches' frequent recourse to revivalism, on the teetotalism of many Lutherans, and on the non-liturgical nature of many Presbyterian services of worship.•

The Baptist-Methodist Hegemony

The statistics for southern religious affiliation by denominational distribution are remarkably transparent to prevailing circumstances.[16] The reported Protestant figure is 42.5 per cent of the total population—a figure which we shall see to be deceptively small. Only 10 per cent is affiliated with the Roman Catholic Church, most of which is concentrated in the areas already named. The Jewish percentage is considerably smaller, 1.1 per cent, and confined almost exclusively to the larger towns and cities.

No section of the country compares with the South on the point of Protestant domination.[17] In the northeastern states, Protestantism's 19.1 per cent figure is less than half as great as the Catholic-Jew aggregate. In the North Central States, Protestantism's 29.9 per cent is not significantly larger than the 23.4 per cent embraced by Catholicism and Judaism. In the West, the combined total of Catholics and Jews outstrips the Protestants 22 per cent to 20.2 per cent. Such information makes it abundantly clear that the Protestant hegemony in Dixie is unparalleled elsewhere. Further, it may suggest (without verifying) the postulate so basic to this study's entire thesis, that the so-called southern way of life is pervasively a Protestant way of life, whatever else it may be.

Intrinsically impressive as the statistics are, their full import is not seen short of the realization that a sizable portion of the religious membership in the southern states is not reported, therefore not included in the sums and percentages at hand. The official count has it that 53.9 per cent of the white population belongs to some religious organization (42.5 per cent in Protestant churches). However, this reckoning leaves out of account a communion which almost certainly ranks third among the

• This contention invites careful researching. Moreover it must be noted that most of the denominations which have strength in the South have always been represented there by their left-wing branches.

southern Protestant families, the Churches of Christ, with a membership estimated to be in excess of 1,500,000, preponderantly in Tennessee, Alabama, Kentucky, Arkansas, and Texas. In addition, as Zelinsky points out, there exists

> an interesting differential between lowland and upland tracts . . . in such states as Virginia, Kentucky, Tennessee, West Virginia, Georgia, Alabama, and Arkansas. The low percentages reported for the poor, remote, and often thinly occupied areas of high or rugged terrain doubtless reflect the difficulties for actual or potential congregations; but they also quite probably indicate the relative importance in such areas of autonomous, rather tentatively organized groups, largely oriented toward the fundamentalist theology and largely unreported in our statistics.[18]

It may be assumed then that a figure in the neighborhood of 50 per cent is more nearly commensurate with the strength of southern Protestantism than the 42.5 official statistic based on reported religious membership.

Still another explanation of statistics is necessary if the massive strength of Protestantism in the South is to be seen for what it is. With a single exception, the front-running regional religious bodies are "exclusive" churches. That is to say, the Baptist, Methodist, and Presbyterian bodies, and the Churches of Christ, have what the statisticians call "confirmed" membership, which means that they exempt from their membership rolls the very young who are the children of adult members and those who attend Sunday School but are not (yet) officially regarded as members of the congregation. Although the Presbyterian and Methodist churches baptize the infants born into families in their congregations, their rolls do not list these as members. In both cases, the rite of confirmation which is administered in the early adolescent years admits to formal affiliation those baptized as infants. Always in Baptist churches and the Churches of Christ, and sometimes among Methodists, incorporation awaits the conversion experience. In view of our aim to discover just how firm the southern Protestant church's grip is, this varied practice of delayed inclusion means that a considerable proportion of Southerners, by virtue of tender age, have not become eligible for official membership in local churches. Notwithstanding the common Baptist practice of receiving children as young as eight, nine, or ten years of age, a host of persons in the region are ineligible.

With these explanations in mind, we are better equipped to view the Protestant hegemony. Accepting 20 per cent (a conservative percentage) as the working figure for children not yet old enough to be members of "exclusive" churches, computation of Protestant membership as percentage of the total white population reveals that the 50 per cent working figure surpasses 60 per cent.[19]

From these facts and figures, the chief inference to be drawn does not pertain to the admittedly impressive Protestant statistics in the South, but to the homogeneous nature of the southern religious population. Many, indeed the great majority of Southerners, are church members. But what is truly significant is that most of this majority is affiliated with the Baptist and Methodist churches. In every other American region, a genuine pluralism prevails, within Protestantism and between the two great Christian traditions, and often among the three classical biblical faiths. Allowing for certain exceptions in some rural areas and a few urban ghettos, we may generalize that the mass of American religious groups acknowledge the presence, if not always the legitimacy, of other groups. Comparatively few citizens can avoid recognizing that their group is one among several or many.

The South presents a decisively different picture. First, Baptists and Methodists are accustomed to living side by side. Neither of these groups regards the other as strange, nor does any Southerner regard these as alien, imported institutions. It is assumed that one will not travel far in any direction before encountering churches identified by these two authentically southern labels. The same applies in a general way to the Presbyterian and Episcopal churches. As relatively sparse as their parish churches

are in rural areas, their existence in towns of any size is expected.
Though they are thought of more as upper-class churches than
as popular, these, too, "belong." The same applies to the Disciples
of Christ in such sections as eastern North Carolina, the lower
valley of Virginia, central Kentucky, and north central Oklahoma; to the Lutheran Church in western piedmont North
Carolina, the lower counties in upstate South Carolina, and
east south-central Texas; to the Churches of Christ in the areas
mentioned; and to the United Church of Christ (especially the
traditional Congregational Christian churches in this merged
body), which has moderate strength in a diffused manner.

Notwithstanding the size and indigenity of several other
Protestant families, only the Baptists and Methodists are almost
everywhere entirely "at home," in town and country, Virginia
and Texas, middle class and lower class, all almost equally.
Certain other bodies are "at home" in towns and cities, still
others in specified areas, as we have noted. But the telling matter
in this respect is that the southern culture is essentially rural,
and a denomination seems to have been able to become an
integral part of the culture almost in direct proportion to its
success in adapting to the rural style of life (with which the
earlier "frontier" style of life has continuities). The two leading
denominations accomplished this as early as the latter eighteenth
century. They entered the southern scene when it was a veritable
religious vacuum, managing to win hundreds of frontiersmen
outright and to proselytize a good many others. As historians
have been fond of pointing out, in the eighteenth century the
one body in best position to envelop the populace of the upper
seaboard South was the Presbyterian Church.[20] Moreover,
Presbyterians were ringleaders in the Second Awakening on the
Kentucky-Tennessee frontier just after 1800. Yet the tradition
of Calvin and Knox was only quantitatively more successful
than the Establishment had been, for the future lay with the
aggressive and adaptive, indeed improvising, Baptists and
Methodists, for reasons soon to be enumerated.

Finally, the statistics themselves are illuminating, especially
in view of the unprecedented gains amassed in the 1950's, most

of which postdate the survey reports being used. In eight states, the Baptist percentage of the total reported religious membership exceeded 50 per cent, while in five states, the proportion fell in the 40–50 per cent span. This domination by a single family appears even more formidable when it is set alongside the percentages held by leading religious groups in other sections of the country—especially where those groups have an inclusive membership and where Protestants are a minority or barely the majority. For example, the Episcopal Church owns a figure of 42.8 per cent *among Protestants* in Rhode Island; similarly, the United Church of Christ (Congregationalist), 34.9 per cent in New Hampshire, 32.8 per cent in Vermont, and 31.7 per cent in Connecticut. The several Lutheran bodies account for 40 per cent of the *Protestant* total in South Dakota, 56.6 per cent in Wisconsin, and 62.5 per cent in North Dakota. Methodist statistics constitute 61.6 per cent of the reported Protestant membership in Delaware, 39.9 per cent in West Virginia, 36.5 per cent in Maryland, 33.5 per cent in Kansas, a figure in the 22–28 per cent range for Ohio, Indiana, Iowa, and Illinois, and so on down to the 15–16 per cent totals in the Pacific States.

In every case mentioned, however, it must be borne in mind that the Protestant share of the over-all religious membership is small as compared with the South: that is, the number of Protestants in the northeastern states is little over half the number of Roman Catholics, and the ratio of Protestants to Catholics in the North Central States is only about four to three. The one divergence from this pattern outside the South occurs in Mormon territory where the hegemony is, astonishingly, far more pronounced than that of Low Church Protestantism in the South. The Latter-Day Saints report 95.2 per cent of the "Protestants" in Utah, 61.6 per cent in Idaho, and 52.5 per cent in Nevada.

Southern Methodist records also are striking. In three states, Arkansas, Maryland, and Virginia, Methodists make up about one-third of the reported white Protestant membership. Only Kentucky's figures fall below 20 per cent, precisely, 16.1 per cent. Each of the other southern states finds Methodists constituting from 20.8 per cent to 28.4 per cent of the white Protestant composite.

Combining the Baptist and Methodist totals, the outcome is an almost unbelievable and seemingly contradictory fact of an American society which glories in its free, pluralistic composition. In six southern states, combined Baptist-Methodist membership runs to upwards of 80 per cent of the reported total, Mississippi's 88 per cent heading the list, with Alabama's 86.7 and Georgia's 86.5 close behind. Moreover, in five additional states the totals surpass 70 per cent.

Finally, if Disciples and Presbyterians, first cousins of the "big two," also are tallied in, the percentages approach astronomical proportions. The total in Alabama, computed this way, hits 90.9 per cent, in Arkansas 88.3, in Georgia 93.0, in Mississippi 93.9, and in Tennessee 87.5. The naked fact of Low Church Protestant, more particularly Baptist-Methodist, domination of the southern white population is dramatically plain.

3
The Peculiarity
of the Southern
Religious Situation

In a circumspect essay published in 1964, an American historian maintains that the fundamental justification for the study of southern history is that "the South's history often diverges from and therefore illuminates the history of the United States." [1] It follows that many generalizations about American history do not apply to the South. This is surely true in the religious realm, for descriptions of the history, orientation, and character of mainstream American religion simply do not fit the situation in the South. Having cited some of the dominant assumptions, attitudes, and statistical features of popular regional religion in the previous chapter, we will now examine differences in the non-religious factors which have conditioned the church in *mainstream* America in contrast to those which have influenced the South.

Studies of American Religion, and the South

The phenomenology of American religion has received an extraordinary measure of attention within the last decade.• Prior to the mid-1950's, comparatively few scholars had concerned themselves with the place of religion in the American tradition. Moreover, most American seminaries and graduate departments of religion gave only peripheral instruction to the nation's scholars of religion (and parish ministers) in this field. Church history was an integral part of the curriculum, but it often stopped with the Protestant Reformation and gave only cursory attention to the history of the church in America.

However, since (and partly because) Will Herberg broke fresh ground in 1955 with his provocative *Protestant-Catholic-Jew* (Doubleday, 1955), much reputable scholarship in this area has emerged, with the consequence that American religious studies have become a discrete discipline. A number of first-rate interpreters, both inside and outside this new discipline—including such prominent names as Ahlstrom, Berger, Hudson, Lenski, Marty, McLoughlin, and Mead—have subjected the religious element in American history and society to rigorous analysis in the interest of the churches' self-understanding or as a contribution to the broad realm of American culture studies, or both.

But the major analysts—without apology—have not even attempted to treat the religious situation of the South. Presumably, a chief reason for this omission is that the South is not representative of America or does not occupy a position on its cultural cutting edge. Another is the relative insignificance of the southern church's participation in world Christianity and the poverty of its theological scholarship.

On the popular level, Northerners coming into the South

• "Phenomenology" comprehends the study of the ways in which religion manifests itself, from theological, historical, and sociological perspectives, without primary reference to the truth or falsity of any or all religious positions.

detect striking differences in the tone of religious life in the two territories. A most convincing illustration of this point from an unpromising quarter appeared late in 1963 in a letter addressed to the weekly journal of the Southern Baptists in Ohio [sic!]. Written by an anonymous native Ohioan, it urged that Southern Baptists in the midwestern state fill the religious void left by the "extremists" who, the letter alleged, control the state's religious life. (The extremists alluded to are "the liturgical churches on one hand and the holiness sects on the other.") Significantly, his plea was to the Southern Baptists to downgrade the importance of "Southern" in their name. More specifically, he advised them to stop discussing the Civil War and referring to "down home" from the pulpit, to refrain from southern idioms such as "you all," and to delete "barnyard illustrations" from sermons being heard by "Buckeyes" who come mainly from urban backgrounds. Although the theological and historical understanding of this evangelical crusader was decidedly limited —he lumped together all Protestant groups from American Baptists on the left to the Episcopal Church on the right as "liturgical churches"—he saw clearly the sociological question at issue: the Southern Baptists in Ohio are markedly southern.[2]

Precise statistical data have not yet become available, but it is an uncontested observation that the troops in the Southern Baptist "invasion" of the North are transplanted Southerners. The members of the new churches in the non-South territories are not natives or long-time residents of Ohio or New Jersey or Washington, but fresh immigrants from Arkansas or South Carolina or Mississippi. Personal friendship with a number of these sons of the South settling in the nation's industrial centers leads one to suspect that many "first-generation immigrants" find primary social identity in the churches, and that their active participation in the churches in their newly adopted home cities is relatively independent of their previous overt patterns in their former southern home communities. In addition, the new churches in northern cities and towns established by transplanted Southerners exhibit the decisive influence of the pattern of church life "down home." One visit to a church in the North molded by these displaced persons goes far toward convincing the spectator of the distinctive tone of southern church life.[3]

If then, as we are maintaining, analyses of American religion at large do not apply to the South, what factors distinguish the two religious situations? And in line with the assertion frequently made that mainstream religion has been victimized by secularizing tendencies which have wrought havoc with classical faith, can it be assumed that the southern church, as many of its members believe, is superior in having withstood the pressure to capitulate to "the world"? On the premise that religion always bears the marks of its culture, we contend that the church in both areas manifests the shaping influence of the particular ethos in which it lives. This means positively, that in both instances the churches are likely to have attained a considerable measure of relevance to the respective situations, and on the negative side, that both are overlaid with cultural veneer.

Profile of the Mainstream Situation

In order to understand southern religion in its distinctiveness, we first need a brief portrayal of religion in the mainstream of American culture. Herberg argues that the church in America has transformed classical (God-centered) religious faith into a seriously weakened, questionably authentic expression of religion. He charges that American religion has become idolatrous, and in doing so offers the gravest indictment possible within the Judeo-Christian context. More precisely, he accuses the American church of placing national goals and values above commitment by faith to God in whom the church lives. Thus classical "high" religion has given way to "low" (man-centered, folk) religion, and the "religion of America," with its own creed and ethic, has supplanted the historic Judeo-Christian forms of religious affirmation. Devotees of the new national faith hold to religious beliefs and practice religious deeds for the sake of national and personal advantage, the beliefs and deeds being founded upon a naturalistic creed fashioned by the American society from the matrix of its unique historical experience.

The rise of this "religion in general" or "religion of democracy" is attributed by Herberg to the social-psychological pressures which weighed so heavily upon the late nineteenth and early twentieth century immigrants, and on their children and grand-children. Millions of Irishmen and eastern and southern Euro-peans, uprooted and alienated, began a new life in the New World, but because of the limitations of their experiences and skills, the transition was often painful. Needing a sense of belonging, of social identification, they turned to the church, the one institution in society which could fulfill three of their basic psychic needs: (1) the church functioned as a reminder of one familiar aspect of life, the religious ways "back home"; (2) it served as the logical center for bringing together all those who were bound by a common language tie, the Italians or Germans or Poles, in a given neighborhood; (3) it helped establish them as bona fide Americans, since church and synagogue were basically accepted institutions in American society, Americans being traditionally reluctant to intrude into so delicate a matter as a person's religious faith.

This was the situation within the first, or immigrant, genera-tion. The sons and daughters of the immigrants, the second, or intermediate, generation, were marginal Americans, neither Old World nor New World citizens in point of identification. On the whole they rejected church and synagogue because they associated them so intimately with the Old World way of life.

The third, or American, generation revived the practice of its grandparents. For not only were these persons exemplars of "Hansen's Law," which states that what the son is eager to forget, the grandson wishes to remember, but in addition they found religious identity as useful a socio-cultural tool as any available. For the immigrant generation, religious identification had been a means to the personal end of achieving social belong-ing in a society in which they were aliens. For the American generation, religious identification served the holy purpose of confirming their Americanness in the eyes of a society into which they were now being rapidly assimilated and which traditionally had accorded a very respectable place to religion. For in this land not only was religious affiliation not suspect, it was regarded by almost everyone as a primary expression of the cherished American heritage.

It is at this point that the analyses of such historians as Gordon Harland, Winthrop Hudson, Martin Marty, Sidney Mead, and Perry Miller become important, inasmuch as the pertinence of Herberg's thesis rests upon the material they set forth. They see the novel and unique character of contemporary religion in the United States as stemming from a redirecting of the covenant theology so determinative for the life of the original settlers of New England. Believing that God had sent them on an "errand into the wilderness" to establish a new Christian civilization, these first Americans reckoned that they were his people, called specially to his service as a kind of new "chosen people," God's American Israel. Like the most sensitive Hebrews of old, the original band of leaders in Massachusetts sought to guard against interpreting this divine vocation in terms of special privilege. As the American experiment passed from success to success, however, the standard (if sometimes unstated) assumption came to be that Americans are a special people in terms of value to God, status before God, and destiny under God. To state the point theologically, national purposes, were exalted above the divine will, or were even subtly identified with it in the minds of masses of Americans. This development was, of course, aided by the steady decline of theological orientation in many of the churches after 1750, an orientation which might well have braked the pell-mell decline by exalting supernatural revelation as normative. Similarly, by default the dominance of an otherworldly concern allowed a nationalistic creed to surge on unchecked in that majority of churches which so long remained in the grip of revivalistic pietism.

Largely as a result of this strong sense of destiny as the new People of God, religion came to occupy a singular place in the American consciousness. In a manner reminiscent of European Establishments, it became part and parcel of the national civilization. The average American reasoned that one really ought to have concrete religious affiliation; if he did not belong to the church or otherwise consider himself religious, at least he ought to affirm religion to be an indispensable part of the national heritage. Small wonder then that the third generation of immigrants saw affiliation with a religious community as an admirably American thing to do. No better means to smaller-group identification, without which personal health is tenuous, could be found than connection with the church or synagogue.

Conceivably the now-assimilated new American might have chosen some other community of identity had not the American temper been so favorably disposed toward religion. The transformed Puritan ideal made the choice of religion as a means to identification more than a legitimate act; it had become in fact as wholesomely and characteristically American as an act could be. In short, Herberg's thesis presupposes the prevailing general tradition that America is God's land and her people his; the value of his exposition is in illustrating an historic American propensity, which long antedates the immigration era but is intensified by it.

Inappropriateness of the Mainstream Profile to the South

There is no urgent reason for challenging the essential reliability of the analyses which attribute the shape of American religion to the convergence of historical and social forces. But what has been described is the situation of mainstream America, and it cannot be thought of as including the South.

In the first place, by no stretch of the imagination can it be supposed that the role of nineteenth century immigrants has been nearly as decisive for the South as for the rest of the nation. Ever since the Colonial era, during which Englishmen and the Scotch-Irish populated the southern territory, a very high percentage of Southerners has been Anglo-Saxon. And although relations between the original English colonizers and the latecoming (after 1720) Scotch-Irish had been often belligerent in their Old World setting, the two groups lived together increasingly amiably in the "back country" of Virginia and the Carolinas. No doubt the formative twin traits, time and space, which everywhere affected the American temperament, facilitating concordant settlement, contributed to the gradual fusion of these erstwhile adversaries into a single people. At any rate, a single culture emerged.

The English and the Scotch-Irish pooled resources to form the normative strain of southern society, which has been departed from only in minor ways. Of course, there have been challenges to this standard pattern of homogeneity. The entry of German peoples into the northern valley of Virginia and the western piedmont in the Carolinas during the middle third of the eighteenth century, and into several east south-central Texas counties in the period 1830–1850, may stand as examples. Although the German subcultures so created were to different degrees isolated and distinct, for the most part their traditional folkways gradually yielded to the unrelenting assault of the dominant British culture. By the present decade few of the dissident folkways have survived in the younger generations. Among the formal vestiges which do survive are certain town names in Texas: Nordheim, Schulenburg, Breslau, Manheim (sic), and others; and the dominance of the Lutheran faith in several Texas counties. The net impact of the German tradition in Virginia and the Carolinas is the perpetuation of a charming but inconclusive heterogeneity in the religious patterns of several counties.

The other openings in the nearly solid wall of Anglo-Saxon culture in the South are well known and have been touched upon earlier. Peninsular Florida and the scattered Roman Catholic strongholds represent the major variations. Simkins' words will serve to bring the matter up to date: "The South since 1865 has failed to attract many immigrants. The growing cities of the New South, enveloped in the rural psychology that surrounds them, have little of the cosmopolitanism that blew from Europe into Northern cities." [4] A hundred years after The War's close, however, this cultural uniformity is breaking up.

Turning from sociological to historical considerations, we find that the factors which conditioned religion in mainstream America were absent from the southern experience. For one thing, the incentives for settlement and the tone of community life in Colonial Virginia differed significantly from the spirit which pulsated through New England life. It is true, as Perry Miller has demonstrated, that the Virginia colonists, like the Puritans who followed them to America, envisioned turning the new continent into the next act in the divine drama of the ages.[5] As a matter of fact it is unthinkable that any extension of seventeenth century English culture, whether as dissent or projection, should have been free from overriding religious assumptions and concerns. But two circumstances played fast and loose with any appreciable realization of a holy commonwealth in Virginia. First, an announced lofty purpose, articulated with consistency during its first years, was effectively quashed after the colony's transference to royal status in 1624. Religious idealism yielded to hard-nosed economic considerations. The second and more telling circumstance was that ardor for the creation of a uniquely Christian society never had burned very high. Unlike their fellow English transplants up the Atlantic Coast, the southern colonists were never consumed by the ambition to establish a new Israel. Their more modest aim was to create an outpost of English society on foreign shores, an aim which automatically carried with it the intention to plant England's church and to labor for the building of a Christian society. The intensity with which the Puritans undertook their religious mission far outstripped Virginia's "energizing compulsion." Furthermore, there was a marked contrast between the energy of the New England colonies and the society that prevailed in the South, especially beyond Virginia. In the Carolinas and Georgia, far less ordered societies existed. Colonizing happened more or less at random in these other areas, there being little corporate planning or social structuring. Thus, whereas certain over-all objectives and plans shaped New England life, in the southern society they operated below the surface or scarcely at all.

Having begun in this less ordered fashion, southern traditions were destined to veer even farther from the culture of the Northeast, and its later (modified) projection on the western frontier. This fact is epitomized by the presence of a corporate sense of destiny in one region and its absence in the other. Hardly more than a modicum of the Puritan spirit of divine calling sifted down from the New England "holy experiment" to the immense, sprawling, southern territory. As a consequence there was little redirecting of the South's primarily commercial orientation. The simple matter of geography also entered into the picture. The southern population was far too scattered and its life too loosely organized for any great corporate aspirations to be fostered until its basic social and economic way of life was threatened by the fight against slavery. Southerners thought in terms of the needs, problems, and destinies of individuals within the society, having little provocation to formulate grand designs for corporate goals. The Colonial Southerner was prone to consider the new land as primarily a place for building a home, rather than in terms of developing property. He was preoccupied with enjoying life as an individual in a context of intimate social relations, not with an indomitable urge to create a radically new world.[6]

Thus if mainstream American religious history reflects a degenerate corporate ideal, southern religious history exhibits an intelligible overlooking of generalized goals and ideals, in virtue of a near-exclusive devotion to the needs and destinies of individuals in a diffuse society.

The hardening of the institution of slavery into the bedrock foundation of southern society decisively reinforced the divergence of the two sections. After 1830, whatever sense of participation in the national destiny had been inculcated into southern thinking was buried by virulent sectionalism, which was reinforced by regional introversion during Reconstruction and its aftermath.

In this way, social, historical, and geographical factors converged to fashion a peculiar southern religious syndrome. The evidence that the South has not been party to the circumstances which have conditioned the church in mainstream America is unassailable. Secularizing pressures have beaten upon it, however, just as they do upon religious life everywhere. We must now examine those forces and pressures and see how they interacted with the South's received theological tradition; only then can we describe the unique belief- and value-system which characterizes the regional church, and later, in what particular respects southern religion is secularized.

4

The Shaping Forces in the Southern Religious Heritage

The famous English cleric William Inge once remarked that a religion succeeds, not because it is true, but because it suits its worshipers. Whatever the implications of this statement, it does point to a powerful ingredient in the historical phenomenon called religion, and more particularly to a profound dimension in the religion of the American South.

On the premise that the religion of the South, no less than that of mainstream America, mirrors (not to mention, transcends) its historical and social heritage, we maintain that the frontier situation, a rural style of life, and cultural insulation have been as influential in Dixie as the transformed Puritan vision, immigrant sociology, and related factors have been elsewhere. It is our purpose now to trace in some detail the emergence of southern religion's peculiar patterns by examining the interaction of various social forces with the received theological tradition.

Religion in the Colonial South

Astounded as an observer of the recent and contemporary South might be by the discovery, the region was not distinguished by the quality of its religious life during the Colonial period. It is of course true that the Church of England was formally established in every colony south of Pennsylvania during all or part of the period. Accordingly, organized religion was paid a certain deference, its existence taken for granted, and its influence felt in broad ways. The religious tradition of western civilization, the faith which had nourished the settlers and their forebears for well over a thousand years, did not lie outside their consciousness. In the historian's words, "a sense of sin and of piety, deeply embedded in people whose ancestors had been devout British Protestants, was not to be uprooted by the liberating circumstances of a new environment." [1] Notwithstanding this fact, the rank and file generally stood at some remove from meaningful religious involvement until the outbreak of a subvariety of evangelical Protestantism in the 1740's and the decades following.

There can be little doubt that religious faith was a crucial element of life for very few Colonial Southerners. Research into the religious situation in Georgia about 1800 yielded the information that "there were not 500 Christian people in all" among 80,000 inhabitants. In 1786, there were three Episcopal churches, each carrying on without the service of a rector, and three churches representing each of three other denominations (Lutheran, Presbyterian, and Baptist), with little health in any.[2] Things were much the same in North Carolina, where Governor Eden referred to the "deplorable state of religion in this poor province" in the year 1717, and where a subsequent governor reported to the Assembly of 1739 that church services were held regularly only at Bath and Edenton, that the state of religion was "really scandalous," and that there was a "deplorable and almost total want of divine worship throughout the province," a condition which he urged the legislature to remedy "without loss of time." [3] To whatever portion of the South in this period one turns, one finds little to relieve the monotony of religious lethargy, and in many cases religious illiteracy as well. It would appear that in the Colonial South "the establishment was simply unsuited to the needs of an expanding population, and only militant home missions of the type developed by the radical wing of Protestantism were capable of meeting the challenge." [4]

There is no honest alternative to the judgment that the Established Church was ineffective in its care of southern souls. Even a sympathetic Anglican historian, despite all his pains to call attention to the differences from colony to colony, is bound to acknowledge "a decline in relative strength and inner vitality." [5] Scarcity of clergy—largely attributable to the fact that there was no American bishop—constituted part of the problem, which was compounded by the generally mediocre calibre of the existing clergy. It has been observed that even when there was a regular clergyman "he was apt to perform his duties in a way so perfunctory as to have little appeal to his parishioners, especially persons of the poorer class." [6] In this connection, a plaque adorning a narthex wall in Christ Church, Middlesex County, Virginia, tells a graphic story: "The Rev. Hefferman, rector between 1795 and 1813, seems to have been a rather dissolute man; more interested in wassail and horse racing than in the souls of his parishioners." The plaque states that, owing partly to his ineptitude, no doubt, the parish was defunct from 1813 to 1840, "and it probably died sometime before 1813 for all practical purposes."

The lack of Anglican strength and popularity must have been generally as it was in North Carolina:

> The Anglican Church was unpopular because it had been established by the royal government and had a close relation to it. Non-Anglicans resented its support by public taxes, its control of education, and its other special privileges, particularly the law which permitted only Anglican clergymen to

perform the marriage ceremony. The forms and doctrines of the church, the "Anglican squat," the church's aristocratic outlook and apparent lack of interest in the common people, its lack of emphasis on preaching, and its lack of emotional appeal met with popular disfavor.[7]

Drawing a similar conclusion, another historian attributes the decline of the Anglican Church to "its lack of vivid affirmations and its preference for common sense and formal ritual, instead of unconventional emotionalism [which] kept it from satisfying the needs of the common people." [8]

Although the church surely was remiss in its duties, the blame cannot be laid there altogether, for many forces beyond the institution's control contributed to its ineptitude and irrelevancy. The unique character of the nascent society struggling for a *modus vivendi* seemed to throw roadblocks before the church's efforts to penetrate with the Christian message, and to require bold new approaches and radical adaptations, perhaps even improvisations, if the church was to communicate and minister to the builders of this new social order.

As far as immediate achievement is concerned, the Anglican communion in the South was served poorly by its inherently conservative instincts. Never before had the Church of England lived in a society which required that it justify itself. In the church's homeland, leaders could assume that the ministrations of the church were intelligible, if not always highly meaningful, to ordinary men. But such was not the case in the American South where a tradition had to prove its worth functionally in order to survive, and where men responded more to the nerve endings of their emotions than to traditions or concepts of forms.[9] Moreover, only once had the Church of England ever been challenged to shift its doctrinal positions and ecclesiastical practices under the stress of radical social circumstances—during the aftermath of the Reformation, in the midst of comparatively stable conditions. Thus it was not inclined either by its Catholic theology (which made it wary of improvisation) or by its concrete history among Englishmen to produce major alterations in position, emphasis, or method. In a word, the strange southern frontier proved too much for England's church in the short run.

In retrospect it appears that the Colonial Southerners, although still within the broad stream of the Christian heritage, would embrace religious faith only if and when there was strong provocation. They did not oppose religion militantly, but neither did they simply drift into faith because convention so dictated.

Moreover, after 1700 a large proportion of southern residents lived geographically outside the sphere of influence of organized Christianity. The nearest church was likely to be a formidable distance away from the small farmhouse or chinked cabin. Clergy were in short supply, especially west of the Fall Line where the population expanded and determinative regional social patterns evolved. Besides, Christian symbols did not impinge upon the daily life, for services of public worship, the reading of the Bible, and, in general, instruction in the Christian way were largely lacking in common experience. One student of the Colonial South has summed up this condition by writing that "thousands were left without the services of any minister at all, while others were forced to content themselves with but one or two sermons a year." [10] The sparsely settled Virginia-Carolina frontier was a dramatically unreligous—not to say, antireligious —area, its inhabitants mainly ignorant of and unconcerned with religious matters. The Reverend Devereaux Jarratt, the evangelical Anglican preacher who was the primary agent in the rise of Methodist societies in southern Virginia, wrote that upon becoming the rector of a parish in 1763 he found religious unconcern and ignorance so appalling that "it was as if the people had never seen a church or heard a sermon in their lives." [11] The young parson Philip Vickers Fithian, while traveling in the back country, was shocked to find that "all the lower classes of people and the servants and the slaves consider [the Sabbath] as a day of pleasure and amusement. . . . The gentlemen go to church, to be sure, but they make that itself a matter of convenience, and account the church as a useful weekly resort to do business." [12] What was true throughout the upper

Colonial South seems to have typified the entire society. The southern colonies formally established a church, but the Christianity it represented stood on the periphery of the people's lives.

The First Great Challenge, and the South's Response

Had there been time, the Anglican Church might possibly have adapted itself to this most extraordinary new setting. However, because religious life was of a piece with that dramatic social change which was the anatomy of the mid-eighteenth century South, the time was much too brief. At this juncture a newly oriented society was born. In one respect—the fact that this new epoch had cultural roots in the British way of life which guided the direction of movement—the new society was not new. In other respects, however, its birth marked a significant departure from the old, and perhaps religious developments during the period of transition illustrate the turn which events took as vividly as those on any plane of regional life. Had the old society survived essentially unchanged, by all odds the one religious institution in the most favorable position to gain the loyalties of the settlers was the church which was part and parcel of that heritage. Yet the Anglican Church occupied that position only so long as Virginia and the Carolinas remained structural transplantations of England (and Scotland). Once the infant society had cut the umbilical cord, it tended to formulate a religious tradition more congenial to its distinctive ethos. Viewed sociologically, it may be said that the earlier society was Anglo-Virginian in the sense that it had internalized the outlook, values, and aims of English society. Now that Virginia was attaining cultural autonomy, however, a new pattern of socialization emerged. In short, the colonists came to adopt outlooks and values of their own making, albeit never severed totally from the Old World heritage, but manifesting ever more affinity to their distinctive ethos.

Following 1740, evangelical versions of Christianity drove the entering wedge into Virginia and North Carolina, soon managing to gain the upper hand, wresting control from the hapless Anglicans and transferring it into the hands of zealous bodies whose outlook and methods were far more congenial to this new breed of Western man.[13] Thus England's church was displaced as the religious center of the colony's life. Once an indigenous variation of Christianity had taken hold, the society which had been indifferent toward the church took on an increasingly more religious complexion.[14]

The years 1740–1741 really mark the turning point. At that time a group of Virginians (of English, not Scottish, descent) living in Hanover County, a scant dozen miles northeast of Richmond, began to hold private meetings in order to read some of George Whitefield's sermons and Luther's *Commentary on Galatians*. Religious fervor soon possessed those whose affiliation had been with the parish church but who now assumed a dissenting posture (and knew of nothing to call themselves but Lutherans). Hearing that a New Light (pro-revival) Presbyterian minister, educated at Pennsylvania's "Log College," the center for the training of revivalistic ministers, was in a nearby county preaching with great success, they invited him to minister in their midst. The Reverend William Robinson gladly came to them for the period of four days. So inspiring was his pious and zealous preaching that a number of others, in addition to the original company of seekers, grew interested, and it was decided that a Presbyterian church should be constituted. A short while later the Reverend Samuel Davies became their minister. Under his leadership, three Presbyterian churches in the area attained a high level of vitality, and a new phase in the religious history of Virginia was under way.

Although Robinson's and Davies' Presbyterian tradition was soon to be numerically outdistanced by other Protestant families, Presbyterian beginnings did introduce Evangelicalism, which with its variations was destined to dominate popular thinking, into southern religious life.[15] Seen in one light it is mildly ironic that the Presbyterians broke the soil from which the Baptists and Methodists were later to reap the greater harvests.[16]

The Separate Baptists

In the decades before the Revolution, the southern back country was filling with former seaboarders seeking land and a new life. Into their midst from New England, in 1755, came a band of fervent missionaries, sixteen Separate (as distinct from Regular) Baptists who, having failed in their evangelizing efforts near Winchester, Virginia, during previous months, constituted a church in the North Carolina piedmont on Sandy Creek, between Greensboro and Asheboro. Their brand of Baptism quickly set its stamp on free-church Protestant life in the South. In fact, this tiny and unpretentious congregation was destined to become, in the words of Baptist historian Morgan Edwards who visited the area in 1772, "a mother church, nay a grand mother, and a great grand mother." With unbounded exuberance he recounted and predicted this church's glorious success: "All the separate baptists sprang hence: not only eastward toward the sea, but westwards toward the great river Mississippi, but northward to Virginia and southward to South Carolina and Georgia. The word went forth from this zion, and great was the company of them who published it." [17]

Basically, the Separates were one variety of evangelical Protestantism, which included most classical Puritans, and has been described as "much more a mood and an emphasis than a theological system. Its stress was upon the importance of a personal religious or conversion experience." [18] Negatively, it was meant to counter any "notion that the Christian life involved little more than observing the outward formalities of religion." The New England Separates, originally Congregationalists who generally turned Baptist, heightened the mood of Evangelicalism to its highest degree, making conversion everything, and finally stereotyping and institutionalizing this conception of Christian experience. [19]

The principal Separate Baptist twist on the Puritan heritage consisted in the transformation of the corporate and social ideal, so important in Puritanism, into an exclusively individualistic concern. The Puritan was no simple Pietist, his objective being much broader than the creation of a redemptive communion between man and God. The building of a holy community was central in the Puritan program. Christian responsibility was thought to comprehend the creation of a Christian civilization. Accordingly these ardent Christians worked for the rule of God over the civil realm no less than the ecclesiastical.

In the hands of the Separates, the range of concern was compressed to the conversion of lost souls. On the eastern Connecticut frontier, they were a people at variance with the world. The southern Separates manifested much the same spirit, concentrating on saving the lost, and failing to assume responsibility for society at large.

About 1750, before the arrival of the Reverend Shubal Stearns—who was baptized and ordained the same day—and his fellow Separates, Baptist presence in the South was restricted to a handful of Regular churches scattered in the coastal sections of the upper seaboard states, with four each in Maryland and Virginia, five in South Carolina, and a dozen in North Carolina. Not until the advent of the Separates, who had been called upon by the Almighty, "to move far to the westward [sic], to execute a great and extensive work," did Baptist numbers accelerate.[20] Whereas their several Protestant predecessors had met with slight success in generating religious enthusiasm, the Separate Baptist expression of Christianity proved to be perfectly at home on the southern frontier, where life was uncomplex. A way of thinking which reduced all of life to simple choice and personal considerations made eminently good sense. Moreover, few forces or needs intruded to disturb this way of thinking. A theological perspective which was uncluttered by larger social goals, or sophisticated doctrine, or principles of biblical interpretation which complicated the "plain meaning" of the sacred scripture, recommended itself persuasively.

At this juncture Baptist growth became truly spectacular from the Potomac to the region of the Savannah, and, following the Revolution, in the trans-Appalachian territory as well, owing partly to massive migration as exemplified by the removal of approximately a quarter of the Baptists in Virginia to Kentucky between 1791 and 1810. Several mergers of Regular and Separate groups between 1787 and 1801 introduced a degree of unity that has in intervening decades become a hallmark of southern Baptist existence. To be sure, both components left their impressions on the denomination, the Regulars the more indelibly on cis-Appalachian developments and the Separates to the west.[21] Measured against classical Baptist standards, it has to be said that the Separates exercised the more decisive shaping power.

H. Richard Niebuhr adventitiously shed light on the identity of the Separates in his observation that Baptist churches in America are "not always the heirs of a European tradition but [are] frequently the native-born children of the frontier religious movements." [22] It is apparent that the Separate Baptist movement in New England had at least as great affinity to the emergent socio-religious temper there as to the classical Baptist heritage. In addition to their most dominant trait, extreme evangelicalism, Separate Baptism contributed three ingredients to the religious composition which became popular regional Christianity. These were: first, dogmatic repudiation of theological creeds and systems; second, hyperconcern with and confidence of assurance; and third, the simplistic outlook of the movement's founders.

Wherever they went, these dynamic Baptist witnesses crusaded in the conviction that all *must* undergo a memorable conversion experience. They held that the experience of regeneration was self-authenticating, and within the power of the preacher to evoke under the right conditions. On the theological side, it is not surprising that they gave central place only to such doctrinal considerations as were implicit in or auxiliary to the theme of conversion. Naturally, there was reliance on, and appeal to, emotional persuasion. These were uncomplicated, devout men who lived life on an essentially emotional level, and whose religion was conceived and practiced on that plane. They submitted little to the tests of reason or tradition, since they lived by the principle that if something felt good, it might well have merit; and conversely, that if something was real and true, the espousal of it would create an emotional awareness within the person. Consistent with this kind of response to life, Virginia Baptist leader John Leland was convinced that "whatever makes for good preaching is *ipso facto* right doctrine." [23] Fully assured that they themselves had been granted peremptory forgiveness of sins, and that the divine blessing was upon them, since "they were obviously more successful than their traditionalist brethren" in other denominations, they forged forward with brazen vigor, devoted to "this one thing," the "primacy of the evangelistic imperative." [24]

Stated briefly, the fundamental Separate belief amounted to two assertions which were standard evangelical ideas more intensely emphasized: The conversion experience is necessary; it is possible. It is *necessary* because the holy God makes only one requirement of men which pales all other requirements, indeed includes all that are of any import, namely, the acceptance of Christ as the Savior from sin and hell. This the Separates took to be the very marrow of Christian truth in terms of one's own standing before God and of Christian responsibility in regard to the mission the converted man assumes.

The *possibility* of the conversion experience was stressed in contrast to traditional theology's insistence that God alone knew who were the elect. Instead, God's saving grace was regarded as immediately available to any and all, flowing into one's life through an extraordinary inward experience which elicited a deep emotional response. Its entry would be unmistakably known to the one regenerated by it. As they saw it, life under God, for all practical purposes, centered in the single moment. Life's spiritual pilgrimage was seen as divisible into two states, being lost and being saved, the two clearly demarcated by the moment in which one knows that the stain of his sins has been washed away, and a heaveny destiny vouchsafed. In so affirming, the Separates altered the traditional Baptist teaching concerning the "security of the believer," which held that no one could be absolutely "sure," by maximizing the importance of assurance and by shifting its base from the realm of divine activity to the realm of immediate psychic experience. To be sure, they were Baptist; the changes they wrought were quantitative—that is, they only accentuated the radical (subjectivist) tendencies inherent in the tradition. But once those changes had been wrought and institutionalization had become a fact, a new species of Baptist life appeared which was significantly removed from the denomination's historical character.[25]

Methodism's Contribution

The variety of Protestant Christianity which the New Light Presbyterians first spawned in the South, Evangelicalism, with revivalism as its technique, was popularized widely by the Separate Baptists. While Presbyterian expansion was stabilizing, the Baptists were planting new churches everywhere. Moreover, once they had penetrated the western frontier, their farmer-preachers spread the evangelical word to the masses in local communities, and their annual associational meetings served on a grand scale as rallying centers for the conversion of the lost.

It was the Methodists who deserve most credit for developing the means of spreading the seed of the evangelical message. Already successful in their labors in the seaboard areas, the western Methodist preachers used the camp meeting and the circuit-rider system to great advantage. Unhampered by such Baptist traits as *local* church ecclesiology, decentralized structure, and residual Calvinist conceptions, all of which conspired to restrain the Baptists from devising an aggressive, grand scheme for mass evangelism, Methodism made great strides.[26] Especially by means of the camp meeting, Wesley's spiritual descendants were enabled to cut a wide swath through the heretofore un-churched frontier population. As a socio-religious institution, the camp meeting possessed several strategic qualities, not the least its social-psychological effectiveness in mitigating the terrible loneliness of the American style of farming; for it brought together for a several-day period many persons who had scarcely laid eyes on any but members of their own families for weeks or months.[27]

Theologically considered, Methodism was enabled to do this

by its conviction that human free will was the God-given faculty which each person could and should activate in voluntary acceptance of salvation. Whereas more Calvinist-inclined theologies, in their urgency to emphasize the primacy of the *divine* initiative in man's salvation, seemed to depreciate the part played by man, the Methodist preachments encouraged individuals to *seek* salvation on the grounds that man's will played an integral part in the act of regeneration. Moreover, Methodism could look back to and re-enact its evangelical experience in England dating from the 1740's. Both theology and experience served to catapult the Methodist movement into a position of leadership in the grand evangelization of the frontier.

Both being evangelical bodies, Baptists and Methodists were one in believing that the church was properly made up of the experientially regenerate only, but the latter turned this conviction into a dramatic and large-scale possibility. Perhaps they were aided in doing so throughout the frontier society by the demise of Calvinist theology there.[28] Explanation for the Methodist success in Calvinist country—quite apart from the seeming incompatibility of Calvinism's utter reliance on deity with the vigorous self-reliance of the frontier mentality—may well lie in the fact that the New Light Presbyterianism had driven a dent in the Calvinist armor, to be followed by the Baptists' further relaxation of their already qualified commitment to it. The decline of the Calvinist rigor, together with the exigencies of the frontier society, meant that after the first decade, nineteenth century "American Protestantism was to be defined almost wholly in Methodist terms." [29] Although this interpretation is intended as a reference to the larger national situation, it applies with special force to the narrower confines of the South where the revivalistic form of Christianity reached a position of unchallenged supremacy over the entire regional culture.

On the trans-Appalachian frontier, beginning with the Great Revival of 1800–1810, vast resources of the considerable Methodist energies were poured into the evangelization of the unchurched lost who made up the large majority of the population, and the Christianizing of a disorderly society. The latter task was decidedly needful, since in their rush for political and economic freedom after the Revolution, settlers "outraced the established institutions of society—the church, schools, courts of law. Not only ignorance but emotional instability resulted, bringing widespread worldliness, immorality, and infidelity." [30] There was a man-sized task to be done in this setting where men were equally dislocated before their God and their fellows. The Methodists rose to the occasion. Streaming through the gaps from Maryland, Virginia, and North Carolina in the period 1785–1810, after a solid beginning in those seaboard states, the circuit-riding preachers blanketed the region. They seemed to penetrate every hollow, copse, valley, and plain, establishing churches and "classes," purifying public morality, and commissioning lay preachers and class leaders to carry on during the many days of the month when the community was without benefit of clergy. Their enthusiastic pietism drove them to relentless labors. It is doubtful that any of their European forebears had generated more zeal.

Like their Baptist neighbors, Methodists conceived of their responsibilities in terms of those facets of their theological heritage which were exacerbated by the frontier environment. They were not fabricating a religion to suit themselves, but their interpretation of the Bible and their selection of major objectives were conditioned by social circumstances. In the hands of these purveyors of popular evangelical Protestantism, as Simkins has incisively stated it, "historic Protestantism was reduced to the consistencies of the Southern environment without sacrificing inherent fundamentals." [31] It would be untrue to say that they forsook historic Christianity, but they did improvise and reformulate, angling the Methodist complex steadily farther away from its Wesleyan legacy. What claimed their singlehearted devotion was the calling to be agents of personal conversion for the lost, and to be themselves practitioners of a purist private morality. In these emphases, as well as other points, they were closely linked to Wesley. Moreover, they perpetuated the forms of church government, discipline, and nurture which he had developed in England (and whose hierarchical nature *seemed* alien to the frontier spirit). For example, converts from the camp meetings who sought membership in the local Methodist church were required to serve a probationary period as well as to attend class meetings for Christian nurture over a span of several months.

Though the continuities with English Methodism at the levels of instruction and discipline endured for a time, the frontier church's passion for spontaneous conversion gradually displaced everything else.[32] Perhaps it was inevitable that the dual components of an experiential religion and the frontier ethos should result in the gradual fading away of the practices of discipline and nurture (class meetings had virtually disappeared by 1900). This was predictable, since Methodism, unlike the other offshoots within British Protestantism during the early modern era with their focus on restructuring the externalities of church life, was concerned about the internalities of faith.

The importance of this near-exclusive dedication to the inner dimensions of organized religion on the part of the Methodists allied them intimately with the Baptists. From their rather different matrices, despite certain real differences, the two had essentially the same face on the southern frontier, thereby creating the climate for popular southern Protestantism.

The Evangelical Conquest

Before the first three decades of the nineteenth century had become history, the reign of the Baptist and Methodist denominations among the southern populace was assured in principle. The traditional churches of England and Scotland (and the colonies) had been relegated to a secondary numerical position, though some of their views had been absorbed in the standard regional patterns. In terms of statistical dominance, the future belonged to the two aggressive revivalistic denominations, and as it later developed, to those groups catering to the lower classes who incorporated essentially the same outlook and spirit.

But, as we have noted, the South was not taken without a struggle. During the Revolutionary era and for a generation following, Protestant revivalism was rivaled by indifferentism and a second religious force, namely, deism, with its attendant tolerance and skepticism. It is true that deism flourished almost exclusively among the upper-class families, but it is important to bear in mind that this sector of the population exercised an influence over the southern outlook out of all proportion to its numbers. Actually, the deistic mentality enjoyed real strength in the region for a considerable period. After flourishing for a generation, however, it gave way to the revivalists' orthodoxy. A foremost student of intellectual and social life in the ante-bellum South asserts that "by 1830 the Southern people had become thoroughly converted to orthodoxy in religion; the skepticism that had existed among the gentry of the eighteenth century, the age of reason, had virtually disappeared." [33] Deism was destined to die out in the southern social context, for the rural masses desired and required a religious approach far warmer and less intellectual.[34]

Despite the fact that before the Civil War, less than 20 per cent of regional residents were church members, there is a curious continuity between this situation and that of the post-War society of which it has been written that "the Southerner found it difficult to believe that any person could be decent in morals and manners who was not a church a member." [35] Only time and outreach by the churches were lacking for Evangelicalism to complete its conquest of the region. The religiously solid South, adumbrated by 1830, was on its unerring course toward realization before the dawn of the twentieth century.

This progress toward converting the entire society snowballed in the early twentieth century. By the 1920's "only the illiterates and the badly isolated in Southern society—white and Negro, had failed to identify themselves with some church, and the eventual progress of education and roads increased the harvest among those unredeemed." [36] The South had come to resemble medieval Europe, in that for persons in both societies it was almost impossible not to own formal religious identification. Not even the advent of industrialization and urbanization managed to impede this development. As a matter of fact, the new conditions simply brought to the cities hordes of country folks (not immigrants, as in mainstream America), familiar with and devoted to the "old-time gospel." Simkins ventures to assert that the fact that "advance of industry, urbanization, and education helped rather than hindered the advance of religious organizations" comprises "one fact about the history of the Southern church, not applicable to other sections of the civilized world." [37]

Thus a society which had successively enthroned or tolerated Anglicanism, indifferentism, Presbyterianism, and deism offered no genuine option to the masses of its people by the 1920's save within the narrow range between Methodist, Baptist, and sectarian versions of the same Low Church Protestantism. The evangelical conquest was unprecedentedly complete.

Cultural Insulation

One of the best-known facts concerning the American South is its comparative isolation from the major changes and developments characteristic of the rest of the nation during the last 150 years, particularly after the 1830's. It is hardly surprising, therefore, that characteristic regional religion has been conspicuously insulated from ongoing process in national and world civilization. This isolation is a major shaping force of the present situation, and leads to the conclusion that popular southern Protestantism is substantially the same syndrome of belief, practice, and emphasis which was born during the formative period, 1740–1830.

Three symptoms of this isolation, from radically different sources, may illustrate its reality. Some months ago a puzzled Baptist minister in the South wrote a letter to the editor of his denomination's state paper requesting a satisfying definition of "fundamentalist." The confusion which gave rise to his almost impassioned request for clarification stemmed from the inconsistency between what he found the dictionary definition of "fundamentalist" to be—one who believes in certain listed doctrines, held absolutely—and the almost invariably low estimation of a fundamentalist he had noticed displayed in publications—"in derision, as if he is something the cat has drug in and should not be mentioned in polite society." This earnest man epitomized regional religious insulation, not because he subscribed to the fundamentalist list of absolute doctrinal truths —this position is by no means peculiarly southern—but in being unaware of any other real Christian option and in having no criteria for producing an objective judgment of the fundamentalist stance.

In a different vein, we note the assessment by a former Californian after two years of residence in the South. A devout Protestant, he had come expecting to find overpowering evidence of a "Bible Belt" society, but saw it nowhere. With cryptic power, he described the South as being not the Bible Belt, but "just a conservative region." By the standards of mainline Protestantism, in terms of which he had been conditioned to evaluate the existence of a Christian society, the South failed to measure up. Largely cut off from classical Christianity, it had developed, as he discovered, its own standards of judgment.

The third illustration grows out of the experience during World War II of a regional seminary whose graduates were serving as military chaplains. When some of these requested transfer from reserve commissions to regular status, their requests were denied on the grounds that their seminary was not accredited. Informed by the United States Commissioner of Education that these graduates of his institution could not be transferred to regular status, the seminary president replied incredulously, "What do you mean, '_____ Seminary is not accredited'? This institution was founded by _____," quoting the name of the school's revered founder, a conservative theologian unknown outside the sponsoring denomination.[38]

But why has the South's leadership not provided local communities, states, and the region at large with visions and plans which would have assaulted parochialism? In other words, especially in recent decades, why have the upper classes not engendered ways of thinking at variance with and superior to popular patterns, thus breaking open the circle of regional isolation? This query becomes the more puzzling when considered in the light of the sociological theory that the relative unity of experience which is typical of simple societies, like the South's, loosens under the impact of "the sharp increase in economic specialization and the heightening of class distinctions . . . characteristic of the new societies." [39] As upper classes begin to form, intellectually inclined persons tend to emerge, persons with more time to observe and compare different human societies and subsocieties.

For some understanding as to why leaders of southern society have not stimulated and fostered progressive thought, Howard Becker's categories (themselves a modification of Tönnies' classic *Gemeinschaft* and *Gesellschaft*) are illuminating.[40] Becker divides human societies into "sacred" and "secular" (in a technical usage of those terms), a sacred society being one which carries a high degree of resistance to change. More precisely, it is "one that elicits from or imparts to its members . . . an unwillingness and/or inability to respond to the culturally new as the new is defined by those members in terms of the society's existing culture." By contrast a secular society is "one that endows its members with a high degree of readiness and capacity to change." [41]

The American South is virtually the paradigm of "sacred" societies in the modern western world. Moreover, it corresponds almost exactly to Becker's description of the three varieties of isolation and impermeability, namely, the vicinal, the social, and the mental. In terms of the *vicinal,* the South's sacredness consists of the "absence . . . of communication, at the level of sheer physical opportunity for culture contact, with persons from other societies." Likewise at the *social* level, for there surely have been barriers to social intercourse with members of societies outside one's bailiwick. The same holds true for the *mental* variety of isolation, there being an "absence of effective communication, at the level of a 'common universe of discourse,' with representatives of other value-systems who are 'physically and socially present.' " [42] The southern upper classes have traditionally been as isolated as the masses, physically, socially, and mentally.[43]

It is this complex of geo-social forces which has conserved the belief- and value-structures of popular southern Protestantism, almost uncompromised, from its formative period to the near-contemporary past. Rapid social change has set in with the advent of the decade of the 1960's, calling for an adaptation of Christianity even more comprehensive than that made by frontier Methodists and Baptists during the formative period (our contention in Part IV). Having noted that social-historical conditioning took place through the agency of various forces, it is now necessary to examine the theological, ethical, and practical essence of popular southern Protestantism.

Part ii
The Essence of Popular Southern Protestantism

5
The Central Theme

Although diversity is a conspicuous feature of southern culture, a "central theme" dominates various aspects of it, including regional religious life. As a result, the several major communions agree on such basic issues as the real nature and primary goal of Christian faith. The southern church "makes all of individual Christianity" and regards the conversion of men as virtually the whole task of the church.[1] It will be the burden of Part II to describe the theological meaning and ethical implications of this central theme.

Denominational Heterogeneity and the Central Theme

The southern church did not begin *de novo*. It inherited a body of tradition, actually four somewhat different theological traditions: the Anglican, the Calvinist, the Baptist, and the Methodist. All of these were born outside America, each under unique circumstances. The Church of England was relevant to sixteenth century England—its *via media* was an attempt to preserve Catholic Christianity while also incorporating the new Reformation insights. The Calvinist Presbyterians embodied the central Reformation impulses to assert the priority and mystery of the divine agency in history and man's radical dependence on God's grace, as well as to remind men that otherworldly focus should include service in this life as well. The Baptists arose from the socio-political revolution which gripped England during the century following 1534. They contended that each man has direct access to the divine and that creeds, ecclesiastics, and magistrates play no essential part in the individual's relationship to God. Methodism sprang to life to overcome the sterility which permeated much of eighteenth century Anglicanism. It labored to restore the personal inner dimension of faith to a central place by emphasizing the reality of the regenerative experience, the ministry of the laity, and the calling to a life of holiness.

The unity of understanding and objective which came to characterize the southern church is explained in part by a salient fact in the history of each of these denominations in their southern career. It might appear that the Anglican, or Episcopal Church, is out of place in the cluster of four, but only if one overlooks its southern experience. From the very earliest days in Virginia, its orientation was Low Church or Puritan. In their concepts of church polity, worship, and morality, southern Episcopalians have had more in common with the popular churches than either their theological heritage or their higher social status would seem to suggest. Of course, the distinction between the Episcopal ethos and the popular churches must not be blurred. Nevertheless, in tone Puritan Anglicanism bore great similarity to groups in the free-church tradition, despite real differences in authority and stated theology.

A second truth supporting the contention that there is an essential southern Protestantism involves the kinds of Presbyterian and Baptist life which entered the South in the middle third of the eighteenth century. As prime movers of the southern phase of the Great Awakening, both fell somewhat outside the central tradition of their respective denominations. William Robinson, Samuel Davies, and most other early Presbyterian leaders had imbibed "New Light" doctrine at William Tennent's "Log College" in Pennsylvania. They were zealous exponents of pro-revival Calvinism, a position which gave priority to saving faith, as against sound doctrine. These were warmhearted preachers who, without despising theology, sought chiefly to set ablaze the fires of vital religion wherever they went. It is of profound and lasting importance that southern Presbyterianism began in this way. Although revivalism had been repudiated outright, or wrenched from the main thrust of the movement, within three-quarters of a century after its beginnings in Hanover County, Virginia, southern Presbyterianism's over-all character had been determined. Ever since, despite its sound theology and good preaching, it has been something less than objectively oriented, generally preferring to emphasize the warmth of relatively informal worship and a high degree of fellowship in the local congregation. In this way Presbyterianism in the South has lain a few degrees to the left of the central stream of its heritage, and by helping create the range of popular southern Protestantism has located itself within sight of the massively popular churches.

Much less obvious is the way in which a particular subtradition within the Baptist tradition helped to contribute to an essential southern Protestantism. For it was eccentric Baptists, the Separates, who won a firm place in the southern religious picture. The Regular Baptist heritage might have been somewhat uncomfortable within the developing southern consensus because it would have wished to retain: (1) the Calvinistic orientation which had prompted the Baptist churches in New England to have little to do with the Great Awakening there; (2) the commitment to an ecclesiology which acknowledged the Christian life as corporate by nature, leading it to reject an individualistic conception of the Christian life; (3) and respect for historic confessions of faith, as distinct from any view which interpreted Christian reality in terms of immediate experience only. To be sure, the Regular Baptist position would not have fallen as far to the right on the theological spectrum as the classical Presbyterian, but its location would have been adjacent to the New Light Presbyterian. The Separate Baptist position was well to the left of both.

The last major factor in southern religious life concerns Methodism. Against the backdrop of historical Christianity, Methodism in general should be placed somewhat to the left of center, owing to its dominating subjective orientation. Although original Methodism was far from untheological or antitheological, its concentration was on the subjective, the "plain truths" of repentance, regeneration, and sanctification, all ramifications of an experiential emphasis in religion. Once Methodism had acquired a certain autonomy in America, its southern branch adapted to environmental circumstances; as its objectives narrowed, squeezing out liturgy and simplifying theology, its left-wing tendencies were exaggerated. In this way southern Methodism came to parallel its companion Protestant denominations in manifesting a leftist leaning, not only within the scope of catholic Christianity, but within the denomination's tradition itself.

In sum, the prevalent diversities within southern Protestantism are minimized by the striking sameness within and between denominations. The radical wings of all four dominated their respective modes of life in the South. The elements of the four heritages which maximized the Bible, informal congregational association, personal holiness, and inward religion—in other words, the most evangelical parties of the four families—early gained the upper hand. An approximate regional consensus was actualized, and in the case of the Baptist and Methodist denominations, a remarkable unanimity of purpose and method resulted.

The Overriding Consideration

All the affirmations of popular southern Protestantism grow

out of one concern, the salvation of the individual. The various religious groupings are not equally intense in their implementation of this concern, nor do they conceive of it in precisely the same way; nevertheless this is the foundation upon which assumptions are made, doctrinal systems constructed, and church programs based.

In one respect, of course, the salvation of individuals has been the goal of every Christian institution; indeed it lies near the heart of Christian meaning as it has been universally comprehended. Medieval Roman Catholicism, Reformation Protestantism, and American Evangelicalism, under their respective forms, alike strove for this goal. Nevertheless, southern religion is what it is because of the near-exclusive dominance of this concern, the particular rendering of it, and the nature of the answer given to it, reflecting its own blending of "Catholic substance and Protestant principle." Overriding everything else is consideration of the ancient question, "What must I do to be saved?" Each part of the question reveals something of its over-all meaning to southern Protestants: the note of urgency as conveyed by the use of "must," the stress on personal decision and action as captured by "I do," and the particular way in which the human plight is posed by this usage of the word "saved."

The operative theology begins with a particular interpretation of the nature of God. The Almighty is conceived as characteristically moral, as One who requires purity and is accordingly outraged over human sinfulness. The quantity and quality of men's transgressions preoccupy the divine consciousness and block any free dispensing of his grace, presence, and power—until certain conditions are met. That is, God is instinctively thought of, firstly and most representatively, as the Holy Judge. Thus, all roads along the Christian pilgrimage lead to the ultimate Day of Judgment. This is not to imply that Southerners regard life in history as merely instrumental. In line with their Protestant heritage, the here and the hereafter, continuous and interactive, are both inherently significant. Yet the deepest layer of belief holds that each individual will one day stand before the Righteous Judge and be required to give account of himself.

This giving account of one's self, in terms of obedience and disobedience to God, is thought to be *what God is primarily concerned about*. The centrality of this requirement owes its place, let us repeat, to the very nature of God himself. Southern churches have declared that there are two sides to the divine nature, righteousness and holiness (a scholastic description which acquired currency in medieval Atonement theology, and was perpetuated by certain schools of Calvinist thought). In this view, the attribute of holiness in deity makes it imperative that satisfaction be paid for man's violation of that holiness. All men have in fact so violated, with the consequence that God cannot abide their presence in relation to himself until that satisfaction has been produced. The all-important work of satisfaction has been performed by Christ, God's only son, by virtue of his death. It is through man's full willed reception of the merits of Christ that the Father is freed to welcome the pardoned into his presence and embrace them, in a real sense now, but principally in the rapture of the life to come. Without the reception of Christ's merit—and its corollary, a new standing before God—there is no alternative to eternal separation from God, which entails excruciating physical punishment in the hell to which God, in virtue of his nature, must consign the recalcitrant.

Reduced to formula, a Christian theology which follows this line of reasoning is of a "problem-solution" sort. The southern church manifests this belief system when "Christ is the answer" is given as a denomination's promotional slogan or as a handy vest-pocket summary of the faith. In so conceptualizing the Christian message, the southern church parts company with medieval Catholicism by considering each man as one effectively set over against God (in which it is Calvinistic), thus obscuring the Catholic teaching that man is inescapably the creature who belongs to God. It diverges from Calvinism by its assumption that man is an effective agent in his salvation (in which it shares Catholicism's instinct, though not its form, replacing reception of sacramental grace with immediate psychic experience). Christian theology so formulated has three components: God, whose nature issues in the "problem"; man, whose concrete disobedience actualizes the "problem," but whose voluntary acceptance of the "solution" makes possible the way out; and Christ, whose death satisfies God's violated holiness and affords man the "solution."

As for man and his experience of salvation, he is described as depraved, incapable of lifting himself, and totally dependent on the mercies of God for his forgiveness. He is exhorted to repent, for if he does not, his ultimate destruction is sealed. God is thought to see him principally in terms of his status—lost or saved, forgiven or unforgiven. Once the person has decided in favor of Christ, he goes on his way rejoicing in his salvation. And his affirmative decision is regarded as his own, a choice he has made in full consciousness in acting upon the either-or proposition so urgently presented to him. In the moment he acts upon the choice given him and experiences pardon, joy floods his soul. The new awareness is emotionally discernible, for it has immediate psychological effect upon him. According to this interpretation of the way in which saving grace is transmitted, the knowledge that one has "passed from death unto life" is direct and clear in subjective experience.

Even in those southern churches where the central theme does not express itself so overtly and dramatically, it nevertheless dominates the theological habit of mind. The necessity of conversion remains uppermost, often creating confusion if the overt manifestation is not called for, and regularly blocking understanding that other Christian concerns might be equally central.

It goes without saying that the southern church does more than convert the lost, a point to which we shall presently direct attention. Moreover, as is so often the case, a people's richness of life far exceeds their statement of belief. But the main practical impact of the southern church's ministry has to do with the conversion of individuals from condemned status before the Almighty to an everlasting reward in heaven, through the merits of Christ's death. This is the gospel in a nutshell. There can be no doubt that popular southern Protestantism rates these intertwined truths as the core of its message and the incentive for its ministry. Every time it tries to say or do more than this, it does so awkwardly, finding itself ill-equipped to expand its primary orientation toward the salvation of souls to include any other responsibility.

Accordingly and appropriately, the ranking church activity is "evangelism." Not only is this task thought to overshadow all other duties, but with even farther-reaching implications, it is presumed to incorporate virtually the entirety of Christian responsibility. We say appropriately, since, given the conviction that its central theme is the essence of divine truth, the southern church could do no better than root its existence in the mission to convert the lost. Its constancy of aim, its single-mindedness of intent, its integrity vis-à-vis the evangelistic imperative, are examplary.[2]

Just how determinative the central theme is in the life of the southern church is seen, for example, when a denomination is promoting fund-raising campaigns in behalf of its colleges, children's homes, and hospitals: again and again, ultimate recourse is made to the evangelistic appeal. The masses of churchmen have been conditioned to see the evangelistic motive as underlying every undertaking, including higher education and care for the ill and indigent.

In a different vein, the central theme also determines the way in which the Bible is interpreted. The total responsibility of churches and Christians is said to be compressed into the final three verses of the New Testament book of Matthew, the passage in which Christ instructs his followers to bear witness in all the world, and called the "Great Commission" (a label by which these verses are not known in all Christian quarters). A number of uncritical assumptions are made concerning this brief passage: that these are Jesus' authentic words; that being his ultimate, or penultimate, saying they are meant to collect all his basic instructions; and that "making disciples" was his equivalent for the southern church's aim of converting lost souls. It belongs both to the southern church's intense willing of one thing and to its method of interpreting scripture so that the biblical message is condensed in a single passage, understood in a specialized way. The fact that the southern church has not seriously questioned its exaltation of the "Great Commission," through a critical exploration of its meaning and by asking what other basic messages the Bible may contain, is some indication of its attachment to the evangelistic imperative.•

Allegiance to the central theme leads logically to the conclusion that evangelism has principally to do with the hearer himself, rather than the message itself in its own objectivity. Evangelism means the individual's conversion—usually in an instantaneous and datable experience, and it is depicted as chiefly negative and future, from sin and hell, for the life to come. A high percentage of southern sermons, naturally enough, are evangelistic in this sense, warning recalcitrant men of their foredoomed condition, and sharing the joyous news that trust in Christ issues in heavenly reward. Everything is geared to bringing outsiders into the ark of salvation. In this setting, the obvious sincerity and decision-evoking powers of the preacher acquire high priority. What he says is far less important than his effectiveness in saying it, for it is what the hearer can be prompted to do through hearing the message that overshadows all else. The preacher, therefore, has little cause for steeping himself in his proclamation; his concern is with effective presentation, taking for granted the truth of the "simple gospel."

It is no surprise that the evangelist is acknowledged as the representative man of religion in the southern culture. For he is that special breed of divine servant richly endowed with the gifts which render him successful in convincing the lost of their need for the Savior. The clergymen whom most young ministers feel they should emulate are the successful evangelists, some of whom labor full time in this work, most of whom are pastors of large churches. As a rule, these men are clever and persuasive speakers, not infrequently in the finest tradition of southern

---

• For example, it is hardly self-evident that the "Great Commission" is more central than Matthew 25, a passage which also deals with the divine judgment, but in a way which links together judgment and the Christian man's ethical responsibility.

oratory. In the case of many, their aim is to glamorize the Christian way. Adept in illustrating their messages with stories which make great appeal to the emotions—to humor and nostalgia, no less than to fear and pathos—many of them are first-rate entertainers, displaying remarkable skills in turning a phrase, in regaling an audience, in attacking evils adroitly, in manipulating emotions. The delivery is usually rapid, free-flowing, and consciously pitched to produce a "verdict" for or against Christ. In the hands of the skilled, southern evangelistic preaching is wondrous to behold. When produced by the thousands of less gifted men, however, it often reflects less refinement of ability (and perhaps of spirit).

There is a second type of preaching done by the evangelistically inclined heralds. Here concentration is on inculcating a commitment to Christ to be expressed through loyalty to the local church, as well as moral obedience in daily life. In sermons of this sort, a great deal is said about attendance at the public services of the church—often three weekly: two on Sunday and one on Wednesday evening—plus support of the church's various organizations.

Despite a possible first impression that conversion could be regarded as an end in itself and as happening in a vacuum, a close relation exists between evangelism and the institutional church. Evangelism of this type considers the church important precisely because it is the place where life's greatest event occurs. Moreover, it is regarded as the primary sphere for one's living out his service to God. Outside the church fellowship itself, the churchman's chief duty, besides the practice of Christian morality, is the winning of souls.[3] In the southern church, there is little sense of one's daily work as a vocation. Similarly, there is virtually no recognition of any responsibility to redeem the secular dimensions of community and national life, inasmuch as life and the Christian life are construed to be essentially individualistic. Being loyal to the institutional church and centering one's social life in church functions, consequently, are promoted as primary expressions of Christian discipleship. Regardless of what man believes himself called to do "in the world," the institutional church remains his principal point of reference.

In addition to the hortatory preaching just described, there is also a mellower style, employed in what is best classified as a type of devotional discourse. Here the message centers on Jesus of Nazareth, his kindly and transforming dealings with his contemporaries, and the exemplary quality of his relation to his Heavenly Father. Expounding upon the perfection of Jesus in his obedience to God's will in subdued and often moving manner, the preacher urges his hearers to imitate the Master in their personal relationships with God and their fellow men.

Few southern preachers can manage to engage in both kinds of address, the hortatory and the devotional, but it is an unusual devotionalist minister who does not invite into his pulpit from time to time a conventional evangelist for the sake of a great "ingathering of souls." By the same token, many a layman who ordinarily finds the "evangelistic approach" troubling, even galling, as steady fare, rationalizes the "usefulness" of an occasional high-powered evangelistic crusade; indeed, he may even deem it an imperative undertaking. Generally speaking, a distinction must be made between Baptists and Methodists on this score, the evangelistic type of approach predominating in Baptist churches, especially in rural and "people's" churches, and devotional preaching in Methodist congregations.

The grip of the central theme on southern church life is also displayed in the peculiar brand of religious liberalism encountered there. If there were greater theological latitude, no doubt unorthodox theological positions would be voiced from time to time; as matters stand, dissonant doctrines, approaches, or emphases are rarely heard. The range of popular preaching is narrow, from evangelistic to devotional, the latter presupposing conversion and proceeding from there in a softer manner. Not since the 1830's has there been, really, any movement which aimed at overturning the regnant theological tradition.

Such liberalism as exists, therefore, is seen in an openness of spirit, not differentiation of belief or method or stress. In one sense, theology has not been important enough to the southern church to become an issue for disputation. This is not only because of central concern for religious experience, but also because of the subtler factor that most ministers simply take for granted the truth of the several articles of faith which devolve upon personal salvation.

What distinguishes the liberal southern minister is his restraint from threatening the recalcitrant with hell or from making abstinence from personal vices the acid test of Christian morality. The chances are that he, too, believes in the reality of hell, but sees fit to make his appeal on the basis of the love of God. Similarly, he is almost certain to abstain from drinking, but he makes sparse reference to such vices. All this adds up to his being a liberal in virtue of what he does *not* do, say, or emphasize, as well as because his preaching is generally of the devotional, or perhaps softly hortatory, sort. He commits himself to long-range, soft-sell strategems. He is a healer by intention, repairing frequently to compromise.

Assurance, the Touchstone

If the "overriding consideration" can be epitomized by the question, "What must I do to be saved?" the central theme's touchstone is the matter of assurance—the individual's yearning to know that he has been justified by the Almighty. It would be difficult to overestimate the importance of assurance to popular southern theology. Whereas this concern has never lain far from the center of Christianity as practiced, perhaps it has nowhere been so determinative for faith and life as in the southern Protestant community.

Calvinist emphasis on the question, How can the individual know he is among the elect? is well known. Both Calvin and Luther had found the ground of their confidence in *objective* affirmations, Luther declaring "I am baptized," and Calvin taking comfort in the fact that his election was determined by the One who alone was qualified to determine a man's destiny. For both of them, the knowledge that God extended his forgiving grace in line with his own standards of justice was consolation aplenty, affording to each man basic confidence.

Calvin was willing to posit three tests for helping one discern his destiny: a correct profession of faith, an upright life, and participation in the sacraments.[4] The later Puritans continued the use of Calvin's first two tests, but substituted personal religious experience for participation in the sacraments. The Separate Baptists went further still in insisting, as we have noted earlier, that the knowledge of one's salvation from sin and hell is conveyed in the experience of conversion itself.

Had the Separates occupied any different position, they might not have gained such widespread success. The rather subtle notion of assurance as willingness to trust God and leave one's eternal welfare entirely in his hands seems to have held little for frontiersmen. Interpretations of the Christian faith which locate assurance in the objective fact of the gospel, or in the objective symbol of baptism, or in the divine election have, as a matter of historical record, found cool reception in popular southern Protestantism.[5] Basically, this fact derives from the southern church's received theological tradition, reinforced by the situation of the frontiersman who, uncertain of everything else, longed to be sure of his standing before God. In seeking fulfillment he resorted spontaneously for his criterion to whether something felt good and right and true in his emotional experience. In W. J. Cash's words, what the average Southerner required was "a faith as simple and emotional as himself." [6] While hearing a preacher who belonged to "his kind" of people portray the Christian responsibility in dramatic, highly personal, and urgent terms, he felt himself stricken then released, remorseful then joyful, doomed then pronounced free of condemnation. He developed the habit of mind of consulting his own visceral reactions to determine the reality and validity of the message he listened to. In fact, whatever entered his experience in any other way was thereby disqualified from a place of importance. The Southerner even concluded that there was correspondence between the flamboyance of the preacher's style and the urgency of the message. As dispensed by liturgical Anglicans or theological Presbyterians, the gospel was something he could take or leave, but in the hands of the experientialist persuaders it seized him as true and urgent. Small wonder that assurance was the pivotal issue in religion. If one did not know that he had got religion—in terms of an epistemology based on emotional awareness—he did not possess it. Nor was it worth having if his passions were not likely to be inflamed when the preacher "broke the bread of life" in his hearing.

Much is owed to the Separate Baptists for formulating a doctrine of assurance which asserted that "genuine faith carries its own assurance," and "if such assurance was lacking, faith was spurious." Doubting on the part of a believer was reckoned as sin, causing one leading Separate pastor in New England to comment that "no Christian who doubts his salvation can perform properly any of his duties to God or man." C. C. Goen's conclusion from the evidence is that the Separates' emphasis on personally experienced conversion was of such magnitude that it developed into "a pietistic inwardness that the early Puritans never knew." [7] Consequently he does not find it surprising that all converts were sternly required to give evidence of their regeneration to others. Nor is it any wonder that they accused many sincere believers, including ministers, of being unconverted or that the Separates branded as impostors and opponents of the work of God those persons who could not (or would not) satisfy the subjective test which they imposed.[8]

The Methodist position on the question of assurance was not greatly different.[9] If assurance was not a subjective reality, it was nothing. Because Methodism is, in Leslie Church's phrase, "Church of Englandism felt," it contended intelligibly that the "acceptance of Christ as Savior must be a definite event of personal decision at a particular moment of time." Equally logical was its notion that conversion is a *sine qua non,* that there "must be some moment in this process which may be indicated as 'instantaneous change.'" [10]

Although revivalistic Methodism in frontier America went well beyond English Methodism in its expression of religious experience through "shoutings" and "fallings," they were at one in their "characteristically Wesleyan insistence that one could *know* his sins forgiven." Both alike affirmed the "gift of assurance

—conscious, sensible assurance." [11] One scholar has underscored this judgment in calling attention to Wesley's avoidance of the word "assurance" when discussing the purpose of baptism (an objective symbol of grace), and of his preserving the term for reference to the "conscious presence of Christ in our lives through the witness of the Spirit that we are pardoned, adopted as God's children and heirs of the promises of salvation." [12]

The Southerner's God tends to be immediately accessible to his emotions; only with the greatest difficulty can he grasp a description of an objective concept of assurance. The note of mystery in the knowledge of God is obscured, inasmuch as the divine presence is reckoned to be near at hand. The Kingdom of God is brought into the present through the miracle of conversion. In some quarters of popular regional piety, relations with deity become "chummy"—God is essentially one's partner, guardian, and benefactor, a sentimental picture which omits the dimension suggested by classical Christianity's "terrible presence of God." In any case, God is deemed knowable under stated conditions. For example, church revivals and mass evangelistic crusades are predicated on the assumption that souls will be saved, on the spot; if congregations pray and witness, and if the preacher is "Christ-centered," men will be born again.

Since the knowledge of God is primarily connected to a man's emotions, southern evangelicals are apt to correlate uncritically the upsurges of a person's emotions with the divine presence. This truth was vividly illustrated by the reaction of an evangelical leader to his visit to a football rally at a church-related college, during which a student led the well-wishers in singing several "gospel choruses": "I have never felt the presence of God more real in any church than I did on that football field tonight." He extolled the vast difference which there can be between a Christian and a non-Christian college, and was undisturbed at the likelihood that the team would lose most of its games, since "character will be developed under such Christian influence."

The paradox of a wholly righteous and transcendent God, requiring basic moral repentance and reorientation, and an accessible God, very near indeed to the emotions of humble and contrite men, highlights southern religious thought-patterns. He demands everything but makes full forensic pardon available, and grants direct assurance that sins have been forgiven and that heaven's gates are open wide. If the position itself is simple, its implications are not, as we are now ready to see.

6
Theological
Fruits of the
Central Theme

A tree is known by its fruits. The observer of the southern church is struck by the way in which the central theme determines almost everything about the manner in which religion functions: what it champions, what it opposes, and what it treats with indifference. In the 1960's, no less than during the formative period and intervening decades, the concern for personal salvation and assurance has colored and conditioned the entire outlook of popular religion in the South—including theological commitments and attitudes.

The Bible and Personal Testimony

The southern church prides itself on its Bible-centeredness. In the official statements of the denominations, in the curricula of the various seminaries, in sermons, in political rallies, in homes—southern life everywhere is self-consciously biblical. With amazing consistency, people in every walk of the society claim the Bible as the standard for belief and practice. Many have facility for quoting numerous texts. Noteworthy numbers of persons with meager formal education undertake perspicacious study of scripture and assume responsibility for teaching Sunday School classes. Few question the literal accuracy of the Bible on matters of geography and history, no less than on matters of faith. This ready acceptance of the Bible "at face value" is consistent with their understanding of proper reverence for it.

As we have said, the southern church's biblicism marks it as fundamentalist—in a specialized respect. Owing to the priority of religious experience, focusing in conversion, a modicum of attention has been granted to comprehensive and systematic theological statement. There has been little acquiescence to doctrinal relativism or vagueness. Firm allegiance to a core of biblical texts and Christian teachings, those traditionally associated with evangelical Protestantism, generally prevails. Differences can be noted between Baptists and Methodists, but they are less significant than those between southern religion and the popular patterns in the other sections of the country where, too, revivalism once dominated.

For example, whereas revivalism imparted to southern religious life a highly particularistic faith issuing in a keen awareness of the transcendence of divine truth, in "Corn County" in the midwest, according to recent research, the "content of the Christian faith is not a pressing and dynamic concern." [1] Nor does attributing this to the absence of "well-defined rival systems" shed light on the persistence of particularism in the South, since there have been even fewer ideological options on the scene there. Revivalistic Evangelicalism has hung on in the South, keeping alive a theological objectivism which comes down heavily on the judgment of God, the reality of sin, the necessity of forgiveness, and the like. There prevails a haunting fear of degeneration to what John Macquarrie has described as a "completely amorphous Christianity that will accommodate every subjective preference."

Thanks to the absence of challenges to its truth-assertions, the southern church has been free to concentrate on Christianity's supposed prime requirement that each individual experience divine salvation, and on those texts and doctrines which surround that experience. Not surprisingly, its constituents have been conditioned to placing personal testimony on a par with (and in some cases, above) knowledge of Christian teachings. Except under duress, such as during periodic threats to orthodoxy, the church has abstained from solid biblical studies or doctrinal definitions.

The place of the Old Testament in typical southern sermons is especially instructive. Among three principal uses, the first is the prophetic "forward look" in support of the New Testament confession of faith that Jesus is the Christ, Messiah. Second, its narrative stories, particularly its biographical vignettes, are advanced as illustrations for practical homiletical points. It is important to observe that in both of these usages, the Hebrew scriptures are not presented in their own light, but are extrapolated from their historical, linguistic, and theological setting in the interest of homiletical usefulness. Third, the Old Testament is treated as a compendium of doctrines—for example, the doctrine of creation, the reality and misery of sin, the prophetic call to godly morality, the injunction to national righteousness, the Lord's claim of the tithe, the moral law, and so on. These ingredients are lifted from such books as Genesis, Exodus, Amos, and Malachi, without scrutiny of many of the great themes which run through these books—to say nothing of the other canonical books. More importantly, the total sweep and massive impact of Hebrew scripture is lost sight of. Because of the southern church's predilection for atomization and selectivity, the Old Testament figures in sermons chiefly in illustrative, instrumental, and supportive ways.

There surely is a tinge of irony in the fact of a greater biblicism among world Protestantism's "liberal" denominations than that which typifies southern religion. One instance of this is the frequency of exegetical sermons in mainline churches, as against the southern church's affinity to topical preaching. This anomalous situation is due to the highly selective usage which the southern church makes of the Bible. And of course the key to this curiosity is the basic conviction that one thing only is needful. The selectivity—which often amounts to manipulation— of those passages which can be turned to advantage in expressing the overriding evangelistic concern is considered eminently justifiable.

In a word, the southern church is biblical in line with its rather specialized interpretation of the divine will. Working from the premise that all else is peripheral to the conversion experience, scripture is combed with an eye for discovering passages which may be brought to bear on the central theme. Therefore, a unithematic and functional approach to the study of the Bible is everywhere in evidence. Few southern churchmen have been offered the fruits of a more expansive and profound exploration of biblical material, nor have they been encouraged by the clergy to undertake such exploration for themselves. And rightly so, since they believe that personal salvation is the near-exclusive interest of the biblical writers. By means of a circular logic, those passages which receive attention are made to say what it has already been assumed they must be saying, and texts which cannot be made into evangelical affirmation or propaganda are ignored.

It should be apparent that the central theme, though possessed of a real objectivism centering on the divine mandate to salvation, has had strong subjectivist undertones. It is not a doctrine to be subscribed to, or an affirmation to be expounded with a primary concern for faithful representation of it, or a proclamation whose chief end is itself. The fondness of southern churches for testimony-type sermons by the clergy and for informal personal testimonies by laymen, in the interest of attracting individuals either to an initial or a renewed loyalty to God, suggests how intertwined the objective and subjective dimensions are.

As everyone knows, personal testimony as a type of Christian proclamation did not originate in, nor is its use confined to, the southern church. What is distinctive in its case is the employment of testimonies as a primary means of public proclamation by the *major* religious bodies, whereas elsewhere its use tends to be confined to the sects or to special occasions sponsored by less prominent organizations. In the South, programs of revival services, rallies, crusades, and conventions are studded with brief presentations on "what Christ means to me" by luminaries from the realms of sports, beauty pageantry, and the movies, and sometimes by celebrities from the business or political world. In the overwhelming majority of cases, these presentations are notable for their simplicity, sincerity, and winsomeness, rather than for any grasp in depth of the substantive Christian message. Nor is it reckoned desirable that they should be otherwise. The celebrated are engaged for these appearances, often at great expense, merely because of their identity as famous persons aligned with the Christian cause, not because of their comprehension of its meaning.

When reflecting on the social-psychological reasons for this preference, the hypothesis that as a provincial, rural people, Southerners are awed by, therefore unwittingly responsive to, the famous or the rhetorically effective has a genuine plausibility. More than most subcultures, the South has been susceptible to control by the celebrated and the demagogic. Behind this is the basal conception of the Christian faith as subjectivist. The believer who can describe his experience of grace movingly is *ipso facto* rated the best exponent of the faith. Since the chief end, making converts, can best be achieved by effective salesmen, personal testimony is valued as a very pure form of Christian proclamation. Those who might impugn the southern church for stooping to utilize inappropriate, or even dubious, means in the attainment of its end should keep in mind that there is a whole tradition within American revivalism that unabashedly selects its means on the criterion of their effectuality in producing the conversion of individual souls.[2] Since the Christian message is conceived in simple, self-evident terms, in the Southern perspective it is right that it be transmitted through the plain, charged words of a pious person whose notoriety has already conditioned an emotionally sensitive audience to receive his words with enthusiastic approval.

Worship

Southern religion's unithematic preoccupation also has decisive implications for its conception of worship. Like evangelism and biblical interpretation, worship is construed as a function of personal and subjective ends. Patterns of worship services do vary—between Sunday morning services and "seasons of revival," between "First" churches and "people's" or rural churches, and in measure between the congregations of different denominations. Yet it is possible to speak of a typical service of worship, in the sense that a kind of (unacknowledged) ritual is in force. What to include in the ritual and in what order to program it are largely determined by custom and convention—though psycho-theological consideration enters at the point of "building to the climax." Early portions are treated as, and often called, "preliminaries." Gospel songs are generally preferred to hymns—although a few familiar hymns enjoy wide currency. Prayers are extemporaneous and informal in tone. Announcements of the week's activities in the local church claim a prominent part. The anthem, or special music, is introduced as a "mood-setter" by way of attuning the congregation to the sermon, and in many churches to the "invitation" or "altar call" at the conclusion of the sermon. If we consider the theory of Christian worship in terms of two forms—the first in which the act of worship is "primarily a matter of feelings," and the second in which it is regarded as "work done in God's service"—it is clear that the first is the standard southern conception.[3]

The gathering which convenes between the hours of eleven and twelve on Sunday morning, called variously the "worship service," "church," and the "preaching service," is not treated by devout churchmen as a service in the usual sense of that familiar term. According to their usage, "service" is virtually a synonym for "assembly" or "convocation," connoting nothing intrinsically sacred. To be sure, what transpires when the congregation is met together in this fashion is sensed to be important. But its importance is conceived pragmatically—as affording opportunity for winning converts, for Christian fellowship, for providing moral instruction, and for promoting the interests of the institutional church by generating enthusiasm. The distinguishing feature of this approach is that the congregation gathers to promote goals, to accomplish stated objectives, to inspire so that particular deeds may result, and perhaps surpassingly to produce an emotional feeling in the individual.

The way in which the selection of songs to be sung by the congregation manifests the tone and value-preference of southern church life has been noted frequently. Liston Pope found that in the mill churches of Gaston County, music is more "concrete and rhythmic" than in the "First" churches. It "conjures up pictures rather than describes attitude or ideas, and it appeals to the hands and feet more than to the head." [4] The son of a famed southern mainline scholar recalled that the church songs of his boyhood experience, mostly products of the great revival waves of the late nineteenth century, were "all about saving souls. That was their one idea." [5]

The note of worshiping God for his own sake, of presenting the act of worship as itself a service to God, exists if at all only subconsciously. In short, the "service" is not a service but a meeting, an assembly with acknowledged aims and objectives, all of which focus on the experience of the individuals present. Vivid portrayal of this is found in the popular conception of the offertory. Although a grateful spirit prompts much of the giving that southern churchmen do, only slight attention is called to the offering as an end in itself, as the symbol of one's offering of himself to God. Here as well as in hymns, prayers, and sermons, what can be *accomplished by an act as a means toward an end* is made primary. On those occasions when givers are reminded that their offerings symbolize Christian self-giving, they are likely to reflect on what the money placed in the plate will do *in the accomplishment of goals,* following from their regular habit of mind which envisions self-giving in terms of *doing* rather than *being* (the ontological issue having been dealt with decisively in conversion).

Corollary to the first demonstration of the reigning functional view is the subjective orientation of worship.• What transpires when the congregation gathers is structured around entreaty, exhortation, and admonition—in a word, the necessity to decide and act. (By contrast, objectively oriented worship is structured around proclamation for its own sake, whether in Word or sacrament or both.) The assumption is either that the substance of the Christian message does not deserve articulation independent of the experience which bears its reality into the recipient's life, or that the germ of the message is already known by the hearer. In this view, all that is missing is the proper decision of the will. Moreover, the individual plays a large part in the appropriation of the divine spirit. Consequently the need is for reminder and persuasion. Focusing on the worshiper himself, the service is geared to remind him of his disobedient acts, his shortcomings, his failure to bear verbal witness, and then to admonish him to embark upon a different course in the week ahead. The tense of this approach to worship is principally past and future, in that it is devoted to the confession of past sins and to spiritual preparation for the week ahead. (Once more, to point up the contrast, objectivist worship means to concentrate on the present through the act of worship as itself a service to God.) [6]

Southern congregations are famous for their informality, not only in their casual "services" but also in their personal warmth. There is public recognition of visitors—especially relatives or out-of-town guests of the presiding minister, and visiting clergymen. Moreover, friendships are cultivated before and after—and sometimes during—the meeting. Non-southern visitors may be struck by the degree of enthusiasm which attends introductions, by the warm handshakes, and by the assurance that the stranger is not a stranger at all, but may consider himself at home. (The notion that some visitors might feel suffocated by the profusion of

• In Chapter 8, a distinction will be drawn between two basic types of subjectivist Protestantism, the ethicist, focusing on moral behavior, and the salvationist, focusing on conversion of the lost. Clearly the southern church deserves classification under the latter.

cordiality, preferring slowly and deeply made friendships, or that an intense worshiper might desire a measure of anonymity would be unintelligible to the ardent southern churchman.) Within the resident congregation, there is a great deal of commingling. Members may exchange pleasantries while the organist plays the prelude. After the service many linger to continue friendly conversations. By contrast with the classical Protestant or Roman Catholic service of worship, where attention is drawn to altar, pulpit, or table, in the southern assembly the congregation itself is the focal point, with every property—minister, sermon, order of service, music, and so on—instrumental toward subjective ends.

As to the more elemental question of how the Eternal communicates himself to men in history, it is clear that southern churchmen take literally the metaphor, the Word of God, believing that the divine self-revelation proceeds through the agency of the *spoken* (and heard) word. In this respect popular southern Protestantism is an extreme manifestation of Protestantism generally, which gets past its strong predilection for the verbal only with some awkwardness.[7]

Yet there is an important difference between classical Protestant and popular southern practices, inasmuch as in the southern tradition the words of the Written Word have been uncritically identified with the content of the Almighty's revelation. That is to say, seldom has the southern church entertained the view that the words of scripture might point to, and participate in, divine reality without being that reality in some substantive sense. The "distance" between heaven and earth, between ultimate truth and human comprehension of it, is narrowed appreciably. A simplistic epistemology has thus entrenched the received theological heritage. The belief that God is *a personal being*—as a "realistic," not a symbolic, description—likewise assists in reinforcing the characteristic view of the divine self-communication as being conveyed through words.

Given this way of viewing revelation, what could be more natural than for the southern church to speak of its place of public worship as an "auditorium," a hall for hearing! Or than the indifference toward upholding theological criteria in planning church buildings so that the place of worship, besides being a presentation to God's glory, may itself excite the multi-sensory spiritual imagination of the worshiper! (The operative criteria are, in fact, acoustical considerations and the planned absence of liturgical symbols.)

The southern Protestant visiting in a predominantly Roman Catholic culture who is conscious of Catholic statuary in public places all about him probably will not realize that his Protestant ethos has produced its own iconography, corresponding to its unisensory (audial) concept of the means of knowing God. He is hardly likely to connect highway signs urging men to "Prepare to Meet Thy God," or warnings that "Jesus Is Coming Soon," with their Roman Catholic counterparts, such as statues of Roman Catholic saints on automobile dashboards and pictures of the Blessed Virgin in subway stations, nor does he see the parallel between home wall pictures of the Sacred Heart of Jesus and Protestant tapestries which importune, "God Bless This Home."

In both instances the reality presented is the Almighty who protects, judges, and saves. Epistemologically, the difference emerges at the point where the Protestant conceives of the communication as striking the mind's ear, so to say, since his primary sense is audial. On the other hand, the Catholic instinctively "sees" God; for him, visual representation best symbolizes the reality. Among southern Protestants one observes an almost complete lack of awareness that the limitation of the Almighty's revelation to verbal agency is not self-evidently defensible. On any showing, the total, if unwitting, exclusion of the other senses as possible means to the knowledge of God is a fundamental and significant fact of the southern religious consciousness.

Accordingly, the Lord's Supper (rarely called Holy Communion) occupies a place of minor importance in southern church life. This sacrament, or "ordinance" as the Baptists prefer, is regularly observed in the great majority of churches, principally because of the desire to be obedient to Christ's "this do in remembrance of me," and by way of duplicating the practices of the early church. Predictably, its interpretation of "remembrance" is literalistic and logical. The sense of communing with the present Christ, of participating in his mysterious reality, is not dominant. As the southern faithful receive the bread and the cup (grape juice), their minds conjure up pictures of the objective individual, Jesus of Nazareth, in his own first century setting. In its salient impact, the observance is construed as memorializing events of the distant past.

It is not that "this same Jesus" is believed to be absent from them, that he does not encounter them in present moments. It is rather to suggest that the medium by which this encounter is conveyed is something other than the Lord's Supper, which in actuality serves a mnemonic function only. Now the southern church does not despise histrionics; it could hardly do so in light of its intrinsic revivalism and pietism. On the contrary, it simply restricts its histrionics to its great moments of the soul, conversion and rededication, when the emotions are sensitized. As a matter of fact, the southern church inclines to viewing the operation of the Holy Spirit in terms of irregular and extraordinary occurrences. On the other hand, classical Christianity has its dramatic moments in *repeated* experiences, with Holy Communion the central one (none being characteristically emotional in nature). As the means of grace, the point of participation in divine reality, and the ground of assurance, the emotional experiences of the religious life are to revivalism what the sacrament is to liturgical Christianity. Southern churchmen, therefore, translate the Lord's Supper into the categories with which they operate, namely, words and ideas. What transpires on that Sunday morning once a month or once a quarter in their experience has more kinship with a lecture in metaphysics or history than with a drama or an opera.

The Place of Theological Education

Given its preoccupation with the subjective in religion, the southern church has had little incentive to engage in theological creativity. It has contributed a disproportionately small share of major Christian thinkers to the theological enterprise, a fact which is little less true at present than in the region's frontier epoch. There cannot be any serious argument for excluding the religious realm from the generalization that the South has produced few intellectual leaders, excepting creative writers. In fact the religious sector is conspicuously lacking in noteworthy attainments. Since theological activity has not been highly prized, outstanding and original output has lagged far behind the "spiritual victories" claimed by the Church. To this day, numbers of flamboyant southern pastors publicly derogate professional theologians. Recently the press carried the statement of one of the renowned southern clergymen who averred that the converts won by today's leading theologians can easily be fitted into "my living room." Granted that this is an extreme example, it does serve to point up the characteristic criteria by which southern churchmen appraise theologians, theological scholarship, and the entire Christian enterprise.

The first thing to be said about the region's denominational seminaries is that the level of their understanding has towered above that of the churches. This is particularly true of the several Methodist-related regional seminaries which have reflected classical Methodism's genuine interest in higher education, thus mitigating revivalism's usual indifference toward the life of the mind. So successful have these seminaries been that some of the foremost Protestant theologians in the United States are professors in them. This fact is not an unqualified good, however, in that it has created a wide gulf between the trained seminarian and the average church, sometimes making for frustration and miscommunication. The strong academic orientation of these seminaries has also presented problems for many entering seminaries from average churches. In many cases the period of theological education does not last long enough to facilitate mature transformation, with the result that large numbers revert to their former stance. This problem is intensified by the fact that a sizable percentage of seminarians are diverted from a single-minded devotion to their training by their responsibilities as weekend pastors of small rural churches. Whether the period of professional training proves successful as an educational venture in extirpating the young minister from popular religious patterns depends largely on the quality of the undergraduate education the seminarian has received (often deficient in the past, but appreciably better year by year).

Baptist seminaries, too, are far ahead of the rank and file of their constituency. For many of their students as well, the disparity between religion as they have understood it in local churches and its deeper meaning as they encounter it in the world of theological scholarship is radical. The net effect of this fact of Baptist life is that for many the seminary education does not "take," despite the generally adequate competence of theological faculties. At the same time, professorial equivocation is not unknown, inevitably since the denomination exercises tight control over its seminaries. A prior commitment on the part of most students, and some professors (at least, emotionally), to the simple and self-evident nature of Christian truth and to the primacy of religious experience renders effective theological education problematic.

Given these facts, it is not surprising that the Southern Baptist seminaries have been on the perimeter of world Protestant theological circles. Their mother seminary (Louisville), however, has long been relatively free from isolation and has done scholarly work of a comparatively high order. This was already noted by a Baptist historian in 1915 when he spoke of it as representing a type of Southern Baptist life "moderately conservative but not aggressively hostile to modern modes of thought." [8] Two recently founded seminaries enjoy similar reputation.[9]

Few scholarly publications have come from these Baptist faculties, a principal reason being the enormous size of the student bodies—four Southern Baptist seminaries enroll over 500 students—with its concomitant, a high faculty-student ratio. Another is the tight denominational control of which we have spoken, sharply curtailing freedom in the area of scholarly publication (much less in the classroom). Further, there is practically no "market" within the denomination for substantive studies. The most significant publishing done has been in pastoral theology, an area not suspect to aggressive ultraconservatives within the denomination—one wonders why—perhaps partly because it is an area with subtle affinities to their own uncritical concern for the subjective in religion. Historically, the most glaring deficiency —and one with unhappy consequences—has existed in Old Testament studies where excellence has been confined to linguistic pursuits.

In the local churches, one sees even more clearly the southern church's relative indifference to any serious content-orientation. Because assumptions concerning the simplicity and self-evident veracity of the Christian faith are held generally, religious education is usually limited to the twin themes of evangelism and morality. Church schools and training classes have rarely introduced members to the critical dimensions of Christian faith. Nor have they been designed, as a rule, to foster open inquiry into the deep meaning of the faith. Not that the teachers are irresponsible or uncharitable persons—far from it. Rather, their teaching is what it is because of the value-preference inherent in the southern church's life. They reflect in the classroom the themes, emphases, and approaches characteristic of the church's understanding generally. Southern Protestant religious education is successful in terms of its aims—to inculcate those patterns of behavior which are related to institutional values. They are less successful in the areas of broader religious values, such as love of neighbor, the proffering of help to those in need, the establishment of racial justice, and, on the ideological side, serious grappling with the nature and meaning of Christian truth.[10]

Thus, whether in worship, biblical understanding, or theological education, the southern church's action betrays its central concerns and characteristic ways of thinking. A common thread runs through all these areas—and through the church's ethical teachings as well.

7
Practical
Fruits of the
Central Theme

John Wesley, who more nearly than any other figure in the history of the church sums up in his own life and thought the dominant traits of popular southern Protestantism, described the Christian life as having two basic components: its beginnings, as represented by the doctrine of justification, which is the foundation; and the "fulness of faith," as represented by the doctrine of sanctification, which is the goal.[1] Our concentration on the former aspect, the foundation, in preceding chapters, is not to be interpreted as suggesting that Wesley's understanding of the goal has been lost on the southern church.

The plain truth is that southern churchmen mean to be a highly moral people, since they see Christian morality as belonging to the very nature of the religious life. Consistently they recognize some kind of genuine relation between justification and sanctification. By definition, the devout in the southern church acknowledge a serious ethical commitment—which is both joyful and unpretentious. They know that the Christian's life is "not his own," that he is called to live in accordance with divinely revealed "ground rules" which are incumbent upon the children of God. They seek to live purely, to hearken to the biblical admonition to "abstain from every appearance of evil," to exemplify in daily conduct the new life they have been granted in conversion. In the words of a favorite southern biblical text, they intend to "come out . . . and be . . . separate," to be a peculiar people, ordering their lives scrupulously about the will of God.

The southern religious picture could scarcely be otherwise, given the shaping traditions in its religious history. From both of its dominant traditions it inherited a passion for personal holiness. The Baptist heritage contributed a yearning after purity, apposite to its stress on the church as the community of the regenerate. Moreover, the influence of the Separates served to intensify this notion of the Christians' walk as serious and disciplined, for their orientation was radically Puritan. Disposed to look with acrimonious disapproval upon "superfluities," those practices that did not directly assist in the establishment of the reign of God over one's own life and the lives of others, they were militant, even belligerent, in denouncing entangling alliances with "the world."

The Separate Baptists' suspicion of worldly enjoyments, especially those associated with middle- and upper-class social practice, led to a very close pruning of life's moral tree. They strove to reproduce the "more scriptural way of the early Puritans," to achieve a spiritual state eminently superior to "the earthlings who groveled among the traditions of men," and were confident of having been successful.[2] In order to put teeth into their expectation that spiritual men would manifest the fruits of the Spirit with undeviating consistency, the Separate churches exercised "strict disciplinary watch" over their members. Their declaration that the church had a back door as well as a front door was no empty threat. Members were "churched" as a matter of regular course. Viewed from any angle, the Separates lived under a compulsion to pristine purity in ethical conduct.

The Methodist devotion to the sanctified personal life is so well known as not to require elaboration here. Throughout its existence, personal holiness has been the hallmark of the Methodist way of life. The recovery of the personal dimension in religion entailed moral responsibility no less than an inner experience of saving grace. Demands were high and expectations great for the saints of God. In this heritage, too, rigorous church discipline was practiced—in America until about 1900. The Christian's walk was known to be serious (and joyous) and the Church, a body with no place for malignant disobedience.

The ethical attitudes of early Baptism and Methodism survive to the present with notably little modification. The old ideas of what characterizes the Christian life persist. It is the precise character of the southern church's ethical understanding to which we must now turn.

Individual Ethics

Southern Protestantism's all-determining attention to the Christian man's *vertical* responsibility produces in the ethical arena a dominant concern for obedience to God in individual deeds and attitudes. Churchmen are reminded continually that their lives must be kept unspotted from evil speech, thought, and act. Like Christians everywhere, the southern man of faith is expected to exemplify the basic virtues of honesty and integrity. But there is a special quality to southern Christian morality, which though not peculiar to the South, illuminates the grip which the central theme has on the regional church in every aspect.

Three occurrences from the recent past illuminate this special quality. In one, a Sunday School teacher, upon being asked by his pupil whether or not Adolf Hitler was in heaven, replied that it was quite possible that at some point in his childhood Hitler had undergone the necessary conversion experience.[3] Admittedly an extreme example, this incident nevertheless suggests the kind of thinking to which southern theology easily leads. There is an effective dissociation of justification, understood as an instantaneous act, from sanctification, interpreted as a gradual achievement. According to the pervasive revivalistic ideology, justification (conceived as forensic) is really thought of as *an act* which is self-contained, having no *organismic* relation to anything else.[4]

In the second incident, a socially liberal editor was pleading the integrationist cause at a high-level denominational meeting, venturing so far as to aver that a person cannot be both a Christian and a segregationist. One prominent pastor, not reputed to be an archconservative, produced a discussion-stopping reply when he accused the editor of making the Christian's ethical responsibility in racial matters "a part of the plan of salvation." This is a characteristic southern assertion, in that it implies that salvation is an act, a kind of transaction between God and the individual, separable dynamically from the life which follows. In other words, salvation is conceived in static terms and along a vertical plane. It is said to be connected with what follows, but the connection is only rational. Life's most basic event is understood to be a forensic pronouncement of pardon, to which are appended certain demands. Predictably, the pastor's "orthodoxy" won the day, for he had appealed to the one concept from which no departures were allowable.

In the third situation, an intellectual in the Protestant mainline became puzzled by the labored argument which a chief executive of a southern denomination's social-concerns agency presented as the Christian case for involvement in the civil rights struggle. The "Yankee" thought the speaker should take for granted the intrinsic relation of the Christian faith to the ethical problem, but the Southerner was well aware that the truth-system by which his colleagues lived did not make such a correlation evident.

The southern church's understanding of evangelism determines its ethical theory. The plane within which one carries out his major obligations includes centrally God and the individual man, set over against one another. The southern Christian does understand that he has duties to perform which involve him with his neighbor and in some sense with all men. But there is no direct line running between the vertical imperatives and his personal duties vis-à-vis other persons. The latter duties are decreed and imposed; they do not belong to or derive from the former.

The individualist, verticalist character of the southern Protestant's responsibilities toward God and his fellows expresses itself in several ethical theorems, of which we shall mention three: the nature of immorality, the meaning of "influence," and the attitude toward the use of alcoholic beverages. As for the first, the southern church shares with organized Christianity in many locales the conviction that sexual promiscuity, drinking, gambling, and the like, constitute almost the essence of immorality. As a recent forceful article has noted concerning American cultural definitions, the term "obscenity" has been generally reserved for the lewd and pornographic, and its scope confined to sex and vulgar language.[5] The proposed counterdefinition is that the obscene is that which "has as its basic motivation and purpose the degradation, debasement and dehumanizing of individuals." In such a framework, "four letter words" would be understood as far less dirty than "nigger" and comparable terms which reflect on the worth and dignity of human persons.

In the South, traditional definitions of immorality are still so uncritically accepted that in 1965 the individualist approach prompted a skillfully organized campaign to rid Hot Springs, Arkansas, of legalized gambling, during a socially critical era when the churches were generating only limited efforts toward establishing racial justice. The churches consistently expend far more energy attacking the passage of pornographic materials through the mails, the liquor industry, and the houses of chance than they do in grappling with such issues as discrimination, disenfranchisement, poverty, and ignorance. By its lights, the southern church is living faithfully before its God. Since it understands Christian morality (like salvation) as essentially vertical, private, and static, its record is commendable. Much of what it sees to be done is done with vigor and resoluteness.

In a similar way, "influence" is defined as pertaining to individualist conduct. Southern churchmen are conditioned to be super-conscious of their influence on other persons, in the sense that they are taught that the Christian has a responsibility so to order his life as not to sidetrack the moral behavior of another, more particularly not to imperil the spiritual condition of the unchurched, who may observe his deeds. Devout churchmen manifest genuine concern to be a positive influence—that is, they resolve to take only such steps as befit the Christian vocation by being instructive for others who may be following. Translated into word pictures, the Christian ethical life appears as two men walking in the snow a few paces apart. The responsibility of the Christian man in the lead is to mark a trail which, if followed by the other, will guide him to righteous destinations.

The kernel of the obligation to be a Christian influence, as thus conceived, is that the operation is performed *at a distance* from the one being led. Secondary importance is attached to etymological "influence," "flowing into" another person. According to the latter interpretation, influence operates at close range as one person seeks active involvement in the other's life. On the former view, major stress is placed on the Christian's obligation not to go certain places, not to engage in certain pleasures, for fear that another weaker soul may see him and fall prey to temptation. Immorality and influence are understood in such a way that the individualist purity of the Christian man and of those whom he touches is regarded as the *summum bonum.*

The use of alcohol stands as the leading moral question for the southern church. Although stringent opposition to the use of alcohol entered the Western church mainly through the sixteenth century Anabaptists (whose direct descendants are the Mennonites and the Hutterite Brethren), the Baptist and Methodist denominations of Protestant Christianity deserve much of the credit (or blame) for intensifying this opposition.

It is a matter of more than passing interest that during the Colonial and early Republican periods of southern history, the populace generally settled for a policy of temperance. After the 1830's and 1840's, vigorous opposition to the production, sale, and consumption of liquor emerged for the first time as a major plank in the popular churches' platform, and total abstinence replaced temperance as the watchword. The rigor of the southern church's opposition to strong drink tightened during the Reconstruction period when, according to Cash's interpretation, the South reckoned its awful plight to be the direct punishment of God. Aspiring to a brighter future, southern society instinctively subscribed to an "ever more Puritanical and repressive" moral code. "Save among the moribund Virginians and the more abandoned poor whites, the fiddle was silenced and limbs grew heavy and pompous; wine vanished from the table, and alcohol became a demon to be eschewed on pain of ruin in this world and damnation in the next." [6] With remarkably few (public) exceptions, regional social customs since that time have not included the drink before dinner or wine with the meal (although recently the old sanctions have begun to give way). Non-Southerners, having heard of "southern hospitality," may be incredulous as to how the reputation was acquired, since conviviality has almost always and everywhere been befuddled by the delicacies of the cup. A satisfactory explanation is easily forthcoming: The popular churches have been enormously successful in inculcating their strictures on drinking into the region's moral code. So effective was its moral influence that the abstinence ethic filtered into the ranks of the aristocracy with much the same strength as it affected the middle class.[7] Pope's inferences from the popular attitudes found in Gaston County, North Carolina, in the late 1930's continue to have fresh relevance. There he discovered that poverty and other social ills were explained in terms of drunkenness and personal shortcomings "rather than in terms of industrial relations as such." The churches' attention was focused on "prohibition as the central social problem, and interest in prohibition legislation became a substitute for nearly all other types of social concern." [8]

In understanding individualist ethics as they operate in southern church life, recognition of a legalistic spirit becomes necessary. A real-life experience, in which four southern churchmen traveling abroad are invited into a pious, middle-class German home for a social evening, provides a typical case. In the midst of an enjoyable conversation, the hostess fetches a bottle of wine and offers each person a glass. The Southerners decline, noticing a mild puzzlement in the host and hostess who, though hardly affronted, appear to wish their guests would see fit to receive this symbol of friendship. No doubt several cultural and religious factors figure in the Germans' drinking and their visitors' refusal. For purposes of our present discussion, what stands out is that the Southerners rate being dutiful to their vertical commitment ahead of all other considerations. They theorize that the Christian's moral duty to God is fixed. To indulge in social drinking would be to compromise right. Reasoning absolutely, the Southerner will suppose that what is wrong in Atlanta is also wrong in Stuttgart and Hamburg. He simply does not *consider the possibility* that joining his hosts in a glass of wine, in the interest of identifying with his new friends through a symbolic act—to say nothing of experiencing the relaxing effects of the fermentation, and of accepting their hospitality—*might be* more Christian than unyielding obedience to a transcendent moral maxim.

His position (although not necessarily his spirit) thus manifests certain legalistic qualities. He tends to exalt a principle, abstinence is right, above another value in the situation, symbolic identification with, and self-giving to, other persons. In the final analysis, his ethic rests on a devout yearning to exemplify the holy life, to maintain purity of body and soul, to stand by convictions about what is right and wrong in the face of any and all challenges—and through them all to exercise a positive influence.

Obviously, not all Christian non-drinkers are harsh legalists, jealously guarding a salvation they are terrified of losing, nor can their motives be reduced to self-righteous indignation. But in the actual energizing propulsion of the southern Christian's individualist ethic, one's duty to God is conceived in vertical terms. When there is a conflict, characteristic southern ethical thinking places "doing right," according to its one-directional understanding, above meaningful engagement with another person. (This truth is not diminished by any lack of awareness that the conflict may exist, or by the prevalence of the region's natural friendliness which sustains many personal relationships.) Although the subordination of a person to a law is hardly conscious or intentional in any malicious fashion, a kind of legalism does prevail.

Personal and Social Ethics

The South's fame as a society of friendly, gracious, and hospitable people is in many respects richly deserved. Personal friendliness is prized, and we have seen that the churches have actively fostered this quality. Helpfulness to individuals in need is also a primary item in southern ethics. Food is taken to homes where sorrow has struck or where the wife and mother is ill. Hours are spent consoling and assisting bereaved families. In a different vein, friends are invited for a sumptuous meal and a pleasant evening, often in gracious style. Amiable conversation is abundant on the streets, in stores, over the telephone.

It may be said that the source of these traits is cultural and not narrowly religious, but the role of the church in exalting personal ethical standards and in promoting good will surely cannot be denied. Of course, friendliness is to some extent a "natural" virtue in a predominantly rural folk society. In the South, a satisfactory dealing with the question is rendered more difficult by the virtual absence of an unchurched sector in the population which might provide some basis for comparison. At least one item of the greatest moment, the relation to Negroes on the part of white churchmen suggests that regional patterns of friendliness have their basis more on natural than supernatural principles. At any rate, culturally unnatural friendships—between whites and Negroes, in the Christian sense of friendship—have been almost entirely lacking, a matter to which we shall soon return.

Breaking down Christian ethics into its three theoretical divisions—individual ("personal purity"), individual personal ("personal ethics"), and social personal ("social ethics")—it is clear that popular southern Protestantism has been conscious of the first two and not the third. The effective neglect of social ethics is a primary and distinguishing feature of popular southern religion and follows logically from the theological verticality of the church's orientation. It has rarely occurred to the churches of the South that there *is* a Christian social ethic. In their eyes the New Testament does not contain one. The Bible-loving churchman discerns no social ethical concerns in the Christianity of Jesus or Paul, since neither is explicitly reported to have lifted a finger to eradicate slavery in the Roman Empire, to foment political change in Palestine, or to advocate society's amelioration of the living conditions of the poor. Accordingly, the southern church argues, Christian congregations have neither example nor instruction impelling them to forsake their soul-winning duties in the interest of so nebulous a task as Christianizing the social order. Absorption in efforts of this kind only serves to dilute the authentic Christian responsibility. There is no time for the church to engage in general civilizing activities when lost souls languish in darkness and despair.

Yet it would be wrong to imply that the southern church never interests itself in earthly affairs. We have already noted the labors of the popular churches in Arkansas during 1965, resulting in the defeat of legislation which would have legalized gambling. Moreover, as recent research has made amply clear, the Southern Baptists in the period 1865–1900 expressed increasing consciousness of their responsibility to society through their organized public assaults on drinking, gambling, and like evils.[9] The southern church has, in fact, repeatedly addressed itself to issues of public morality, but almost exclusively in terms of its verticalist theology and an accompanying individualism in ethics.

In their study of the role of churches and church members during the heated 1957 racial disturbance in Little Rock, sociologists Pettigrew and Campbell ascertained that the city's Protestant ministers felt themselves unprepared to cope with social crisis. Trained for and lodged in the roles of evangelist, pastor, and church administrator, they were overwhelmed by the awareness that some extra skill was required of them in this situation. Clearly what was happening was affecting the most private sectors of life for all citizens. Something needed to be done. Yet the "called" servants of God were ill equipped in terms of training, experience, and criteria of success for the role of social reformer. As one said, "Actually, we've been taught that controversy is un-Christian." Another remarked, "I knew I should be doing something, but I'm afraid I simply did not know what to do." [10] In theological terms, their inadequacy to bring some Christian perspective to bear relevantly on the crisis stemmed from their evangelical doctrine of the Kingdom of God which operates with the conviction that "the human unit is the individual." The only life crisis it was geared to meet was *death*. Quite logically, such a conception has few resources for dealing with social crisis such as open social conflict and the misery of human groups.[11]

In this respect, one is reminded of the congruity between the southern religious outlook and the social philosophy of the classic evangelical minister of America's "Methodist Age," the century beginning with the Great Awakening of the 1740's. The means of reforming the nation is the conversion of individuals. Moreover, the church has no responsibility for making impact at any level other than that of the individual.[12] Nor is there any other way to change things. It follows that the minister is not a priest with duties to all persons in the wholeness of their lives, but a "consecrated functionary"; for the conversion of souls is everything and the minister's work is judged by the degree of his success in this task.[13]

It has been argued that in mainstream America the Methodist Age soon fostered massive social reforms, owing to its person-centeredness, its repulsion to evil, and its great stress on sanctification.[14] One asks why southern Evangelicalism has possessed the same features *without comparable results*. Whereas verticalist theology-ethics was transformed into a social ethic elsewhere in the nation, it held fast to a salvationist objective in the South. Manifestly, extra-religious factors were at work, re-enforcing Evangelicalism's grip. Among these was an ignorance of the immediate bearing that laws, customs, social change, and social problems have on individuals. This was a natural consequence of the rural and uncomplex society of the South. Population was sparse and scattered. Economic life consisted largely of independent, self-supporting family units. There was no other way to construe evils and problems but as individual and personal—certainly not social, either in origin or ramification. Altruism meant personal services to friends rather than the more complicated forms of altruism peculiar to interdependent societies. Neither the ante-bellum nor the New South produced a Walter Rauschenbusch, because circumstances did not prompt southern moralists to channel their reformist energies toward social salvation. Prior to the recently begun demise of the rural, folk-society South, Southerners had no occasion to doubt that all that can and need be redeemed is individual persons, or to suppose that social conditions profoundly affect the welfare of the human spirit. Perhaps this situation accounts for the persistence of the South's hallowed tradition that religion was to "mind its own business," given over to saving souls and abstaining from meddling in politics, a tradition described insightfully by Weaver:

> Although Southern clergymen occasionally invoked the word of God to defend Southern institutions especially when these were being assailed, as a general rule they were overwhelmingly opposed to the use of the church as a tool for secular reform. The evangelical sects aimed at a conversion of the inner man; the conservative ones at the exposition of a revealed ethic, but both regarded themselves as custodians of the mysteries, little concerned with social agitation, and out of the reach of winds of political doctrine.[15]

Not until the last decade or so have conditions developed which arouse the southern church to see that a re-evaluation of the Christian ethic accordingly might be called for.

The regeneration of human hearts remains the primary goal of the southern church. As William McLoughlin has observed for American revivalism at large, the logic of its theology "disparaged and even deplored collective efforts at reform."[16] What he says of Billy Graham and Charles G. Finney applies also to southern evangelicals: They prefer "to make all social reforms an appendage of revivalism and to subordinate all other activities to soul-winning," holding out "the promise of utopia through supernatural eradication of personal sins." [17]

Bewildering as the attitude is to Christian leadership outside the region, the southern church still fundamentally believes that involvement in the great social crisis which overshadows all else in the contemporary South is not actually its responsibility. Southern churchmen insist that they are friendly to Negroes. "Some of my best friends are Negroes," is a phrase often heard and sincerely meant. They are among the majority who deplore the unsettling of "harmonious relations between the races" resulting from the agitation of "outsiders," declaring, "We have provided for the Negroes, why is there dissatisfaction?" It is true that *in terms of the South's traditional categories of understanding,* friendships between whites and Negroes have been real and relations harmonious. Consequently they have had no cause to consider whether they regard the Negro as human, hence the white man's "equal," and if so, whether the social traditions and structures take account of and implement that humanity. In view of the church's detachment from the gravest crisis the South has experienced since the Civil War, it is dramatically clear that the central theme maintains an extraordinary, almost mesmeric, power over the southern church. Individualistic evangelism and morality are all it gets excited about, notwithstanding the headline-making events which occur under its nose almost every day.

Part iii
Classification of Popular Southern Protestantism

8
Southern Religion
in Relation to
Historical Christianity

We have seen that the southern church diverges substantially from mainstream American religion. Without committing ourselves to a historical-cultural reductionism, we have attributed this divergence to the peculiar historical and cultural situation of the region. Despite the genuine yearnings of the religious people to be "pure," non-religious factors have left a heavy imprint.

We turn now to classifying regional religion in terms of historical Christianity.[1] Of course, despite all the modifications imposed by their peculiar ecology, the various bodies have retained basic kinship ties with their parent families. The southern Methodists are detectably Methodist, the Southern Baptists detectably Baptist, and so on. In tone, emphasis, doctrine, and

organization, continuities persist. Moreover, each of the southern
bodies has continued to be affected in varying degrees by the
wider communion to which it belongs. For example, southern
Presbyterians, although organized into a regional church, none-
theless have significant interaction with other branches of Reformed Protestantism. By virtue of membership in the National
Council of Churches, all the major southern Protestant denominations (except the Baptist), whether constituted as regional or
national bodies (as with the Methodist and Episcopal bodies),
are affected by "outside" influences which do provide a system
of checks and balances. The Southern Baptists alone are self-
contained to a decisive degree. Even here the isolation is not
total, for the Southern Baptist Convention is a constituent of the
Baptist World Alliance. Furthermore, a growing number of its
younger ministers are sensitively in touch with the larger Christian world.

In addition to these formal denominational connections, popular southern Protestantism exhibits affinities with general sub-
movements or typological varieties of historical Protestantism
which are not embodied in a single denomination; for example,
Puritanism, the English phenomenon of the early modern period,
and Pietism, a slightly later development primarily associated
with Germany. Also the southern church in some of its impulses
resembles movements with which it has little or no direct relation,
a common cultural occurrence. That is, in the American South
as everywhere, concepts, concerns, methodologies, orientations,
and the like may simply be "in the water," coming to the surface
at random times and places. Moreover, so dynamic a historical
force as religious faith is always prone to erupt with fresh interpretations, and push off in new directions. Accordingly, there is
no intrinsic reason why a version of Christian faith which
emerged, say, in seventeenth century Germany should not sprout
in America a century later among churchmen who had not had
direct or even indirect contact with the earlier movement.

To summarize before proceeding: Popular southern Protestantism is composed of uniquely southern factors, received theological traditions, and general typological varieties of Protestant

Christianity. To the last two we now turn, in the interest of juxtaposing popular southern Protestantism with the many other subtraditions of the historical church. We shall also examine briefly several facets of southern religion to see whether they are traditional or radical, liberal or conservative, orthodox or heterodox.

The Southern Central Theme and "Historic Religion"

We have seen that the southern church's "central theme," as a doctrine of the Christian faith, is neither novel nor peculiarly southern, inasmuch as the overarching concern that individuals be saved from the punitive consequences of their disobedience toward God the Righteous Judge has been prominent throughout Christian history. Moreover, the bewildering quantity of variations on this theme, in the Roman Catholic, Protestant, and Anglican communions, should not be allowed to obscure the major place which this complex of truths has occupied.

In an instructive schematization, in which sociologist Robert Bellah divides Western religion as a historical phenomenon into five stages or periods, the Protestant Reformation is described as marking the fade-out of "historic religion" (stage 3) and the birth of "early modern religion." The former was distinguished by a dualistic conception which derogated the value of the "given empirical cosmos," and issued in the popular notion that human life has two places of abode, the earth, and heaven or hell after death.[2]

"Historic religion," so characterized, lasted longer and more influentially in precisely those varieties of European Protestantism which gave American religion its original shape. For the Church of England and Calvinism, while certainly making no greater differentiation between the Creator and the created order than Lutheranism, were both more geared to a conscious "fleeing from the wrath to come" than Lutheranism and Anabaptism.[3] On this score, Anglicanism, largely by intention, and Calvinism, unwittingly (as we shall maintain), reveal closer affinity to "historic religion" than do Luther and his posterity—despite the fact that the Lutheran position was generally more conservative than the Calvinist.

As a first step in demonstrating the genealogy of popular southern Protestantism, we note briefly the way in which Reformation theology cast the doctrine of justification in a very different mold from that of medieval Catholicism: (1) Protestant teaching took justification out of the faith-and-works orientation it had had in Catholic thought, and strongly maintained instead that one trusts God for the gift of forgiveness, quite independently of any striving to attain salvation by good works; (2) In the comparative theologies of the sixteenth century (irrespective here of the courses each may have followed since), Protestant thought veered toward a greater interest in the personal meaning and social application of justification in the here and now, as against Catholicism's residual orientation toward the life to come; and (3) The reality of justification was mediated through the spoken word, chiefly, in the Protestant view, with response to the proclamation of the Christian message being given the place participation in the sacramental mysteries had held in Catholic life. Obviously, the southern church's central theme harks back to the Reformation interpretation of justification, in its proclamation of *sola gratia,* in its insistence on the immediate relevance of justification—revivalism's notion of conversion is a radical adaptation of this—and in its giving central place to scripture and preaching. Yet in its particular twist on the Reformation affirmations, the southern church came to maximize the legacy from "historic religion," going even beyond Anglicanism's and Calvinism's disposition in this respect. To this day, it remains almost entirely unaffected by the two most recent stages, the "early modern" and the "modern."

The English Protestant Heritage

Southern religion's direct continuity is with British Protestantism, not Continental.[4] The question before us is: What is there about early British Protestantism, during the period when "historic religion" was shading off into "early modern religion," which became central to southern Protestantism? Briefly, the answer is the dominance of the concern for "fleeing from the wrath to come," the common preoccupation of Anglican and Calvinist thought with man's dislodgement from the favor of the Eternal Judge.

Owing to its deliberate conservation of many portions of medieval Catholic life, the Anglican Church from the first acknowledged the "forgiveness of sins, the resurrection of the body, and the life everlasting" as cardinal truths, and conceived of them as making up the church's imperative mission to the world. Divine grace must be mediated through Word and sacrament *so that* sins may be forgiven, reconciliation realized, and life everlasting vouchsafed. Though the here and now took on added intrinsic significance, there remained a strong pull to the hereafter. Anglicanism's most illustrious child, the Methodist tradition, retained this concern for the salvation of individuals in similar soteriological terms. Although Methodism modified its Anglican heritage at this and numerous other points, a perceptible thread runs from medieval Catholicism to the Church of England to Methodism.

The same holds true for Calvinism, whose several branches gave priority to the way in which the redemptive might of Christ overcomes man's hopeless alienation from the God of Justice. Here again the question of man's guilt before God overshadowed every other claim and responsibility. English Puritan, as well as Scottish Presbyterian, thought and life reflected the Calvinist genius by drawing attention to the decisive moral cleavage between the Holy God and depraved man.

South of the Tweed, the Calvinist interest in man's standing before God was reinforced by the general English tradition that this was life's greatest issue—thanks to both Catholic and Anglican influences. The climate of the national culture made one feel that nothing else mattered half so much. Added together, the various subtraditions within British Protestantism afford the impression that the air all Britons breathed was supercharged with the question of one's status before the Holy God who granted forgiveness, but who punished eternally those whose sins went unrequited. As Paul Tillich has commented, life's one critical question at the time of the Reformation—and in many cases for a considerable period thereafter—was the question of guilt. Although Luther himself is the archetype among those so possessed, the full impact of this question's implications operated nearer the surface for the Calvinist groups.

The next stage in historical development brings us close to the theological bloodline destined to inform the life of the southern church. This is the shift from a high doctrine of divine election, shared in different forms and contexts by both Anglican and Calvinist teachings, to a generally greater confidence that the identity of those elected to salvation can be known. The introduction of this note of confidence, whether as probability or as absolute certainty, marks a dramatic alteration in Protestant theological patterns.

The problem of knowing who are the elect, always a knotty one for Calvinists, was not intense for the Church of England. One reason is surely that for Anglicans theology as such—in this particular connection, the theology of the fall, the atonement, and hell—received less stress than sacramental participation in the mysteries of divine grace. That is, the Anglican faithful were exposed far less to verbal warnings about the awful anguish of hell than to "holy communion" with the triune God in liturgy and sacrament. Further, the Anglican temperament does not seem characteristically to have excited passionate religious disturbance of the kind which would exacerbate longings, fears, and dire preachments concerning the life to come. Transplanted to the southern colonies, the Anglican church produced a similar effect on its new surroundings.

The elevation of interest in assurance did not occur within Anglicanism itself, but awaited the eruption of Methodist revivals, which achieved a large following among the southern masses following 1765. It was natural that this Anglican offshoot should declare the need for forgiveness, justification, and reconciliation to have primary importance, given its high place in the entire Christian tradition and more particularly in the life of the denominational parent. But two new teachings which helped precipitate Methodism's birth entrenched the classical doctrines and brought them into the open in a manner unknown to the parent tradition. The first of these was the confidence that one who has been pardoned will be granted a profoundly inward and immediate knowledge of it. The would-be regenerate was to consult his own experience, not the objective Word and sacrament of the gospel, though of course he believed that the source of his forgiveness lay outside himself in the objective work of God. In this way the Methodists relocated the ground of confidence—not to say, the source of their salvation—transferring it from the realm of objective declaration and signification to the level of personal experience. The second feature was the Arminian strain within Methodist thought which had the effect of conditioning each man to believe that the possibility of divine salvation, in some sense, lay within *his* grasp, if *he* would act gratefully and claim God's freely offered grace. If in Anglican life the soul's welfare was an ever-present matter running through the whole, in Methodist practice this concern was overtly paramount. As the Methodists saw it, the issue of individual salvation not only *had* to be dealt with, it *could be resolved*—in a manner which was mysterious but self-verifying.

As for Calvinism, we have earlier suggested that its dualism and its concern for one's status in life after death manifested a dimly concealed continuity with the medieval outlook. Calvinism did more than cling to the classical doctrine of predestination; it inflated that doctrine's importance by regarding its truth as the *means of assurance*. To the perplexing question, how can it be known who are the elect, Calvinist theology affirmed that God alone knows (and determines) who they are.

Once Calvinism had been transferred to the American scene, this understanding of the means of assurance seemed to elude the more subjectively oriented Protestants and to have little appeal for frontiersmen, who lived by their emotions. With certain modifications, however, the Calvinist heritage did filter to the level of the masses in the New World; the tight hold of predestination was relaxed, and the confidence that men could distinguish the elect spiraled. In the case of English Puritanism, modification was real, though not radical, in the direction of a simpler, more inwardly appropriable variety of faith. The "superfluities" of elaborate worship were denounced and curtailed. The direct mediation of God's grace to the soul, independent of liturgical banalities, was vigorously affirmed. More importantly, the maximizing of the moral demands of a "streamlined" Christian life free from wanton and frivolous behavior, claimed a great amount of attention.

All the religious bodies which were under the sway of Calvinist theology maintained the clear dualism of "historic religion." In a more forceful manner than Lutheranism, the Calvinist theology radically separated depraved man from the merciful God inasmuch as its teaching about assurance was less personal and dramatic, more intellectualized. Among Calvinist groups there was less personal awareness and assurance, *in dynamic, subjective terms,* of the direct relation between the individual and transcendent reality. The direct relation in this context tended more often to be a scholastic statement, or at least a comprehensive theological affirmation, than an inward act of trust.[5] In all fairness, it must be noted that Calvinist theology did shift, *by intention,* from status concerns regarding the life to come. At the same time it did not provide the personal or dramatic *inward* dimension that the masses of men, particularly in America, seemed to require for assurance that they had been granted an escape from the everlasting anguish of hell.

Two aspects of this description of this Calvinist anatomy are integral to the South's regional Protestantism. In the first place, Calvinism helped bequeath to regional religious life an overarching dualism and an attendant concentration on status concern. The acknowledgment of man's separation from God determined the shape of the churches' proclamation and their conception of personal ministry. Second, the subvariety of Calvinism which first made its way south had already undergone a process of adulteration at the point of its teaching about assurance. The Separate Baptists in particular claimed to know with certainty who were the saved, on the basis of personal experience in conversion. These then joined forces with the Methodist revivalists to guarantee that inward awareness would be the region's mode of assurance. As far as the tastes of the southern masses were concerned, the Separate Baptist Calvinists and the Methodists had a sympathetic approach to the question of assurance.

The Anabaptist Strand

In addition to the British antecedents, two Continental Protestant movements, Anabaptism, which dates from the 1520's, and pietism, which flourished from 1650 to 1750, parallel southern developments and in certain ways directly impinge upon them. Although there are very few genuine descendants of the Anabaptists in the South—mostly the Mennonites of the northern valley of Virginia—the southern church bears interesting resemblances to Anabaptism. As a particular approach to what is important in the Christian faith, and as a way of life, historic Anabaptism looks very much like southern religious life on many sides. This indirect kinship further demonstrates that popular southern religion, distinctive as it is, is far from unique.

Restitutionism

Foremost among the Anabaptist traits pertinent to southern religion is the zeal to recover primitive Christianity. There is an important difference, however, between this objective as enshrined by the Protestant Reformers generally and its place in Anabaptist life. For one thing, the Anabaptists manifested a greater innocence that restitution could be accomplished—and quickly. For another, they sought as passionately to restore the *forms* of New Testament church life as its central message. In addition, they took the literal character of scriptural text to be part of the Book's essence; if the biblical text knew nothing of altars, crucifixes, surplices, and crosses, neither would they.[6]

Although in this attitude the Anabaptists shared the animus of English Puritanism, the two movements possessed different dispositions. (In its emphasis southern revivalism generally resembles the Anabaptist more closely.) Anabaptism was distinguished by its intense subjectivity in religion. Whereas the

Puritans were engaged in a running battle with "popery" and Anglicanism's "papistical" retentions, the Anabaptists, more withdrawn from cultural institutions, were not disposed to joust with any state church, and devoted themselves to the individual's direct religious experience.

More than this, the restitutionist principle inclined them toward a radical rupture with the post-biblical history of the Christian church. Unlike the English Puritans, who were too English to consider divorcing themselves completely from the past (of institutional Christianity in this case), the Anabaptists cared little for the heritage of the previous eleven or even fourteen centuries. As they saw it, what had happened in that millennium-plus should be discarded as a mass of extraneous accretions to the divinely launched ship of faith.

The southern church manifests an equally disparaging spirit toward the patristic and medieval periods (and in many cases a total ignoring of post-biblical history). Especially among the Baptists, there is only contempt for medieval developments.[7] Methodists have ignored the past with a less easy conscience. As for the southern branch of that family, at the popular level there is no sensitivity to the subapostolic origin of some of its usages, but the denomination does possess a residual catholicity, never too far below the surface, which comes to light when alert leaders analyze Methodism's essence. The masses of southern Methodists and Baptists alike, however, are prone to believe that recovery of New Testament forms as well as message is both a possibility and an obligation.

Voluntarism and Synergism

The stress on the voluntary nature of religious faith provides a second parallelism between Anabaptism and southern religion. According to both, each man must believe for himself, else he has no faith. As the Anabaptists read the Bible, no one is to be baptized who has not affirmed his personal faith in mature years. Hence paedobaptism was rejected, and the church conceived to be a gathered community (as distinct from a national corpus). In English Independency, similar conclusions were reached by somewhat different routes, with correspondingly different implications drawn. A key distinction merits mention, however, in that in Anabaptist practice, voluntarism gave rise rather naturally to a notion of synergism. Because of Anabaptism's explicit doctrine of man, its version of synergism puts it somewhat closer to the southern church's position than is the Arminianism of classical English Methodism. It maintains that both God and man play real and necessary parts in the reconciling relationship which binds them. Man is not declared totally depraved, hence he is regarded as able to choose, with that choice determining his eternal destiny. Thus a man's conversion to Christian faith was seen as *integral* to justification. It was otherwise for the Reformers who made the act of God prior, indeed exclusively constitutive. For instance, Luther made much of this theme, *simul justus et peccator,* interpreting Paul's confession in Romans 7 about being in bondage to sin as describing the state of his new life in Christ, while the Anabaptists were apt to attribtue this outcry to the apostle's preconversion life "under the law." Although mainstream Anabaptist thought did not unequivocally declare "sinless perfection" to be a possibility, it saw little or no tension between divine righteousness and human righteousness. The theology implicit here gives a high rating to man's moral capacities, when—and only when—those are enlivened by the active agency of the Holy Spirit. Sin can be truncated. Clearly, the Anabaptists and the Reformers entertained two different conceptions of the nature and profundity of sin, with devout encouragement to the faithful to live the wholly pure life the main impetus of the Anabaptists' teaching. They were willing to assume the possibility of such living in history.[8]

A similar spirit of optimism in regard to man's moral and religious potentialities has permeated southern theology. Indeed, revivalism, in the South or elsewhere, could be justified only by this or a similarly simple, perhaps sanguine, understanding of the relationship between God and man. From the vantage point of both Anabaptism and revivalism—historically the former has never given rise to the latter—the epistemic gulf separating God and man is not so difficult to bridge. Yet the two bodies of theology are far from identical. Anabaptist voluntarism-synergism is morally oriented. What it exalts is the necessity of the Christian's separateness from the world *in his moral conduct*. Southern revivalism is soteriologically oriented (after the manner of Calvinism), for it exalts the necessity of conversion—the experience of entry into the state of being saved. At this point, the discrepancy between ethical subjectivism and salvationist subjectivism emerges clearly. At a fundamental level, nevertheless, presuppositions of the two movements are the same: what God primarily requires he makes readily possible to those who will only act upon his demands by willfully receiving what he offers. Both are relatively free from theological complications. Both show signs of anthropological optimism and espouse a concept of the relation between faith and works which puts man in a favorable position.

Spirit of Urgency

The Anabaptists believed that the demands of Christ laid an urgent claim upon them, making the Christian self-conscious about his identity. As a people, they have been well described as possessing an "emboldened sense of personal answerability both before God and man" and further, a "fresh awareness of covenantal responsibilities." The heart of their spirit is captured in the observation that "the cumulative effect of their testimony is that Christianity is not child's play, that to be a Christian is to be commissioned." [9] This intensity of commitment stirred the Anabaptists with a missionary zeal, an impulse which marked them as distinct from what George Huntston Williams calls "the magisterial Reformation." They set out to witness to Christ in the world, showing slight inclination to reform the church as such, having "glimpsed the mission beyond Christendom." [10]

All of this helps account for the absence of theological sophistication in the ranks of the Anabaptists, and in fact for some of the tendency to heresy of which they have been accused. Since, to borrow Hans Hillerbrand's words, their "zeal for a life of obedience to God" differed from "Luther's quest for a merciful

God"; since their emphasis was on "man's commitment to live a holy and devout life" in preference to the Reformers' emphasis on the "divine forgiveness of sins which would be apprehended by faith," their failure to produce astute theological writings is readily understandable.[11] The positions of Anabaptism and popular southern Protestantism are not identical, but each is more consciously devoted to working out the practical demands of Christian discipleship than with refinements and apologetical formulations of Christian truth.[12]

Attitude Toward the Present World Order

Historic Anabaptism has consistently expressed itself in explicit, though not usually hostile, rejection of human culture at large. The reasoning is that since the kingdoms of this world are not the Kingdom of God, participation in them must be minimal, with great care taken lest the servant of God compromise his convictions or misplace his loyalties. The Anabaptist sought to emulate Christ in a life of thoroughgoing love and sacrifice. He knew that "suffering . . . is the unavoidable fate of a true Christian on this earth," and that "whoever seeks seriously to put Christian love into action meets unavoidably the opposition of worldly powers." [13] The revivalistic Protestant of the southern United States has also been unable to make peace with the world about him, in theory at least, for he has been conditioned to making an issue of obeying God rather than man, because of his conviction that there is a vast difference. His antiworldly animus has not put him in the same radical position relative to his surroundings as the Anabaptist, however, because revivalism has concentrated somewhat more on the conversion of individuals to the God above culture than on personal morality. This value-preference has shifted the focus partially away from culture as the foil against which one implements the Christian life. More important by way of explaining the difference, the southern churchman has lived in a culture so shaped by and so accepting of him and his position that the foil he might have found himself arrayed against has not been noticeably present.

We may conclude that although their actual historical linkages are tenuous, Anabaptism and popular southern Protestantism have much in common. The major distinctions between them are evident at the point of ecclesiological emphasis and relation to society. Anabaptism's characteristic urge has been horizontal, or ethical; southern religion's, vertical, or salvationist.[14]

Pietism

A final historic Protestant movement having continuities with popular southern Protestantism is Pietism. Historically, the link was provided by John Wesley, who was influenced by Moravians and who bequeathed to his spiritual descendants a vision of Christianity which was essentially pietistic. Wherever we touch the pietistic tradition—within state churches, in sect groups, in Methodism—we find the same essential heartbeat: profound inwardness of Christian faith, joyful experience of personal knowledge of the Savior, and a tendency toward doctrinal minimalism. Characteristically, pietism's emphasis has been on the need for emotional, devotional, or spiritual emphasis in faith and worship more than on intellectual considerations.

One quality of pietism which is emulated by southern Protestantism is its vertical orientation. Christians of this sort revel in "seeing" God, in experiencing the Savior's love through the deeply inward awareness that they have been pardoned and justified. Accordingly, the Christian life is seen as a way of soft and gentle love, the kind which issues in man's raising paeans of praise to his Redeemer. The conscious focal point of his life and the conscious source of his purpose and joy is the precious Son of God.

This quality of sweet inwardness in Pietists does not cause them to deprecate the world about them, but rather to live as members of society within culture, performing their duties in that context. However, the religious life is conceived as something to be carried on in an essentially separate compartment of life. That is to say, the one point of direct connection between faith and the world is that religious people live in the world. It is *not* their aim to *transform* culture in the name of Christ, but rather *to enjoy* the gift of divine salvation, to exemplify love in all dealings, and to purify the church from within. In terms of its relation to culture, their faith is passive.• In terms of relationship to God, it is active through joyful inward communion with the Savior's love.

The second quality is Pietism's special ethical urge. It is true that the Pietist makes his peace with the world, that he entertains no program for assaulting the secular order in any systematic fashion. But he does not leave the matter there. He entertains a quiet hope that through his faithfulness to God he can flavor the church, and epiphenomenally the society, by giving concreteness to Christ's description of his followers as the salt of the earth. Again, he so concentrates on the gift of grace and the practice of purity appropriate to it that he quite logically believes that the Christian responsibility consists primarily in those great matters of the soul. The ethos of his religious life is the sphere in which he has personal intercourse with the triune God. Further, in concrete historical terms, it is simply a fact that Pietists have maximized the responsible life (as they understand it). Indeed their tradition has trailed off into legalism and moralism more often than into antinomianism. Their ethic has been self-conscious and decisive, although limited in scope to the private personal relationship with God.

Subjectivism is Pietism's third salient quality. It stresses the inward, the personal, the experiential. Its tone is affectional, not scholastic or formal. The intensive inner knowledge of divine grace with corresponding emotional impact is what really matters. On occasion an excessive emotionalism has pervaded pietism, and to outsiders it usually appears as a sentimentalized version of Christianity. At the same time, historic pietism has pointed to the subjective as an appropriation of objective revelation rather than as a substitute for it, and in its revival of the doctrine of the Holy Spirit has emphasized that the church, sacraments, and Bible were the objective media used by the Spirit.[15]

• In this connection history reminds us that for all its verticality and asceticism, classical (German) Pietism did produce Spener's thisworldly eschatology and Francke's philanthropic and missionary endeavors.

Popular southern Protestantism manifests all three of these qualities in one way or another. Its verticalism is evident in its commitment to the absolute priority of the soul's relation to God. To whatever extent this vertical orientation is "soft," that is, gentle, deeply joyful, emphasizing the inward solace felt by the redeemed, a variety of pietistic Christianity exists. Much of Methodism abounds with this, as does some Baptist life, especially among laymen in rural and small town situations where aggressive, highly institutionalized approaches do not dominate. A strong pietistic undertone prevails *among the laity* even where "hard" verticalism reigns supreme—although one surmises that the rural psychology of the people is as effective as the influence of pietistic Christianity in the creation of this attitude.[16]

Moreover southern Protestantism possesses the same kind of keen ethical sensitivity as Pietism. The cultivation of a life of exemplary purity is, of course, explicit in Methodism, where sanctification is placed high on the list of Christian doctrines. It has been said that Wesleyan (and historic Methodist) ethics has seen sin as "individual vice and laxity," as "sensuality rather than selfishness," and that its social ethic was one of "philanthropy and humanitarianism." [17] The appeal in Pietist-influenced Methodism is to a life filled with love, in a more or less sentimental (that is, non-aggressive) way, and demonstrating abstinence from the so-called personal vices. Out of a somewhat different heritage, the Baptist denomination has formulated much the same mandate. Church membership is restricted to those who affirm regeneracy; it follows that their lives are to manifest the reality to which their church membership is a testimony. In both cases personal purity, rather than social ethics in the conventional sense, forms their ethical impulse. Revivalism is aggressive with its vertically oriented concerns for others (that is, for their salvation) but not inclined to be aggressive in its relation to others at the level of ethics, save in love for them as individuals, and in the desire to "influence" them.

Subjectivism, Pietism's third quality, also characterizes the southern church's life. Without repudiating the objectivity of

Christian authority, the churches maximize those experiences in which the reality of divine grace is inwardly known with intensity. The formidable strength of Pietism in the South is evident, from a negative standpoint, in the manner in which Methodism has veered from its classical heritage by stressing warmhearted religion *at the expense* of biblical, theological, and sacramental objectivism. Schaff saw this in 1854 when he wrote that American Methodism "really little understands the use of the Sacraments though it adheres traditionally" to them, and that it "has far more confidence in subjective means and exciting impressions than in the more quiet and unobserved but surer work of the old church system of educational religion." [18] Surely this description applies to southern Methodism, confirming the impact of pietistic subjectivism on its life. The effect of pietism on Baptist life has been quite different. For to its stress on experience of the dynamic presence of Christ is joined a second stress, of another order of knowledge: the call for assent to the propositional truths taken as the heart of the biblical message. Notwithstanding the ambiguity of the call to two commitments, the awkwardness created by its failure to set one in subservience to the other, the Baptist denomination shows strong ties of kinship with the pietistic spirit.

Doctrinally Traditional or Radical?

Because the southern church intends and claims to be a courageous holdout against modernistic encroachments and devitalizing tendencies in world Protestantism, whether it is traditional or radical, orthodox or heretical, is of more than passing interest.

From the outset, American Protestantism has been radical by all the standards of traditional Christianity. Its left-wing character consisted mainly in its shift from stress on the objective reality of Christian truths to their internal realizations, and from church government by designated authorities to life determined by the Spirit's guidance of ordinary Christians. Southern religion took up these positions, with even greater intensity, during the Great Awakening of the mid-eighteenth century and has held them ever since.

The subjectivist bias of the southern church has expressed itself in numerous ways which classify it as radical. One is the partial or even wholesale rejection of traditional external forms in public worship, on the grounds that they are both an impertinence and a possible obstruction to true religion, which is deemed to be of the heart. It follows that, although the Word and, less enthusiastically, the sacraments, are affirmed, both become in practice wholeheartedly given over to their subjectivist function.

Granting individuals the right to interpret Christian truth is another radical propensity. Whereas in classical Christianity, trained theologians and well-chosen councils and commissions are assigned the task of exploring substantive issues facing the church, the southern church generally regards the "grassroots" popular will as the primary locus of the Spirit's operation.

A subjectivist commitment likewise appears in the placement of greater stress on human decision than on divine grace in southern sermons. Although the historic church has generally opted to affirm some version of the doctrine of divine election as an instance of the Almighty's free sovereignty, the southern church has paid more explicit attention to man's role in the context of his freedom and responsibility.[19] The same disposition is revealed in the church's enthusiastic emphasis on the divine call to the ministry—a fervor which is not duplicated in considerations of theological education as an integral part of the ministerial vocation.

Although these features mark popular southern religion as untraditional in intent and attitude, it stands nevertheless as one of the most conservative varieties of Christianity in modern history. This corresponds with its basic yearning to restore the primitive faith. Confident that such a goal is possible, formally as well as spiritually, it struggles to preserve the original, equated with the essential, from doctrinal and moral erosion which would compromise the "old-time religion" in the alleged interest of being up to date.

However, southern religion arrays itself on the left flank of the historical Christian spectrum in its stand on several theological issues which can only be touched upon here. In its preoccupation with individual salvation, it invites the charge of being "gnostic," although clearly the two conceptions of the nature and means of salvation differ sharply. A "fulfillment ethic" animates southern religious life to the extent that attention to one's own status needs in relation to a judgmental deity is pre-eminent. It certainly deserves classification as "Arminian," because of its clear assumption that men are quite realistically responsible for, and capable of figuring in, their salvation. The implicit suggestion in southern evangelical activity is that men save themselves through choice. Moreover, this variety of Christianity is open to the accusation that it is "man-centered," given its optimism over what men can accomplish and its heavy stress on the advantages which accrue to those who align with Christ and the church. Again, the near-obsession with salvation from sin and hell has led the southern church to border on the "docetic" heresy, wherein the "divine nature in Christ" is upheld for the sake of safeguarding his atoning death, at the virtual expense of orthodoxy's affirmation of his true humanity. Lastly, it clearly espouses a practical "Marcionism," holding that the Old Testament depicts God as legalistic and judgmental, whereas the New describes him as gracious, and regarding the message of the former as hardly more than a function of the Christian scriptures.

In conclusion, the southern church is a modern embodiment of many historic themes and ways of thinking about Christianity, brought together in a fascinating configuration. Everything considered, it stands in the tradition of the left wing of the sixteenth century Continental, and seventeenth century English, Protestantism. This legacy itself marks it as in many respects "innovationist," although a number of its positions are classical and the majority of its impulses are conservative. At the same time, its peculiar experience has resulted in the modification of its received tradition so that its intended and asserted orthodoxy often turns out to be heterodoxy even in the context of left-wing developments. The distance between Wesley's near-Calvinistic view of free will and the southern church's stark Arminianism, and between early Baptism's exclusive ecclesiology and the Southern Baptists' inclusivism, establishes the point beyond refutation.[20]

9
Church-type
Sect-type

It is widely acknowledged that one of the most fruitful instruments for perceiving the real personality of religious institutions is classification according to sociological type, developed more than a half-century ago by Max Weber and Ernst Troeltsch. As is well known, Troeltsch devised the classic formulation of two major types, the church-type and the sect-type. We submit that the application of salient features of this theoretical device to southern religious phenomena is as instructive for comprehending regional religion as any single methodological tool.

Troeltsch's description of a church-type religious group refers to a "type of religious organization that accepts the social order and is at peace with it." [1] By contrast, a sect is a group which is "at odds with prevailing cultural values develops a subculture and remains relatively isolated and insulated from society." [2] The heart of the disagreement of the two types consists in their divergence on just what sphere of mundane reality is to be brought under the domination of the "supernatural aim of life." In the case of the church-type, the objective is to relate the "whole of the secular order" to the divine rule, whereas the sect-type, Troeltsch theorizes, seeks to "refer their members directly"—that is, as individuals, irrespective of their involvement in society—to this supernatural aim. Clearly he meant to include in the sect classification all groups which incline toward withdrawal from the larger society in order to create self-consciously religious groups emphasizing the personal element in the Christian faith. Equally clearly, he placed all groups which make peace with the world, or at least presuppose its life as the general background, in the church classification.

Our question now is, Is the regional church hostile or indifferent to its culture or accepting of it and at peace with it? As a corollary to this question, we are endeavoring to determine what values and attitudes the churches inculcate in their members regarding their responsibilities toward society.

One of the difficulties faced in any such endeavor is the disparity in modern secular societies between the theological substance and intent of a given religious tradition and its actual practice. On one side, the devout churchman and the theologian are frequenlty prevented from seeing their church as it really is, because of their commitment to realizing the ideal. This is graphically illustrated in differing assessments by two reputable students of the Baptist movement with respect to the "distinctive feature about Baptists." Henry Cook, learned denominational leader in Britain, found the essence of Baptism in its "emphasis on the supremacy of the New Testament in all matters of the Church's faith and practice. . . ."[3] Historian W. T. Whitley declared alternatively that the "distinctive feature about Baptists is their doctrine of the Church."[4] It would appear that whereas Cook saw the Baptists in terms of a controlling ideal principle, Whitley viewed them in clearer historical perspective relative to what has actually distinguished them. In the case of the analyst of society, however, too great attention to empirical data may blind him to the operative norms of religious belief. In other words, he may fail to perceive major causal factors in personal and social life through lack of familiarity with religious ideology. To correct this myopia, we must investigate the intent and theological animus of the southern church. In order to set right the misimpressions of the former, it is necessary to assess the historical and present practice of the church, independently of any primary reference to ideology.

Theological Intent of Historic Baptism and Methodism

No one could dispute the point that the character of the Baptist and Methodist denominations has been significantly modified over the years. Yet it is instructive to see the original form, for the sake of understanding the current form which has continuities with it, and in the interest of discerning the fundamental animation, genius, and, presumably, intent of each.

The Baptists

The appearance of the people called Baptists about 1610 marked the logical penultimate stage in the entire English Puritan movement. Puritanism's characteristic rejection of a socially comprehensive concept of the church, replaced by the notion that the church is a limited community comprising only the gathered elect, found its most strenuous expressions in Baptist (and later Quaker) ecclesiology, which restricted church membership to confessing adult believers. From its infancy the Baptist movement was preoccupied with the church's own life. The purity of local communities of faith was the burning issue to which the Baptist interpretation was offered as a specific resolution. By its very nature, this incentive for commencing a new Protestant subgroup turned the focus of the Baptists toward the church itself. That is to say, the Baptist personality was introspective, bent upon seeing that the church measured up to the purity God required of it. The Baptist people did cast their eyes outward, but chiefly in relation to other individuals for whom they longed to be instruments of regeneration.

This is not to intimate that the founding fathers of Baptism did not care for the human community outside their small conventicles. For the most part, especially among the Particular Baptists, they were not hostile toward the world. As a matter of fact, feelings ran higher against the Established Church than against the social order as such. They entertained no well-structured notions for the conquest of the social order and produced no classic treatises dealing with the relationship between church and society. Instead they gave themselves to the lofty ideal of forming a pure church and of winning to membership such as their divine Lord would redeem, all the while awaiting (not passively) his ultimate victory over all historical men, nations, and institutions at the time of his triumphant return. Because of their eschatological expectations, they could not be ebulliently confident of the success of their labors. But whatever the reasons, the theology which informed their life did not lead to the interpretation that they were called to subjugate the social order to the rule of God. The creation, preservation, and advancement of pure communities of believers took clear precedence over any passion for overhauling society at large.•

When we recall that the Baptists were a people's movement, lacking powerful and influential founders and in general a leadership class, the early Baptist personality begins to take on a certain concreteness. These were ardent Christian believers from the lower classes who would scarcely have been able to wield social influence had they possessed a theology compelling them to try. Nothing about the character of this movement (which was insignificant, really, in seventeenth century English society) rendered it capable of assaulting society in Christ's name. They and their leaders did not operate with a habit of mind which would have inclined them toward a comprehensive social concern, nor was

---

• Students of Christian history will be struck here by the unconventionality of Baptist social theory. The Baptists were anything but unconcerned for the secular realm, but their conception of their relation to it departed from Luther's dualism, Calvin's transformationism, and the Anabaptists' rejectionism. Probably the Baptists' lower-class orientation had more to do with their inactivity in the social order than any explicit ethical suspicion of it as in the case of the Anabaptists.

their theology sufficiently aggressive or expansive to impel them toward that objective.

Given the historical circumstances of its origin, the Baptist penchant for a pure church constituency is intelligible. The Baptists were caught up in the prevailing tides.[5] In their own judgment they were only pushing to full fruition the reformation of the English church desired by the Puritans as a whole. The restatement of ecclesiology to conform with the biblical teaching as they viewed it and the full realization of it in practice were their consuming passions. Comparative examination of the Westminster Confession of Faith, the Presbyterian creed, and the classic Baptist confessions in both England and America discloses striking similarity, bordering on congruity. Only on the doctrine of the church is there notable Baptist departure from mainline Calvinism.

Since the Baptists are better described in terms of their positive churchly goal than in terms of a negative social objective, it would be misleading to refer to their tradition as massively sect-type.[6] More accurately, they were sect-type but within a society dominated by the Establishment. It was their single-minded dedication to the practice of pure (biblical) churchmanship in a society which thought them irresponsibly radical that has led to a somewhat exaggerated interpretation of their sect qualities. Easily overlooked are the absence from their policies of the antimagisterial feelings so prominent within the Anabaptist ranks and their formal acceptance of the central body of Protestant teaching in the Calvinist vein.

It may be that these ambiguities in the Baptist emergence help to account for the insufficient concentration on Baptist beginnings in discussions of church-sect typology. Classification is difficult, at best. Nor has the appearance of many remarkable varieties of Baptist life in subsequent history made the task any easier. Two firm conclusions do seem compelling. First, the local church instinct of Baptist life was sectlike in the most fundamental sense of that term, for the church was conceived as a "gathered" community, composed of adult believers only, as distinct from the parish church whose membership is conterminous with the local population. This characteristic is so patent and so well known that awareness of it has tended to obscure the second conclusion, that the Baptists were a one-doctrine people. They were dedicated to the reformation of the Christian church in England at one fundamental point, that of the proper constituency of the local church. Neither the repudiation nor the transformation of the secular realm could lure their vision from that goal.

All of this has great relevance for our study of the southern religious situation in which the Baptist people, uniquely in all Baptist history, have arrived at statistical pre-eminence. That this has happened at all would seem to be symptomatic of the comparatively irenic temper of the Baptists toward the social order. Imbued with Calvinist attitudes, Baptism reveals a measure of balance in being mindful of some responsibility to society as such. In addition, it is a tradition with a solid theological context and heritage, even though this fact has often been obfuscated, especially in the American South, because of its passion for evangelism and piety. Summing up, the substance and intent of the classical Baptist tradition call for its placement to the left of center along the spectrum of historic Protestantism, but still inside the magnetic field of the mid-point. Its comparatively mild radicality helps to explain the way in which the denomination has made its peace with the southern society, and has assumed certain responsibilities not usually associated with sect-type bodies.•

The Methodists

Intriguing similarities at a number of points make Methodists and Baptists first cousins in the Protestant family. Yet Methodism

---

• The somewhat different character of the *Separate* Baptists, whose ways rubbed off on Baptists in the South so decisively, is germane to the present discussion. They stand significantly farther to the left, deserving description as sectarians in the accepted American sense. This distinction is captured in Richard Niebuhr's insight, quoted earlier, that the Baptist movement in America has in some of its expressions been native-born rather than characteristically British.

is a product of a different history, and has its own traits. Numbers
of scholars have sought to classify Methodism by means of
Troeltsch's categories, but with only partial success—no doubt
because of the inherent ambiguity and dynamism of the movement, which possesses both church-type and sect-type elements.
The Reverend John Wesley, priest and presbyter of the Church
of England and founder of its Methodist societies, himself epitomized this ambiguity.

In a manner reminiscent of the Baptists, Wesley and his fellows
in the faith were consumed with the belief that the Christian life
centered in inward experience and personal holiness.[7] Yet it can
be argued that there was a more profound individualism implicit
in this theology than the Baptists had embraced—at least this is
what came out in American Methodism. The manifest concern
of the eighteenth century Revival was for the personal experience
of saving grace, inwardly identifiable. The passion which flooded
the souls of these religious zealots was for immediate inner awareness of the divine spirit. Somewhat less explicitly than the original
Baptists of the preceding century, they were committed to a new
conception of the church, the corporate order of Christians. After
all, the Methodist societies emerged as a movement *within* the
Church of England; their doctrine was essentially that of the
Mother Church, the difference being at the point of emphasis.
And as is well known, Wesley instructed the members of the
Methodist societies to attend communion in Anglican churches.
Profound confidence of pardon, subjectively communicated, fol-
lowed by the rigorous practice of personal holiness in terms of
abstinence from personal vices, characterized the Christian life.

It is clear then that Methodism was not brought into being
either to overturn the social order or to herd Christian believers
together into a cloistered existence. Rejectionism of the Anabaptist sort did not run strong in Methodism. Rather, Wesley
and company gave themselves to the fundamental and positive
task of regenerating men. If their policy resulted in the absence
of any aspiration to reorder society, this was partly because of
their wholehearted concentration on another task, and partly
because of the sociological fact that their earliest victories were

among the lower classes—even though the new movement's appeal was not confined to them. In the words of one scholar, "it is clear that to 'join the Methodists' meant withdrawal from much social life and the necessity to find one's pleasures among the faithful members of the local society." [8] Wesley himself did not manifest a basic hostility to society, nor was he a denizen of the lower classes to whom opportunities for social leadership were closed.[9]

From the start, ethical considerations were significant in Methodist life. Methodism's ethic left little implicit. Albert Outler has written of Wesley that he was haunted by "the old ghost of antinomianism." [10] In his clashes with both the Moravians on the left flank and the Calvinists on the right, he contended for the absolute centrality of sanctification. Rejecting quietism and any form of preoccupation with "religion" (as contrasted with ethics), and abhorring the concept of predestination, Wesley came down on the side of the gospel's demand for *actual* righteousness. What has pertinence for our investigation of southern religion, however, is the *kind* of ethical orientation present in the tradition, and its understanding of sanctification's relation to justification. In this framework, ethics was personal morality, hardly ethics in the more comprehensive sense of "relation to ethos."

If it is legitimate to refer to the original Baptists as a one-doctrine people, original Methodism may be termed a one-sentiment denomination.• Everything was made secondary to faith as inner awareness. The transformation of institutional religion into personal, of sacramental into inward, of theological into experiential—this was the goal of Wesley's half-century of intense labors. Though far more theologically conscious than much subsequent Methodism has been, Wesleyan religion was distinguished by its maximization of the dynamically subjective. Outler illuminates this truth on two counts. First, Wesley was

• Sentiment is used here (with no pejorative connotations) as a more subjective contrast to the rather objective and rationalistic "doctrine" and does not mean "sentimental." The usage was first suggested to the writer by a sentence from George G. Smith's history of Methodism in early Georgia in which he averred that "Methodism was a sentiment before it became an ecclesiasticism."

not a theologian's theologian, since his interest lay rather in a folk theology. "Theology, for Wesley, was always to be vindicated in its service to the Christian life." [11] Secondly, for Wesley, "grace is always interpreted as something more than mere forensic pardon. Rather, it is experienced as actual influence—God's love, immanent and active in human life." [12]

In their respective origins, then, neither Baptists nor Methodists were, in general, church-type, since their areas of concern were less expansive than those of churchly institutions. A wholesale war was not to be waged against the social order, nor were the regenerate encouraged to withdraw from it. Methodism was restrained from such a policy by its interplay with the Established Church; Baptism, by its residual Calvinism. Neither *renounced* the culture-dominating instincts of their respective parent traditions; the prevalence of the social order was simply taken for granted. On the other hand, they were clearly sect-type in certain basic characteristics. This is most tellingly true in the dimension of the church-sect typology wherein a church is defined as a religious body which supports the integration of a society, and a sect as one which aims at satisfying various individual needs.[13]

The Southern Church in Its Formative Period

Once Baptism and Methodism had been surrounded by the circumstances of the unsettled American environment, both emerged as overwhelmingly sectarian bodies, manifesting few of the qualities expected of church-type institutions. As we have seen, both traditions were essentially—although ambiguously—sectarian from the beginning. Perhaps the recessive church-type instincts within each would have come to light in America, but conditions for this did not materialize until well into the nineteenth century, even in Methodism after it organized itself into a self-contained, centralized American body in 1784.

Earl Brewer, in his astute analysis of the nature of early American Methodism, first notes several respects in which it retained church-type features—for example, its general support of the Federal Government, the founding of schools and orphanages, the organization of preachers into conferences, and the requirement that a ministerial candidate be voted into the conference of preachers. His conclusion, however, is that the tradition was predominantly sectarian.[14] What possessed its adherents was the yearning to draw other individuals into a "highly emotionalized process of repentance, salvation, sanctification, and Christian perfection." [15] Conversion into the life of "scriptural holiness" was their major objective. They existed in small, scattered congregations, held together by class meetings. Because they required that the individual have experienced personal salvation, they possessed the means for distinguishing between members and non-members. This sectarian concept of the church naturally led to the practice of disciplining—on occasion expelling—profligate members. Lay preachers were authorized to carry on between the visits of the peregrinating ordained preachers. The preachers themselves, although encouraged to read and sell books, were not required to meet any set educational standards. Emphasis was placed on the "call of the Holy Ghost to preach." Excesses of all sorts were inveighed against and a number of prohibitions prescribed. The formal liturgy of the Church of England was rejected in favor of "informal worship and preaching services, with simple revivalistic songs." [16] This spirit gave rise to their "decided opposition to rented pews, cushions, crosses, stained-glass windows and other so-called excesses of the church-type religious institution." [17] Most members were from the lower class, and the places of meeting were "homes, brush arbors, simple chapels, and in the open fields," where collections were received after strong emotional appeals.

Constructing a church-sect continuum with five stations on either side of the zero mid-point, Brewer locates the American Methodism of the primitive decade, 1780–1790, at station four from the center on the left, the sect, side. He justifies his interpretation on the grounds that the classical traits of sectlikeness dominated: "appeals to the New Testament and the Primitive Church as ideals," "radical individualism in religious experience," and "redemption through subjective experience rather than through objective grace." [18]

Certainly the eighteenth century American Baptists also deserve placement well to the left of center. A distinction between the Regular Baptists, those directly descended from classical English Baptism, and the more radical Separates must be drawn in any attempt at sociological classification, however. In the context of that age, the Separates surely warrant placement at the leftmost station. The Regulars belong one notch farther right, and we suggest that Methodism should stand at station three, by virtue of its centralization and rather better leadership.

The Baptists shared with the Methodists those definitive traits which Brewer assigns to sectarian groups. The urge to reinstate primitive Christianity was conscious, powerful, and all-determinative. If anything, Baptism outstripped Methodism in this objective, owing to the more emphatic nature of its devotion to *the text* of the Bible, an impulse imparted to it by Calvinism. Moreover the Baptists came to rival Methodism in embracing individualistic subjectivism—both because and in spite of its particular ecclesiology. For, it must be emphasized, the Baptists' one doctrine was highly subjectivistic. The church was affirmed to comprise the regenerate, and the regenerate were identified as such by subjective experience. The early southern Baptists believed that it followed from this emphasis that no "superfluities" were allowable either in the moral life or in worship. Accordingly the place of worship was starkly simple. Sacramental forms and visual symbols were excluded. Baptists sought to uphold only one objectivism, the Word, which was to be subjectivized in the inward regeneration of the individual. The individualism which was characteristic of both bodies at first enjoyed a higher priority in Methodism, though later the Baptists embraced revivalism more ardently than the Methodists.

The Baptists also held in common with their Methodist neighbors their concern for personal holiness and the lower-class orientation of the great majority of communicants. There were also several features which distinguished Baptists from others on the American scene: their acrimonious clashes with public authorities, resulting in persecution and imprisonment; their basic unconcern for education and theological knowledge on the part of the clergy as well as the laity; and their almost total lack of a leadership class which could command public respect and grasp the wide dimensions of the church's social responsibility.

Thus, after the advent of the nineteenth century, both Methodists and Baptists were sect-type. The Methodists and Regular Baptists possessed certain qualities which made transference to churchlikeness a reasonable possibility. The more influential Separate Baptists had virtually no traits which would incline them toward assuming a churchlike stance, short of miraculously novel sociological conditions. One of the singular events in the history of Christianity is that those miracles did occur.

The Transformation Process

The key fact is that Baptism and Methodism, historically nearer the sect classification, have gained a place in southern society where they are the dominant religious groups in the region and are looked to as the principal resources for the spiritual and moral life of the society at large. By their very success they have acquired the responsibilities classically associated with the church-type bodies. In other words, they have been thrust into a role whereby their sect intentions have been obscured through their responsibility to be *the* religious agencies in the society. Conception of themselves as isolated and intimate small religious groups has been out of date for many decades now.

A recent analytic theory by Bryan Wilson illuminates the process by which southern Methodists and Baptists shed many of their sectarian qualities through its contention that these sects, the so-called "conversionist" sects which seek to convert "outsiders" are the most likely to surrender their status as sects.[19] At any rate, this is an accurate description of the southern "big two" which have aggressively campaigned to convert every person in the society, and which in so doing have increasingly assumed the identity of denominations.* This is true because those groups which support evangelists and missionaries seem increasingly to feel that they should train those whose tasks are regarded as important enough to support. As these leaders and emissaries are trained, the group moves "up." In addition, the conversionist sect by its very design cannot remain altogether aloof from wider culture precisely because its burning passion is to "reach" men in the secular world for the sake of bringing them into its fold. Furthermore, unless it takes pains to erect extremely high standards of admission, the sect is likely to experience an erosion of its spiritual quality "through the impact of recruitment," that is, through the fact that its new converts are "incompletely socialized" from the sect's point of view at the time of their entry into it.[20]

The way in which this type of sect articulates its doctrines is not significantly different from the doctrinal statements of the denominations. When the conversionist sect's standard of admission, the "simple acceptance of a Savior," is joined to it, there results a doctrinal indistinctiveness that produces difficulties, especially within the conscious religiousness of the second generation. Finally, since such a sect is only relatively self-contained and inward-turned it inclines toward exchanging sectarian identification for denominational. Conversionists, unlike other sectarians, have a concept of brotherhood which somewhat relaxes their self-consciousness as sect members and the rigor of their standards as exhibited by their longing to include persons outside the immediate group.[21]

A quite different kind of sociological theory, by Milton Yinger, sheds light on this process by suggesting that whether a sect develops toward denominational status—that is, in this connection, social acceptance—is determined by its original impulses,

---

* A "denomination" is not identical with church or sect. It resembles the church-type in that it is stable, respected, at peace with its society, and firmly established as a part of ongoing life. It is not in any historic sense an "Established Church," officially approved and governmentally subsidized. In a word, a denomination has a relation to the religiously pluralistic society without Establishment which is comparable to an Established Church's relation to its society.

either social or individualistic.[22] The unequivocally individual-istic drives of the early Methodists and Baptists, according to this theory, should have turned them toward denominational stand-ing, which is certainly what happened.

Once Baptists and Methodists in the South fully embraced and substantially relied upon revivalism as the central element in their institutional life, they took on the character of conversionist sects. Historic Methodism had always been, on balance, a conver-sionist sect. The Baptists had been somewhat more conservative because of their aversion to free-will doctrine and their rigorous standards of admission and discipline. It will be recalled that they did not embrace the technique of revivalism without equivocation. Both Baptists and Methodists moved out to the people; indeed they were part and parcel of the popular society. There was no Established Church, not even dominant alien religious patterns which they might have felt compelled to attack or withdraw from. Effectively speaking, all that lay outside their ranks was an unregenerate society. There was nothing to contend with but sin and sinful persons. Highly motivated, armed with revivalism as a pragmatic technique, free from the stifling influ-ence of principalities and powers, the southern church went to work filling the vacuum, feeding the unfed sheep in a sprawling population. Thus theology, history, and sociology conspired to transform these conversionist sects into denominations.

On to the Present: Sect-Type

In spite of the powerful historical and social forces which have tended to strip the popular churches of their original qualities, much of the intrinsic impulse toward sectlikeness has endured, especially in the way in which overarching attention is given to meeting the needs of the individual.• This preoccupation may take quite different forms, but it is rarely sacrificed to the universalizing sentiment of the church-type.

• The definition of sects as religious groups which are oriented toward meeting the needs of individuals is Yinger's. Troeltsch's definition has more direct reference to their emphasis on personal religion.

An insistence on the necessity of directly experiencing God underwrites expressively, and in some sense causes, the negative attitude toward the world which is characteristic of sects. The southern church has so insisted—the Baptists along the line of requiring a conversion experience, and of asserting that the Bible's message is known to the faithful reader immediately; and the Methodists by a warmth of spirit (which in practice is sometimes detached from any forceful objectification). This subjectivist bias, the bedrock quality of the southern church, serves to entrench its sectlikeness the more firmly. It does so by leading southern churchmen to believe that the richness of each individual's religious experience qualifies him to interpret the Bible and Christian theology normatively. When this way of thinking is stretched to denominational proportions, it means that theological truth is determined by consensus. The scholar or ideologist of the faith is accorded little authority in the task of discerning Christian meaning. Because of this subjectivist mentality, the southern church is confident that God has entrusted divine truth to its keeping in substantially pure form. Thus churchmen proceed to declare it uncritically, rarely reflecting on its veracity in the light of norms which transcend their own consensus. This combination of subjectivism, ideology by consensus, and the notion that the in-group has a corner on the truth can hardly be called anything but sectarianism.

The virulent self-consciousness of Christian identity within many southern churchmen is another indication that the sectarian mentality keeps its firm grip. They deplore "casual religion," regarding the very term as a contradiction. The devout southern Protestant has been conditioned to think of himself as first and foremost a citizen of the Kingdom of God. In this connection, empirical research has disclosed that members of "differentistic" religious groups (sects) are more likely to identify themselves by their religious affiliation than are members of "conventional" (church-type) groups. For the sectarians, religious affiliation is a primary point of reference.[23] By its very nature the sect must emblazon on its members and the larger society the rationale for its existence. The extremity of some of the southern churches' protestations (against drinking, the continental sabbath, the ecumenical movement, etc.) reveals its sectarian spirit by suggesting that it may labor under a compulsive need to demonstrate the peculiarities of its mission. This conscious striving to be different continues as a prominent feature of the Southern Baptists, notably, who frequently view their Convention as the chosen remnant in the midst of a "modernistic" Christianity and a secular world.

Finally the intensity so evident in the southern church's life clearly reveals its sectarian character. Its vigor and vitality produce a frankness of affirmations, an aggressiveness in evangelistic outreach, and a rigor in its moral programs not often found in Christendom. It sets its sights high and perseveres toward its goals. Afire with enthusiasm and optimism, it will not be daunted in its mission to win the world. Long ago Troeltsch associated this trait with the sects: "These are also the groups in which an ardent desire for the improvement of their lot goes hand in hand with a complete ignorance of the complicated conditions of life, in which therefore an idealistic orthodoxy finds no difficulty in expecting to see the world transformed by the purely moral principles of love." [24]

On to the Present: Church-Type

In his article cited earlier, Brewer has demonstrated that by 1940, American Methodism, although it was still in "sect-type conflict with specific activities, such as legalized liquor, drinking, and gambling," had become, in general, church-type.[25] Surely the enormity of the body and its acceptance in southern society is *prima facie* evidence of this fact. Many decades had passed since members were persecuted or ostracized or had felt any inclination to withdraw from society. Moreover, the modern Methodists came from all classes. Little distinction was made between members and non-members. The memorable experience of conversion was relegated to the periphery or discarded altogether, and entry into the local congregation was increasingly stylized. Church life had undergone modification from the "relatively simple local societies and conference of preachers to a highly differentiated bureaucracy" with a multiplicity of boards and committees, so that in many cases secondary relationships replaced primary.[26] Educational standards for ministers had been elevated. Formality in worship had increased, as seemed appropriate to the mammoth, elaborate church buildings now adorned by visual symbols and clergymen in vestments.

Concretely, Brewer has placed American Methodism of the decade 1930–1940 at station two to the right of zero—in contrast to its clear sectarian status in 1780–1790. Although he does not distinguish between national and southern Methodism, we deem it responsible to locate southern Methodism one or two stations to the left of the larger collectivity. Moving to the present decade, if mainstream American Methodism stands at position two or three on the church side, rurally oriented Methodism stands at station one on the sect side, with the midstream southern congregations at station one on the right.

The Baptist story is much the same. By all external appearances, more precisely in its institutional life, the Southern Baptist organization is church-type. Instead of small, intimate fellowships, informally structured, as they were until this century, Baptist congregations are large, not infrequently gigantic, and usually organized to the hilt. They meet in extensive, expensive buildings. In a growing number of cases their ministers are recipients of seminary training. This is particularly true of the larger churches in which churchlike concepts of official leadership, church property, and internal structure tend to be associated.

Differences do persist, however, between Baptist and Methodist attitudes. For one thing, the Baptists still talk a great deal about restricting church membership to the regenerate. Overtly at least, their goals surpass the Methodists' at the point of ecclesiological purity. Further, the Baptists continue to look askance at the use of worship forms. Markedly absent from their services are robed ministers, traditional visual centers, and notions that the place where they gather is properly called a "sanctuary."

The attitude toward the place of theological education in the life of the churches may be the most suggestive of all southern religion's traits relative to church-sect typology. Baptists and Methodists share the consequences of accentuating the "call to the ministry" and of the regnant or residual revivalistic theology. Seminary products within both groups are apt to be relatively unaffected by the three years' exposure. Yet there is ever mounting respect for the necessity of the educational experience. On this level, the sect ideal appears to have been modified, perhaps largely dispelled. Although theological education is not yet an earnest component of the churches' actual life, as would be the case with truly church-type institutions, both denominations pour impressive sums into the maintenance of many seminaries, a number of which maintain high quality, and none of which is obscurantist in basic outlook. As a matter of fact, in the case of the Methodists, most seminarians go to distinguished divinity schools—Duke, Vanderbilt, Emory, and Perkins at S.M.U. (noteworthily, all associated with leading "secular" universities), three of which are supported directly by the denomination.

The passage of the southern church beyond unequivocal sectarian status is also demonstrated by the peculiar form in which it has routinized charisma. In their organizational structure, at local, territorial, and comprehensive levels, both denominations strive for consensus and discourage diversity. Within Methodism, because of the almost exclusively administrative nature of the episcopal office, as well as among Baptists where rule has come naturally from the "bottom up," the desire for consensus has the practical effect of muffling the prophetic element which has been native to their respective heritages. In both denominations the "personality figure" has assumed the role normally reserved for the prophet, a predictable eventuation given the precedence of institutional solidarity over the responsible quest for truth. The leaders accorded the greatest following are those who are best equipped by personality to further the institution. Methodist bishops and Baptist executives alike are expected to implement the will of the people by dint of suasion. Standing in judgment on present patterns of church life and charting new courses therefore are tasks felt to lie largely outside their charge. The authority of office is not derived from God so much as from "pragmatic legitimation." By being successful in advancing the institution, they win, then justify, their leadership roles. Though both the Baptist and Methodist traditions are "voluntary societies" by declared intent, with strong prophetic strains from their past, their leaders are generally "quasi-charismatic" figures who are apt to have gotten where they are on the strength of striking personalities.[27]

The position of the southern church on the place of the Negro in southern society is the most dramatic instance of its church-likeness on the question of the relationship between Christ and culture.• By all odds the surpassingly important issue of the day in the South, the integration movement captures little of the church's concern, formally or informally. Leaving aside the significant theological incentives for this neglect (discussed in Chapter 7), it is clear from a sociological standpoint that the southern church has taken over the values of the culture in which it lives. The religious institutions have made their peace with the social tradition of the region which long relegated the Negro to an inferior and alien place.

Caught in the vise of factors which are at once sociological and theological-ethical, the southern church manifests church-type traits on this gravest of all issues in contemporary regional life. In other terms, southern society is a "folk culture," as distinct from a "state civilization." [28] Wherever a society is characterized by folkways and folk mores, wherever social change is gradual and primary institutions and community predominate as in the South's folk culture, religious institutions find little leverage for analyzing and criticizing the culture or for divorcing themselves

---

• It will be recalled that Rufus Spain has demonstrated that between 1865 and 1900 the Southern Baptists became increasingly conscious of their responsibility to society. However, this responsibility was conceived in terms of a narrow ("biblical") code of personal morality. Spain notes that as with all accepted religious institutions, the Southern Baptist organization supported the basic structures and outlook of the society in which it flourished—in politics, race relations, economics, and other areas. This situation has not changed in the meantime.

from it. Instead of profoundly transcending the culture in its value-orientation, the church is closely identified with it. Needless to say, perpetuation of sect-type qualities is far easier to achieve in a state civilization, where culture somehow transcends the people living in it, than in a folk culture. The southern situation has precluded the emergence of a concept of leadership that would grant leaders genuine freedom to evaluate, criticize, and reconstruct religious positions.

All of this helps to explain how, in the face of historic Baptism's and Methodism's classical insistence on church discipline, standards for admission to the southern church have all but disappeared. Since popular religious teaching is a folkway, it is simply taken for granted that virtually every citizen assents to that teaching, and that he will, later if not sooner, own up to his responsibility to act on it. Needing little convincing as to the veracity of the teaching, he awaits only the moment of truth at which there surges through him the impulse to cast his lot with Christ and the church. Even the rigors of the Christian life *cannot* quite sound rigorous to him, because the culture around him seems to subscribe to the same moral tenets. In short, the nature of the culture and its domination by the religious institutions have worked against the preservation of the "pure church" ideal, even when that ideal has been articulated most forcefully. Only such a group as the Moravians of early Salem, North Carolina, which was transferred intact from Germany and kept itself apart from southern society by self-subsistence and tight communal self-regulation, managed for long to retain a classical sect-manner. Unlike the Moravian communities, the dominant southern bodies were unable to demarcate a value-system distinct from that of the surrounding folk culture.

Finally, the southern church was encouraged to embrace a church-type role by the absence of any powerful, dominant ecclesiastical colossus against which to protest. Back in England, Baptist and Methodist societies struggled to birth in reaction against the imperfections of existing churches. They drew identity and vitality from the obligation they felt to rectify the errors of and indifference within empirical institutions. But since foils,

without which sects cannot be sects, had largely dsappeared from
the South by 1800, it was inevitable that the southern church acquire a mentality which stamped it as church-type in the Troelt-
schian sense. Especially because the original Baptist and Methodist sectarians were of the conversionist stripe, they changed character as their task became less reflexive and more initiating. The
combination of their particular make-up and the southern cultural setting would not let them continue to be what they had
been born to be.[29]

Part iv
Beyond Analysis:
The Church in a
Changing Society

10

The Uses
of Religion
in the South

Wherever religious faith pulsates in the human spirit, it helps in fulfilling, motivating, and directing human lives. Personal belief and religious institutions have been as richly meaningful for Southerners as for men of faith in other societies. In addition to these standard benefits, however, religion has offered Southerners a distinctive set of advantages and usages in line with the peculiar social and cultural setting of the region.

We should remember that the religious factor in southern society did not serve the function of providing a rallying-center for immigrants of the same ethnic stock, or afford a small-group identification for unassimilated immigrants, as it did in other sections of the nation. Similarly, religion has not played so significant a role in producing or reinforcing the stratification of southern society as it has elsewhere. To be sure, the Episcopal and Presbyterian churches have been composed very largely of persons in middle class and above, but the Baptists and Methodists, which began as people's churches, have shown an amazing capacity for winning and keeping individuals of means and privilege—notwithstanding the tendency in more complex communities for local churches to be identified with a particular class, such as the mill village church, or the "First" church catering to the higher classes.

A paramount feature in the unusual meaning the church has held for Southerners is the intensity and vitality which is its hallmark almost everywhere. One of the many visitors to the South who have taught it so much about itself, Sir William Archer, an Englishman traveling in the region just before the turn of the twentieth century, ventured the judgment that "the South is by a long way the most simply and sincerely religious country that I was ever in. In other countries men are apt to make a private matter of their religion . . . ; but the Southerner wears it on his sleeve." [1] Popular southern religion is anything but casual about either its business or its self-identity. Whatever else this vitality indicates, it surely demonstrates how much religious faith means to those who profess it. If this criterion counts for anything, it means that the Southerner's faith runs very deep and lies near his center. This has been true in both the psychic and the social dimensions of his life.

The Psychic Dimension

Personal Christian faith is nothing if it is not supportive to those who hold it. Millions of persons across the expanse of southern territory in all periods, from the Colonial to the present, have been uplifted, sustained, and encouraged by faith in God and the fellowship of the local congregation. They have been enabled by this faith to meet crises, of which Southerners, individually and corporately, have had a seemingly disproportionate share. They have experienced joy in the knowledge of sins forgiven and their consequent heavenly destiny. They have found warmth, friendship, and release within the circle of the congregation. In another vein, many have received from ministers and other concerned churchmen stimulation to pursue an education or to set their sights higher. Horizons have been enlarged and visions lifted through Christian influence.

There is an enormous number of southern men and women, many of them coming from confining, uninspiring, even hopeless settings, who are profoundly grateful for the light made available to them by the southern church. Accordingly, only one reared among them, who has experienced something of the same encouragement and support, is prepared to understand the hurt and revulsion many of them feel when their church is criticized. For all its faults, it has been a "life-saver," in several senses, to millions of the sons of Dixie. There should be no surprise that they defend it, even against objective analysis. Because of faith's profound meaning for their personal lives, many of the devout are suspicious of criticisms of southern religion which have begun to be voiced against its provinciality and alleged irrelevance.

Any discussion of what the church has meant to the South which overlooks its constructive role discredits itself. "Outsiders" disposed to deprecate southern religion are simply required to take it on faith that, whatever the appearances, the church has wielded a strong positive influence on millions.[2] Yet it is equally clear that the church has had some deleterious effect on the region and its people. Not infrequently, furthermore, religion has played a predominantly secular role, without either the institutions or the people being conscious of it. More importantly, millions of southern people have found in religion the meeting of needs which have little to do with, and sometimes are antithetical to, the church's intended ministry. The requirements of ordinary honesty and of the church's obligation to measure up to its calling demand open-eyed scrutiny of the wide range of meaning which religion has for the southern people.

To begin with, we may recall the way in which, in the setting of the frontier-rural South, religion served the high purpose of affording relief from loneliness and monotony. The periodic warm-weather camp meetings and revivals, as well as the occasional local church services, provided social opportunities to many who only rarely saw anyone outside the circle of their own families and closest neighbors (who were apt to live several miles away). In the mill villages which sprang up before and after the dawn of the present century, religion helped relieve the repression of the mill workers whose jobs were beset by sameness and poor working conditions. Pope has described this memorably:

> Religious services . . . help the mill worker to transcend his daily life through providing excitement. All ministers acknowledge that mill workers need a strong emotional outlet because of the damming up of self-expression by the conditions amid which they live. The company-village system pre-empts nearly all their fundamental choices, and jobs in the mill are highly mechanical and routine in character. When his day in the mill is over, the worker frequently feels the need of a vigorous emotional massage; he finds it in hair-raising movies and emotional religious services, among other outlets.[3]

Just as all societies structure periods for the purpose of throwing off restraints, so every man has the need for bursting the bonds which hold in his emotional urges, and in one way or another religion has offered itself as the most accessible means for providing this occasion to vast numbers of Southerners. The "sensual and physical thrill" of dramatic religious experience characteristic of southern revivalism accounts for a measure of its attraction and "usefulness" to the masses of people. Of all the institutional arrangements available to southern society for coping with the multiple deprivations—social, economic, and psychic —afflicting a host of its citizens, religion was by all odds the superior candidate.[4] Countless individuals found in religious experience and congregational life welcome and adequate resources for filling gaping emptiness in their personal lives.

Other less noble psychic needs, however, also seem to have been supplied. For example, the urge to spirited competition expressed itself powerfully on the frontier in cockfights, in fist fights, in horse races, later in organized sports—and not least in intersectarian competition. There is ample evidence that many found no greater delight than in public debates "proving the superiority" of their denomination over others. In fact, many of the debates and polemical essays in this genre seem to have been produced with tongue in cheek. The competitive exchange was an end in itself for many frustrated spirits; it did not matter ultimately what the subject area was. It is an item of considerable historical moment that among the Baptists, what may well have commenced as little more than a pastime, escalated into an ardently defended dogma, a theory of "Baptist succession," the so-called Landmark movement. Flamboyant claims and fanatical allegiances gave bored men something exciting to live and fight for, even if truth and tradition had to be handled deviously.

One infreqently recognized service which religion has rendered to the southern psyche consists in affording great numbers of people confined to farms and small communities the only direct association they have had with a vast and powerful institution. Few have belonged to labor unions, and farmers' Granges have lacked the qualities of massiveness, dynamism, and cosmopolitanism necessary to satisfy the longing to be a part of something big. While it is true that almost all Southerners have been Democrats, politics is far too complicated and the party's constittuency far too heterogeneous to provide most Dixie Democrats with any sense of intimate belonging. The religious denomination remains as the only "big outfit" with which the average man has been able to identify.

The annual meeting of the Southern Baptist Convention, to take the best illustration, is a magnificent sociological experience. For here are gathered under one roof (few buildings in the South are sufficiently cavernous to contain this assembly) thousands of individuals normally isolated from the power structures of any organization but very much a part of an immense, destiny-conscious, muscle-flexing institution in which the accents and concerns of the leaders, because similar to their own, are intelligible. Complex issues which transcend their grasp and concern, when raised at all, do not stay on the floor very long. This is a people's convention, where the leadership is attractive, persuasive, and smooth-tongued, but cut from the same cloth as the

average pastor or layman in attendance. Consensus rules. Here
"scripture-based," emotionally attuned opposition to a progressive
measure which is strange-sounding to the "messengers" can
produce a tabling or an adulteration, with a resulting emptiness
surpassed only by its acceptability to a tradition-bound and
unity-obsessed assembly. It is remarkable how these annual
meetings have so effectively brought together institutional gran-
diosity and the psychology of an agrarian, inferiority-ridden
people. With or without the personal experience of the collectivity, the southern churchman derives buoyant support from
belonging to something as vigorous, successful, and ultimate as
his religious denomination. It has done what no other connection
has, namely, put him in touch with something which manages
to transcend the simple patterns of his own life while retaining
the tone of the folk society apart from which he is threatened.

The ministerial role is still another function of religion's
meaning for the South—both for those who are ministered to
and the ministers themselves. We have already called attention
to the positive impact which many ministers have made upon
southern people. They have guided, helped to orient, donated
needed funds, given time and encouragement, healed interpersonal disaffections, and championed public morality. The
exalted status enjoyed by the clergy throughout much of southern
history—in some respects, they have been like an untouchable
caste—was partly deserved, owing to the quantity and quality
of their services to the people. In many a community, the minister
was one of a very few persons, perhaps the only person, from
whom any sort of stable leadership could be expected. Accordingly, it was natural that he should be turned to and respected.
More than this, he was the "man of God" in a society that
entertained scant notion that God might not exist, or that God's
existence had no urgent bearing on a man's behavior. That is,
the figure of the local preacher incarnated what was ultimate
for an uncritical society. Small wonder that such a society should
vest him with an authoritative role.

Painful as it is to say so, the unique features of the socio-
psychological climate of the South have issued in some important

distortions of the ministerial role, especially in the tendency of the ministers to overrate their own authority and in the acquiescence of many laymen to a supposed gradation of callings. One sensitive layman, who doubtless speaks for many, not long ago admitted to a kind of role victimization during an address to a gathering of seminarians in the following candid remarks: "I grew up believing that a layman had no right to question . . . [the minister's authority]. Since a minister was a man who had received a call from God, his position was equal to the one claimed for the pope. His judgment was presumed to be not his own, but that of God." So deeply rooted in the southern consciousness have these assumptions been that few have been able to perceive the pattern for what it is and declare with this layman that "subsequent events have altered these youthful views."

It may be, however, that in the long run the greater distortion has occurred with ministers themselves—the prospective as well as the full-fledged. For an important proportion of the clerical leaders of the southern church have been astute and ambitious politicians. The pastoral office has been one of the most direct paths to fame and power in southern society.

Two conditions in southern life have made the ministerial vocation attractive to the ambitious: first, the ideological consensus which left no doubt that Christian truth, as communicated by the "man of God," was to be taken *prima facie* as absolute; and second, the sense of hierarchy endemic to the Colonial South and only just now decisively crumbling, which graded society by roles as well as by class of birth.[5] For these and other reasons, the ministerial vocation has enjoyed a high status. Doubtless, there is a correlation between the unchallenged leadership role shared by white and Negro Protestant clergy in their respective subsectors, especially after the Civil War, and the fact that among all the professions, the South had an abundance in only one, the ministry. Its percentage of clergymen per 100,000 of the population exceeded the national average by 135.6 to 121.2.[6]

The large majority of southern ministers appears to have been dominated by a purer desire to serve. Nevertheless, the search for ego gratification, no more acute in the South than elsewhere, but more difficult to achieve, seems to have been a factor motivating men to choose the ministry, especially within the past forty or so years under conditions of rapid growth and large-scale bureaucratization. The political maneuvering behind the conferring of Doctor of Divinity degrees upon southern clergymen is some index of this. As far back as the 1830's, Alexander Campbell observed "a hankering after titles amongst some Baptists." [7] Even at that date regional colleges awarded honorary D.D. degrees. This situation is not peculiarly southern, and the practice is rife in other professions as well, but one is impressed by the deference paid to the system in the South. The pastor of a sizable congregation, who owns a D.D. degree and enjoys an approved standing among his peers, is automatically a revered figure in southern society, even though he gives little evidence of a concern for learning.

Rapid social change has already introduced a new situation concerning the prestige of the ministerial role in the South. On all sides, one hears indirect comments concerning the declining influence of the clergy. A series of interviews conducted by the *Charlotte Observer* in the winter of 1963 indicated that younger persons feel markedly less obligation than their elders to accept the opinions and positions of their ministers. Moreover, the heightened specialization of skills in community leadership, as well as the lessening of automatic peer status, is a threat to the minister's central role, unless he takes steps to qualify as a leader in the changing communities. To date, few southern ministers have acquired the requisite expertise. Nor do they now possess an honored station which grants them automatic entry into high councils. A generation ago the pastors of the most prestigious churches in a city would be called in by the mayor as consultants on key matters. This is increasingly less often the case. Ministers are still likely to be paid a certain deference, and to be applauded as hail fellows. Day by day, however, the latter image is becoming more of a liability in communities where men who deal in issues, problems, and ideas are in far greater demand than the once-hailed charismatic personality.

The Social Dimension

Southern Protestantism's individualistic posture and strong sectarian leanings, real as they are, have not prevented it from making a decisive difference in the social fabric of the South. As a matter of fact, religion has penetrated areas of life far beyond the church walls with its outlook and values. Besides the social impingements we have already observed, the southern church continually views its mission in social terms in various ways, for example, by calling attention to the judgment of God upon the whole society or an entire denomination. It speaks of the destruction which is perpetrated upon the society at large by the minority who indulge in crime, delinquency, debauchery, and the like. Although the southern church has never devoted its energies to the redemption of the social structures, and certainly warrants no identification with the "social gospel" tradition, it has not been blind to the relation between the Christian faith and a number of social currents and responsibilities.

One of the most obvious social functions of southern religion was noted by Frederick Lee Olmsted during his 1853–1854 sojourn in the South, namely that church buildings were used as "places of assembly for all public purposes." [8] Some eighty years later, Pope found that transplantation to industrial communities had done nothing to remove the church fellowship, organization, and building to the periphery of social life: "Group life in the mill villages needed focal centers around which to integrate itself; the church had been the most characteristic institution in the rural background from which most of the workers came, and it was quite natural that they should desire a similar rallying point in their new industrial setting." [9] Likewise, Poteat could assert in the decade of the 1930's that the "church has been and still is the center of much social interest and activity, with the annual revival meeting or Homecoming Day the social highlight of the year." [10]

It is hardly surprising, therefore, that according to informed estimates, 78 per cent of the social participation of a sample of rural people in North Carolina (which in this respect must be close to typical) was through their churches, only 22 per cent coming through all other community organizations. Moreover, it is important to point out that these descriptions pertain to the "better classes" as well as the lower. In the South it is the poor and uneducated who are likely to be ecclesiastically dispossessed, not the more privileged. Timothy Flint's analysis of the audience at camp meetings in the 1820's is instructive: "The ambitious and the wealthy are there, because in this region opinion is all-powerful; and they are there, either to extend their influence, or that their absence may not be noted, to diminish it." [11] Although the motivations of the higher classes need not be viewed with so much suspicion, it is true that they, too, have found religion "useful." In sum, it is not too much to say that the entire range of southern society has considered the church an indispensable institution. More than the school, the church has been the one aspect of community life which, as its unchallenged center, comprehended a wide variety of functions.

At a deeper level, the churches have been a mighty force in the generation of the society's values. Indeed this statement is a truism. Religious values aided immeasurably in taming a boisterous frontier and building a public morality. The church has been a powerful contributor to the inculcation of such personal virtues as sobriety, integrity, and friendliness. Southern Christianity's record with respect to the last, however, is less positive in the area of white-Negro relations. A dissonant admixture of genuine good will and depersonalization, the church's ambiguous influence is due to being so closely identified with the society that it has difficulty sitting in judgment on it. This means that the minister, called to be a prophet, is restrained by the social-psychological situation from violating the values in terms of which the congregation understands itself. At the same time, however, the groundwork which the church has laid for a Christian conscience affords the greatest hope for change. As one sensitive Southerner has observed: "An appeal to that conscience does mean something; until now it has not been turned toward race, but the change is coming." [12]

The Southern white says he has genuine affection for the Negro, means what he says, and is accurate, *in terms of his particular definition of affection where Negro-white relations are involved.* He is often kindly, protective, even generous in his dealings with his black neighbor. He has yet to see, however, that Christian love is not present when kindliness, protectiveness, and generosity are extended toward another on condition that he is not to be regarded as a full person—that is, when the other's inferiority of worth and potential is taken for granted. This does not mean that there are not many in the South who can be won over on the basis of an appeal to Christian conscience.

As the final item in a brief cataloguing of some of the major roles, both positive and negative, which the church has played in the South, we must mention the assistance it has been to thousands making the transition from an agrarian to an urban style of life, in the last half-century especially. In the early years of the population movement the religious life with its appurtenances succeeded in molding the farmers into stable, contented, and sober citizens.[18] At that demographic stage, the prohibitionist crusades of the churches did contribute to the well-being of a society which could easily have "come loose at the hinges." By providing moorings, a sustaining fellowship, and emotional outlets the church rendered invaluable service to the recently transplanted.

The role of religious values and institutions for tiding over the "uprooted" during a period of structural change in society is not confined to industrial workers. Many within the middle classes as well have experienced social disruption, and because of their rural and small-town orientation have sought security in the church. The patterns of conversation and social organization in southern city churches to this day betray the simple background from which the older adults of the churches came to find work and a new life.

Perhaps the churches' role in the South's transition today will be a compound of short-run value and long-run obstruction, with the prospect of the latter not entirely bedeviling the good qualities of the former. More specifically, in an age when seemingly everything which has been the Southerners' is being taken away—politics, the law, schools, and social customs, all heretofore conducted in the southern manner—some conserving yet bridging institution may be needed by a people beset by disruption and dislocation. For all kinds of good and poor reasons, the popular church is singularly well equipped for such a role. The deep psychological hurt in southern hearts today cannot be stressed too much. Assistance in making the transition to a different southern society, one that is significantly incorporated into the national mainstream, is urgently called for. It may well be that one or more of the South's major religious groups will be partially in the service of Providence by remaining essentially rooted to the past. Such an interpretation contains a modicum of realism and moves with considerable good taste toward salvaging something positive from the realities of a religious situation which is on the whole distressingly unpromising.

11
The Threat
of Rejection

The passing of each year witnesses a further intensification of social change in the South. More than a dozen years after the decisive Supreme Court ruling designed to eliminate segregation at the public school level, previously unbelievable alterations are now visible in southern life, and the end is not in sight. The time has come when the southern church must either reconceive its ministry in terms of the social change swirling all about it, or abdicate its responsibility, except in terms of limited and short-run tasks. The relationship of the southern church to the persons and society it seeks to serve is being drastically recast.

Implications of
Social Change for Religious Life

It may be that contemporary events in the American South disclose nearly as far-reaching and revolutionary a stage in that culture's career as comparable movements in Asia and Africa. For the South is currently in the throes of transition from semicolonial status (in which it judged reality by provincial standards, lived an essentially uncritical existence, and was cut off from wider civilization) to a position of involvement in world culture.

Numerous elements in this transition have immediate consequences for the church. High on the list is the shift of the cultural center from farm and small community to city. On the assumption that the desire "to preserve the family farm . . . has symbolized our national roots" and the American consciousness has regarded farming as more than a business, "it has come to symbolize moral values as well as economics. Consciously or unconsciously, *religion and agriculture are regarded as inseparably related.*" [1] There can be no doubt that this way of thinking has a firm hold on citizens of the South. The personality of congregational life, the rhetoric of sermons, indeed the church members themselves, many of whom are either farmers or first- and second-generation emigrés from farm life, are convincing testimony. The emergence of an essentially urban South is exciting a clash of civilizations.[2] Whereas southern cities in earlier periods were far from urbane and only marginally urban, now those same metropolitan centers and other newer ones, greatly swelled in size and complexity, have more in common with similar centers outside the South than with the regional communities of which they were formerly little more than enlargements.

What does the confrontation with (and the inevitable triumph of) the urban character of life mean for the life of southern churches which remain effectively oriented to rural values and assumptions? Sociologist Gerhard Lenski, in treating the transformation which the introduction of urbanity as the way of life brings about, remarks that for one thing people of *diverse backgrounds* are brought into constant and close association with one another. This destroys the old pattern of homogeneity. Again, in urban living people find that "they are obliged to cooperate in the production of goods and services, the maintenance of law and order, and a variety of other tasks essential to the well-being of the total community. As a consequence, they find it necessary to ignore the differences which divide them, at least while they are engaged in those activities requiring cooperation." Thus "norms of *tolerance* and secularism [religious neutralism] inevitably arise in urban centers." [3] By definition, life in the modern city differs significantly from life as previously known in country or country-town; life in the urbanizing South can be no exception.[4]

In terms of urbanism's impact upon southern religion, the emergence of tolerance and religious neutralism as prominent traits within the city dweller is decisive. The urbanite is apt to be less dogmatic in his religious pronouncements. Inevitably he confronts other ideological alternatives, at least some of which will strike him as having a certain plausibility and perhaps a greater meaning for his life. More likely still, he finds that work and leisure, as efforts toward making a better, more enjoyable life on the naturalistic plane, supersede supernatural considerations. Caught up in pressures—and dazzling opportunities—he may turn from the values of heaven to those of earth, from the rule of God to the immediacies of a materialistic existence.

Correspondingly, the new urbanite's social-moral habits are undergoing alteration. The use of alcohol, because it is considered fundamental, affords the richest illustration. After growing up in a rural or semirural environment, where the use of alcohol to any degree was alien to social practices and the *bête noire* of the preachers, he now finds himself in a climate where the cocktail hour and wine-adorned dinner table are standard social practice. Nor do these customs, or the persons who observe them, strike him as irresponsible—certainly not as bawdy—as he had been led to expect. His resistance weakens, due partly to the impulse to conform, but also perhaps because he discovers that the psychological effects of alcohol are pleasant and relaxing. Before long he is a regular social drinker. He may begin the practice also because of an inchoate conviction that Christians have a duty to become a part of the interests, needs, and desires of others; therefore, he should join, not stand apart from, persons in this symbolic act. In a word, he may shift allegiance from one guideline, "Dare to be different," to another, implicitly biblical:

"To as great a degree as is consistent with your ultimate commitment, join in with other persons in the fulness of their lives." The principle becomes, persons before rules.•

Whatever the exact nature of the process, assimilation into the mainstream of urban life does alter social practices. A recent survey of Mormons, a people more strict than southern Baptists and Methodists, revealed that with reference to the use of tea, coffee, tobacco, liquor, and beer, *"rural* Mormon families were significantly more orthodox than were those of *urban* Mormon families."[5] Sociologists repeatedly have observed that it is difficult for religious people to maintain their peculiarities from generation to generation in a large city "where public education and other nonfamily socializing influences tend to modify 'radical' practices of cultural subgroups."[6]

It would appear that since World War II several patterns of social adjustment have been prominent among religious Southerners who are becoming urbanized. Two had simultaneous currency from the mid-1940's into the present decade. Using drinking practices as the focus of the discussion, one pattern reflected a transfer of the old social ideals into the new setting. Among these people, unyielding abstinence from drinking characterized the behavior of the minority, who were gradually thrown into social circles where drinking was standard. The somewhat larger subgroup that had no contact with liquor or occasions where it was served—except with the lower-class drunk who sometimes made a public spectacle of himself—uncritically maintained the traditional rural value-structure. The younger adults, including many men who had spent years on military reservations and battlefields, "had it both ways." They continued to be loyal Baptist or Methodist churchgoers, never abandoning Christian truth-claims or dropping their institutional ties. At the same time, they adjusted to surrounding actualities: social drinking,

---

• We have not meant to suggest that the use of alcohol presents no problem, or that no Christian case can be made against it. Our interest has consisted in pointing out that drinking is the prime evil in the eyes of the southern church, that the alcohol issue is not identical with the southern church's understanding of it, and that the essential legalism of the southern church's ethic is well exposed by its attitude toward drinking.

alternative modes of life-orientation, and secular influences in general. This group was not without compunctions of conscience, nor without some awareness of the discrepancy between the moral positions they accepted from the pulpit and their activities at parties and on business trips. Yet they *could* "have it both ways," we are suggesting, because on the one hand they gave allegiance to Christianity in good faith, while on the other they unreflectively sensed that much of what the church had branded as evil was actually inconsequential to Christian life. Of course, they must have rationalized some or much of their conduct. Nevertheless, fundamental changes in attitudes concerning the Christian ethic were taking place. The desire to share in the lives of friends, which having a drink together both symbolized and accomplished, took precedence over adherence to a conservative moral code, drafted by a preacher who was not likely to have been in social company where the issue presented itself.

Now, however, the arrival of a new social situation prompts a different response to the church's moral attitudes. The southern businessman and the southern intellectual may feel no obligation to "have it both ways" any longer. The old disparity between "church morality" and actual morality, which operated below the critical level, is giving way. Now the disparity is rising to the surface, and "church morality" is being rejected—not so much because it is out of date, we submit, as because it is trivial. The age in which the preacher's dicta were taken as equivalent to the voice of God has already come to a close for many. Moreover, alternate world views and moral principles are live options. Young Southerners, collegians especially, are no longer constrained to embrace Christianity by the power of certain sanctions, such as the assertion that life in the church is the best or only avenue to truly joyful living, and the threat that hell awaits the disobedient. Orthodox southern churchmen have tended to interpret rejection of these sanctions as signs of sheer recalcitrance; a more astute reaction would note that *positive* concerns contribute to the rejection. For example, some seem to have become aware that a trivial morality, a rose-colored view of life, and a threat-based appeal to conversion are incongruous

with Christianity *on its own terms* as conveyed by depth understanding of it.

Even though the southern church partially acknowledges that
relevance and intelligibility are essential to its ministry, it continues to be wary of adaptation and reformulation. In such a
revolutionary age as the present, it must learn to see that the
Christian faith can, and must, carry all its *basic* principles and
spiritual values in the process of adaptation.[7] But up to now the
obligation to adapt and reformulate has not been fulfilled, nor
has a tension between the transcendent and relevant dimensions
of the faith been achieved. One explanation surely lies in the
fact that the South's upheaval has been partly "imposed" upon it
by the Supreme Court, inasmuch as social change is much more
dislocative to a society when its agents are imported and not
indigenous. All things considered, what is happening today in
the *white* South is not by its own choice. This is certainly true
of the church right up to the present, for the pressures to change
have come principally from beyond its ranks, only gradually
infiltrating southern whites themselves.

The distinguished sociologist of the South, Howard W. Odum,
could write as late as the 1940's that the South, the first western
frontier, was, in the twentieth century, "still a frontier country,
even though it had been 'first' in the development of America." [8]
One historian stated in 1964 that "in time . . . the South passed
through the same economic and social upheavals as the rest of
the nation, but usually 50 to 75 years later." [9] Alterations in
the southern style have continually occurred, and are occurring
today with dramatic power—*except* in the regional religious
institutions. The incredible growth experienced by the churches
in the 1950's is not to be taken as a sign that the church had
become relevant. Actually, the people had not changed significantly by the 1950's, and the church was still purveying its
ministry in terms of the so-called "old-time religion":

Religion in the fifties perhaps to a greater degree than in
previous decades was a potent conservator of the Southern way
of life. . . . General assemblies of clergymen urged the

churches to abandon segregation . . . as undemocratic. But the actual emphasis was on the old-time religion. This meant absorption in other-worldliness with little or no concern over the social problems which worried a few progressive pastors. . . . The strength of the Southern Baptist church stemmed from the same cause as that of the Roman Catholic Church: its utter refusal to compromise with the liberal tendencies of other churches.[10]

The old-time religion persists—in a new time. Barely adequate for the old time—a mixture of good and bad qualities—it is ludicrously out of step with the new. Today it is unthinkable that, without a major overhauling, the southern church can be faithful to the God in whose name it ministers or the people who are the objects of its service.

Southern religion's rigidity is paradoxical, since historically it derived some of its shape, much of its relevance, and most of its success from the factor of adaptability in the formative period, 1740–1830. Today, faced with the eruption of a new social order, it tragically refuses to forsake apparatus given to it by a culture which is presently dying. Two centuries ago it improvised an approach to Christianity when the existing culture-forms could no longer carry traditional Christianity; now it faces its second momentous opportunity. Having been by-passed by much of "early modern religion," completely out of touch with "modern religion," it languishes in a patently obsolete semi-medievalism, calling it "timeless."

It is axiomatic that every responsible institution in human society is forced to be aware of, and in some sense to adopt, the categories of its age. If it is responsible, its problems are the problems of the time and place it serves. The applicability of this maxim to religion has been described as follows:

Each time there is a revolution in the area of knowledge—such as we have seen over the last four hundred years—the relationship must be reappraised. It is incredible that anyone should think the revolutions inaugurated by Copernicus, Darwin, and Freud would not radically revise the Christian understanding and interpretation of life. Never has the work of theologian and philosopher been more difficult than now.[11]

Southern religion has been virtually untouched by these revolutions, and only recently have young ministers for the first time been exposed to their implications in seminary. Young lay Southerners are being exposed to them on a much larger scale, in fact with such frequency that they have greater occasion than before to ponder the bearing these currents have on their own society. At the moment three courses of action are open to this new generation. First, they can attempt to conform to the diverging values of both the church and the contemporary world. Second, they can violate intellectual honesty and live in the world of the church. Third, they can practice integrity and reject the church. It is encouraging, however, that should the church become responsive, a fourth path will lie before them, one which recognizes compatibility between the internalized values and outlooks of their ethos and the framework within which the church affirms its message and lays its claim upon their lives.

Identification with Simplist Mentality

Since all religious movements face periodic protests, cries for the reformation of the southern church do not attest to an exceptional situation. Nevertheless, there is something startlingly unique about the protests beginning to rise from that alert minority sensitive to the implications of social change for the southern church. To a high degree, the protesters intellectually are the *upper* classes, the cosmopolitan citizens in the new society. Historically, in the South and the nation generally, protests have come from the disinherited, the down and out, the economically and psychically deprived. By contrast, the current plea for revision comes from the "above" groups and is directed to the "strategically influential elites" within the religious leadership, the segment which shapes the "formation of those values and definitions of the human situation in terms of which policies and decisions are made," on the grounds that they have failed to grasp the "significance of the new developments taking place among the laity." [12]

The novelty of the present situation is not surprising, however, in view of the demise of the old "sacred" society, and since the impassioned voices, if not yet the regional leadership, belong to the post-New South generation. In effect, their clamor for change pertains to the simplist orientation of the church's thinking. These critics are apt to recognize that the southern church's history has rendered improbable any other kind of orientation up to now. They know, too, that poverty victimized the southern populace and that, accordingly, "both leadership and response carried the stamp of intellectual backwardness." [13] Practically none of the circuit riders or farmer-preachers of the frontier era were educated men. As a matter of fact, only a minority of southern ministers received any college or seminary training until after World War II.

Even now, in Baptist ranks, it is estimated that between two-thirds and three-fourths of the ministers come from rural churches—which, in the regional context, implies a mentality somewhat less than cosmopolitan. Generally, these clergymen have been, and are still, restricted by a provincial angle of vision. In portraying the historic differences between northern and southern Baptist people, one historian described the Baptists of the Middle Colonies and New England, as they moved west in the early years of the Republic, as "largely an educated middle-class group." By contrast,

> in the rural areas of the South and on the southern frontier there was no middle class and there were few opportunities to secure an education. Consequently, outside the few urban centers of the seaboard, where Baptists had long maintained an intimate relationship with their northern colleagues and shared their interest in education, the Baptists of the South were of low economic and social status.[14]

By the dawn of the present decade, millions of Baptists had

changed, but their churches had not. A recent survey of the occupations of the fathers of 481 students enrolled in a progressive Southern Baptist seminary disclosed that of 394 fathers living and employed, only 19 were engaged in occupations which generally command high incomes and great prestige. Farmers comprised the largest group, which numbered 72. The other occupations, whose separate totals exceeded 30, were textile workers, merchants, ministers and missionaries, and finally, machinists, mechanics, metal workers and repairmen. This evidence corroborates other indications that from the 1750's to the 1960's the Baptists have been a people's denomination.

Recurrently in the twentieth century the Baptists and Methodists, immense and wealthy bodies, have spoken of their responsibility to the lower economic classes who generally have been either unchurched or aligned with the sects. Significantly, a great deal less has been said about the upper classes, who, despite their smaller numbers, compose a potential "mission field" in the eyes of many who regard the "higher" denominations which tend to attract the upper classes as nominally churchly. Baptist and Methodist interest in the unchurched lower classes and inattention to the upper classes afford a glimpse into their characteristic ways of thinking. As Christians with genuine concern for persons, their more poignant concern for the down and out than for the well heeled and prominent is at least understandable. "Nonreligious" incentives, however, are probably also prevalent. One is the denominations' (especially the Baptists') collective inferiority complex, issuing in a kind of "underdog" mentality that enables them to identify with the dispossessed. Another is their unarticulated confidence that they can speak successfully to the lower classes. Still another is the considerable size of the lower classes, an important consideration in a numbers-conscious ecclesiastical approach.

But we submit that the most revealing reason for the denominations' failure to engage in ministry to the socially or intellectually elite is a haunting awareness that they are not equipped to communicate Christian meaning intelligibly to the intellectuals, or relevantly to the opulent. At any rate, excessive deference is paid to the rare intellectual or scion in their membership, and disproportionate use is made of others of his kind in the program of denominational meetings.

Already there are signs that the popular churches are experiencing frustration in their encounter with unprecedented rejection by particular strata. Until recently they had good reason to believe that they could do what they set out to do, that the world was theirs for the winning. Now, for the first time they seem on the verge of acknowledging that real obstacles impede their success, and even that some of those obstacles are of their own making. They would be well advised to listen to analyses of the effects of social change, such as, for example, a recent inquiry into religious involvement in Great Britain, in which Rodney Stark found that within the ranks of church members, the middle and upper classes are more likely to *do* their religion, whereas the lower classes are more likely to *feel* or *believe* their religion.[15] From this the southern church could ascertain that so long as their orientation is heavily weighted toward religious experience, they are likely to make negligible appeal to those persons who could be eminently sensitive to Christian meaning and responsibility.

If the popular churches are to have any hope of ministering to the leadership elite in the post-New South, they must perceive that the higher classes, too, experience deprivation. As Glock so penetratingly argues, *ethical* deprivation, which exists "when the individual comes to feel that the dominant values of the society no longer provide him with a meaningful way of organizing his life, and that it is necessary for him to find an alternative," is no less dire or acute in its consequences than the kinds of deprivation suffered by the lower classes.[16] The southern church has exhibited little awareness that ethical deprivation exists, to say nothing of concerted efforts to eradicate it.•

Now that Southerners are developing critical faculties, many

• "Ethical" here refers to the entire *ethos* of one's life, including its relation to ultimate reality and basic values, and thus has a far larger meaning than "moral." In terms of Christian theology, it incorporates the vertical dimension as well as the horizontal.

are, predictably, rejecting the church outright, or shifting from the popular denominations to those which are more alert to Christianity's over-all and long-range relevance. The reduction of the faith to single emotional moments, trivial moralisms, and sanguine institutional loyalty, so often characteristic of the popular churches, neglects to offer to the critical mind cogent meaning concerning either God or man and his world, or their relation. The symbol-system of the traditional southern church is utterly irrelevant to an expanding segment of Southerners. Their understanding of reality requires infinitely more "differentiated, comprehensive, and rationalized" formulations (Bellah) than the southern church is now capable of producing.

Of course the southern church employs symbols in the prosecution of its institutional life. Familiar examples are "groundbreaking ceremonies" when construction of a new church building is begun, "note-burning ceremonies" when a church debt is retired, "installation services" for newly elected church officers, and "homecoming services," annual fellowship days when streams of former members of a given church, now living elsewhere, return. But on its theological side, the southern church is scarcely aware that its affirmations are symbols, so confident is it of the exact correspondence between the words which it speaks about God and ultimate truth itself.

To this ineptitude is added the liability of a theory of leadership which holds that the leader is the properly representative agent of popular consensus. As we have noted, this has been as true of Methodism with its episcopal polity as of Baptism with its congregational polity. The bishop has rarely concerned himself with speaking authoritatively on substantive issues. Similarly, Baptist leaders are prevented from perpetuating the biblical-prophetic tradition by the fiction that the spiritual convictions of a provincial, rural, uninformed constituency are equivalent to the will of God in matters requiring information and rich insight. In both cases, well-meaning piety has interfered with responsible effort to apply the Christian faith across the wide range of extraordinarily complicated human problems. The world is thus presented with the spectacle of a provincial leadership making decisions on isues which confound the world's most revered leaders, and justifying them by glib recourse to the biblical text. In the name of devout reliance upon the Holy Spirit cultural traditions and personal whimsy are cloaked with divine sanction. As sacrilegious as it may sound to southern churchmen, it is of very limited value to "rely on the Holy Spirit" in treating substantive issues.

The essentially priestly posture of southern church leadership is another major stumbling block for the ethically deprived. Hearing much talk about prophetic Christianity, they find, instead, church leaders committed to a policy of building security in turbulent times and of aggrandizing the existing institutions. In so doing, the popular denominations default on their responsibility and discredit themselves in the eyes of many. Enlightened younger Southerners are already being revulsed by the likes of oft-heard catch phrases, "keep sweet," "don't rock the boat," "stay in the middle of the road." When the church acts as if "peace" was a more important Christian virtue than ministry to persons in the form of leading insiders to become responsible and serving outsiders, it forfeits much of its integrity. Regional crises have not yet driven the southern church to assume a prophetic stance. One measure of this is the penchant of Baptist seminaries to appoint, even since the outbreak of the social revolution in southern life, safe if competent men to their faculties. As for ministers, we have seen that to be "successful" means to "produce results" in terms of numerical and financial increase; one must also have "a good personality," able to blend in with the situation as it is.

Finally the simplistic way in which personal and social transformations are viewed deserves some treatment. Earlier we sought to discredit the supposition that a life turns on the emotional impulse of a single (ahistorical) moment, the hallmark of southern revivalism. It can be claimed that "simple faith" *is* simple in the sense that no precocity of any sort is required for one to participate in it. Yet any truth-system which brings together in its theory and practice the One who is affirmed to be Lord of all truth with the concrete lives of men who are enmeshed in history and conditioned by a congeries of social forces can scarcely be regarded as simple. At every turn it encounters the menace of limitation, distortion, and obfuscation, in both its meaning and its application.

The inadequacy of a simplistic mentality for a previously closed society as it becomes caught up in rapid social change has been graphically portrayed by Father Desqueyrat in *La Crise Religieuse des Temps Modernes*. A lengthy but unabridgeable quotation from a recent recounting of that story follows:

> [In the story] it is supposed that a new pastor is appointed to the parish of Ars, famous for its earlier incumbent, Jean Baptiste Vianney. What would this new pastor find? The same village, the same houses, and so on—apparently much the same as at the time of the saint. But he could no longer use the pastoral approach of the Curé d'Ars, which was that of a rather simple man. The saint had discovered that there was one sin at Ars—dancing. His pastoral duty was clear: to get at the cause of this evil, and the cause was obviously the violin player in the village; without music, there was no dancing, and therefore no occasion of sin. The Curé d'Ars simply paid the volin player to go away—to provide an occasion for sin in another village.
>
> Father Desqueyrat asks what change the new pastor would find today. One decisive change is that there is a violin player in every house—that is, there is a radio (and increasingly television). One cannot pay this violin player to go elsewhere; he is already inside. It is as if the village were actually living in a big city, by means of the radio. The modern world uproots men because of the power of its mass media in communicating ideas and images. The closed society of the village no longer has to come to the city to be overwhelmed with distractions and contradictory appeals; even in the country he participates in the life of the city.[17]

This picture could equally well comprise the confessions of a perceptive Baptist or Methodist pastor in almost any town or village of the American South. Even the choice of the "issue," dancing, is pertinent, since this and the other "finger sins" continue to claim a great deal of attention among southern Pietists.[18]

Identification with Reactionary Values and Interests

The likelihood that the working classes will reject the church in the post-New South may be as menacing as the exclusion of the leadership elite. In the past the southern working class was made up for the most part of small farmers and non-unionized textile mill employees. Now, however, an organized industrial segment is arising to dominate the labor scene. Although conditions in the industrial South are likely to be more conducive to the acceptance of religion than in those societies which became industrialized more than a century ago, the new laboring classes are sure to look upon life in ways very different from the outlook of Southerners in all previous eras.[19]

One of the surest ways for the church in any society to invite rejection is for it to identify itself with reactionary values and interests during major periods of social transition.[20] In the case of the lower classes of white Southerners, the church's traditional alliance (by implication, at least) with the economic status quo, with management in its endeavors to keep southern industry as union-free as possible, is not calculated to enhance its image. Not that the southern church has actively striven to bring what it considered Christian principles to bear on large-scale economic disputes. It is the inactivity of the church, its detachment from economic probems, which stamps it as out of step with global economic movements. Furthermore its tacit association with many leaders of business and political communities who actively support laissez-faire theories of government may tarnish its luster in the eyes of the new industrial classes. The increasing unionization of industries and the regular introduction of new governmental agencies and programs could spell irrelevance for the church; it could show up the church's conservatism as inertia in an age much taken with "liberal" causes. At another level, unionization could begin to gratify many human needs which in the past were met by religion. The church for so long has ignored the welter of social-economic-political problems which have confronted the South that today's new situation may drastically curtail its opportunity to serve.

The Negro's stake in the new society cannot be a primary subject of inquiry here; only time will reveal the response of the Negro community to the church as Negroes attain first-class citizenship. Several factors work against the church's remaining a significant factor in Negro life: The record of the white church in using religion as a means of keeping Negroes docile and oriented to life in the next world; The record of the Negro church in reducing faith to mere emotion; And the Negro church's obsequious dealings with the (white) community power structure. If these recollections stand out, the church will have become obsolescent for the new Negro. Also, wherever material and political deprivations sear the Negro's spirit, and Christianity is confined to otherworldly concerns, the church will be spurned. On the positive side, the fact that the church has often led out in the civil rights cause may augur well for its future. Negroes may see that the one platform they have had, their churches, often has supported them in the hour of their brightest hope. Thus, the identification question has yet to be answered for the southern Negro community.

Another frightening prospect, perhaps especially to the white church, is the possibility that religion will be viewed as having been a principal "drag" on regional life, that is, as a major conservator of the ways of the traditional South. We have noted that the church stands as the most rock-ribbed of all the old southern institutions during the current social revolution, a fact which persists right into the mid-1960's. Rapidly burgeoning segments of southern people, especially in the younger generation which will provide tomorrow's leadership, "know in their hearts" that desegregation (if not integration) is legal, just, and right.

Some of them may well conclude that the church was the one regional institution that should have instigated this revolution, which aims at vouchsafing dignity, respect, and opportunity—in a word, humanity—to southern Negroes. Having kept silent on this crucial issue, it may be seen by them as a monumental failure.

Inevitably, many thinking persons will find serious fault with the church for its grievous negligences. In view of its record of reactionary and sub-Christian conduct toward Negroes, repudiation of the church will seem the only authentic reaction to those who perceive the massive corporate guilt which rests on the shoulders of the region's Anglo-Saxon peoples. If the southern church continues to concentrate its energies on "saving souls" and denouncing personal vices, it will further discredit itself as the world moves on and social revolution erupts everywhere.

Nothing in its experience, and little in its theological understanding, prepares the southern church to meet the crisis of irrelevance—its first major crisis—now pressing in upon it. Tragedy is in the offing. For here is a destiny-struck, successful church which is wed to a fundamentalist theology with nothing substantive to recommend it to critical persons, and cramped by a subjectivism acutely dangerous in the context of a "sacred" society.

The Christian church has four major responsibilities. If it fails in *any one* of them, it jeopardizes the mission which it is divinely commissioned to carry out. In fact, the measure for evaluating its faithfulness consists in the degree to which the church devotes itself to the achievement of *all four* objectives. The first responsibility is to perpetuate Christianity by casting it in forms and structures, and equipping it with authority, so that it can abide the corroding and eroding forces of time and circumstance. The second is to bring the gospel's meaning and power to bear upon all individuals in every society across the entire range of human needs and problems. The third is to review Christianity's truth-claims constantly in the interest of theological statement at once rooted in transcendent revelation and practical relevance. The fourth is to bring about the transforming and healing relation of all persons to the God of Jesus Christ.

Obviously the four are intertwined, but they are four distinct tasks, and none is dispensable. The southern church has been in "God's hurry" to accomplish the fourth only. It is under judgment for its failures in the other three areas and for partializing the one task it has undertaken. Its irresponsibility in these respects forms the subject of inquiry in the final chapter.

12

The Danger of
Irresponsibility

The threat of rejection, although a serious matter, does not compare in gravity with the question of whether the church is being faithful to the transcendent norms and mandates by which it understands its existence. Whereas in the previous chapter we examined the southern church's unresponsiveness, that is, its irrelevance, to the new cultural situation, here we are asking: Is it alert and obedient to the ground of its being, God revealed in Jesus Christ? Is it carrying out the mission on which the Christian scriptures declare it to be sent? Does it give itself to the *essential* tasks, and does it give itself to *all* of them?

In Relation to the Full Christian Mission

Perpetuation of Christianity

The popular southern churches believe that they have achieved a more nearly exact duplication of primitive Christianity than other branches of Christianity. Taking into account the propensity of all human groups to exaggerate their own importance, we must still ask why the southern churches' self-assessment is so high. The answer lies in the swashbuckling vitality which characterizes their life. Looking around, they see no other religious bodies in America or Europe unleashing torrents of activity comparable to theirs and no other denominations so statistically successful. Moreover they discern (correctly) that few Christian groups, apart from the sects whose devoutness they admire, are as inclined as they to identify themselves, openly and self-consciously, as Christians. By southern standards, most other churchmen appear to be culpably nonchalant about their Christian profession. Thus, they regard Christianity in the hands of the liturgical churches, the established churches, the objectively oriented bodies, and the social-action groups as cold and stagnant, and, most important, as diverted from the main goals by peripheral preoccupations. It is principally the southern church's *vitality,* more particularly its vitality about *evangelism* (according to its peculiar understanding), which stamps it as superior in its own eyes. The popular southern churches know what they are about. Armed with selected scriptural texts taken to be the gospel in miniature, they march into the world to rescue the unsaved from the onslaughts of the enemy and bring them into the fortress of divine salvation.

Vitality does abound, although let us hasten to add that vitality, in and of itself, is not the Christian *summum bonum.* Within the past few years, an analyst of the southern church, while drawing essentially negative conclusions, could speak of its great promise, which he located in "the vitality of a committed faith." [1] Vitality is exhibited on every hand and at every level, in the form of huge church buildings, immense budgets, intricate organizations, aggressive programs of outreach, and bustling self-confidence.

It has been observed that American Protestantism, on its way toward dominating the national culture in the nineteenth century, although "shot through with vitalities and validities," nevertheless " 'just growed' in the environment" where it was supported by law and untested by alternatives.[2] This description applies to popular southern Protestantism with astonishing exactitude. It, too, "just growed," unrestrained by any forces but its own inertia, unchallenged by rival truth-systems. To its great credit, it did not wither and die in so favorable a climate. Once centralized denominations emerged, the southern church took on an increasingly militant character. The more powerful it became, however, the more it institutionalized its abundant vitality. Ironically, vast success detached it from the same divine judgment to which it appealed when enlarging its membership rolls, highlighting the arrogance of its claim to be a reconstituted first century church.

The great tragedy related to this vitality is that so many sound instincts are largely wasted. By Christian norms, the southern church is right in meaning to submit to the biblical message as its authority, in taking the Christian mission seriously, in stressing the importance of personal decision and personal faith, in insisting that conduct must be commensurate with profession, and in its sedulous vigilance against compromising Christian truth. The tragic waste results from its severe partialization of the Christian message, which is no light matter but, rather, the very essence of heresy. In the southern church's hands, the Christian affirmation and claim are reduced to a mere shadow of their massive, dynamic reality. Likewise, the *means* by which the message is said to be appropriable are simplified to emotional moments.

Winning the World and Serving the World

The simplism and partialization inherent in the southern church's understanding of its mission come to primary focus in its all-consuming aim of "winning the world to Christ." Even where the "secondary" ministries are performed, there prevails an abiding watchfulness, almost a suspicion, lest the "social gospel" encroach on the primacy of the "evangelistic imperative." It often appears that a choice must be made between the "evangelistic" and the "social." Accordingly, the southern church tends either to devalue the "social" ministries or to treat them as means to the "evangelistic" end. While this is not always the case—many eleemosynary institutions are sponsored—it is a fact that the "evangelistic" responsibility alone is viewed as ultimately important.

On any interpretation of Christianity, the impulse to "make disciples" is an extremely sound one, and for exposing its nerve endings to this mandate, the southern church deserves commendation. What has to be asked next is whether this is the only primary commission given to the church, or, viewed differently, what is the relation of this charge to many other concerns traditionally construed as Christian responsibility? Also it must be asked whether the southern church's motives and means for "winning the lost" are as sound as the impulse they are meant to express.

At the level of motives and means, the evangelistic appeal characteristically has been based on the prospect of heaven and the threat of hell. New generations of Southerners, however, are far less likely to be swayed by portrayals of heaven and hell. As modern men, they are less dogmatic about life after death than their ancestors; they may forthrightly reject a God who is represented as not free to accept men until some need of his own has been satisfied; or they may take the road of avowed secularism. When "scare tactics" are used, even if mild, the hearer's conception of the Almighty is likely to be dominantly judgmental. Of course, the lives of many devout southern churchmen transcend the articulated theology, especially its crude conceptions of God's judgment and Christ's atonement. Nevertheless, serious damage has been wrought by the contradiction involved in founding the evangelistic appeal on affirmations which are inconsistent with the stated goal of reconciling alienated men to a loving God. As Richard Niebuhr has said, "The character of a religious movement is probably more decisively determined by its definition of the sin from which salvation is to be sought than by its view of that saving process itself." [3]

The world church today is rediscovering its role as the *servant* church, with the understanding that it was called into being for the sake of serving men across the variety of their needs. Its model is Christ, who is described in the Bible as loving *men* as whole persons, and giving himself for them, not for an abstraction such as their sin-debt. "Saving" men remains a major concern, but in the etymological sense—to make whole. One vital aspect of salvation, seen this way, is the incorporation of the "saved" into Christ's Body, the church. When salvation and incorporation are so interpreted, the notion of "preaching at" persons, from a distance and in a staged setting, as it were, for the sake of inducing a single experience and decision, is found to be theologically and morally distorted. Instead of concentrating on "inviting people to church," with the formal church convocation conceived as the primary locus of divine activity, contemporary churchmen see their calling in terms of being emissaries to people in the world where they live and in the whole variety of their needs and situations.[4]

Let us repeat that the servant church, too, longs to incorporate men into Christ and his Body, having found in him the gift and meaning of life. But two basic features differentiate it from the southern church's characteristic stance. The first is that the servant church seeks to incorporate them through setting the message of Christianity within the framework of a ministry to them as whole persons, that is, to their physical, material, economic, political, and social psychic needs—*all seen as fundamentally spiritual.* The second is that such a church seeks to serve all needy persons (all persons) irrespective of their affiliation or unaffiliation with the institutional church. Consequently, it does not take a "religious census" of the community in an attempt to discover who needs the church. Its direct objective is service. As a result, it forever runs the risk of adding few, or no, new members to church rolls. It serves its Lord, trusting his promise that against the church "the gates of hell shall not prevail. . . ."

The southern church is nonplused by this grasp of the church's calling, owing partly to the relatively simple social setting of its life, but more importantly because it conceives of the church as a function of the divine preoccupation with the cancellation of the sin-debt in the moment of salvation. Those who would seek God must find him within the church building itself or through directly "religious" witness by churchmen. The Christian's obedience consists in being an instrument for beckoning individuals to the institutional church and the conversion-oriented salvation it provides.

At least two distortions of the Christian responsibility may stem from an undue stress on this "vision of God" theme. One is the degeneration of the valid Christian belief that the life of faith produces transforming power into the naive judgment that the conversion experience will rectify all individual and social ills, and by itself humanize life. The second is the tendency to overlook persons and their needs unless they are "prospects" for membership in the local church—with the partial exception of the care provided for orphans, the sick, and the aged.

Finally, it is worth recalling that the southern church inflates one portion of the biblical message into the whole, concentrating on the Great Commission and correlated passages. "Making disciples" is translated into "converting the lost," and the all-important moment of conversion is dynamically separated from the rest of life. Such serious deficiencies in its notion of Christian service can be overcome by the southern church only if it achieves a more profound understanding of the truth-authority under which it stands.

Theological Astuteness

Despite its unyielding allegiance to Christian truth as popularly understood and the particularism of its message, the southern church lacks theological depth and sensitivity. Its very genuine intention to be theologically responsible is curtailed by the narrow limits within which it allows theology to move. With child-like innocence the southern church speaks of "timeless truths," which, when examined, turn out to be very much dated—the products of medieval and early modern scholastic movements in the western church. To this inheritance have been conjoined piety of a special (revivalistic) sort, and the pragmatism and optimism so characteristic of the era in which the religious southern patterns were formed.

One of the decisive criteria for the southern church's principle of theological selectivity is whether a given article of faith can be emotionalized so that "results" can be virtually guaranteed.

One suspects that many a religious leader has been gripped by fresh, perhaps unconventional ideas, insights, or interpretations but has squelched them on the grounds that the old constructions were working so well. New formulations suffer from the double jeopardy of being strange sounding to southern ears, and unsuited to spectacular institutional success.

Nor is the southern church's theology in any way erudite—an element in our reluctance to describe this theological program merely as "fundamentalism," since historically this term applies to groups which are rationalistic in orientation, and often produce scholarship directed toward elaborating and validating propositional revelation. Concerns of this sort have been quite peripheral for the massive southern denominations.[5] Outstanding scholarship has not been entirely lacking in the seminaries, but since role-expectation for the clergy places far higher premium on personality than on familiarity in depth with Christian meaning, the ability to persuade rates well ahead of skillful interpretation. It is not surprising then that the "liberal" label has been reserved for those clergy who were liberal *personalities,* that is to say, tolerant, benign persons. "Liberal" has had only the slightest reference to a man's theological position, in terms either of openness to new truth, or of entertaining views foreign to the popular tradition. This glossing over of issues and concepts, so characteristic of the recent history of the southern denominations, today stands as a great liability in a South where educational levels are rising, rival truth-systems are beginning to compete, and social problems threaten the stability of the entire society.

One of the fascinating features of the southern church's theology, as we saw in Chapter 8, is that at several important points it is historically heterodox: in its docetism, the heresy that stresses the divine nature in Jesus Christ at the expense of his real humanity; its Marcionism, by which the Old Testament is effectively sidelined by being made merely functional; and its paradigmatically heretic quality in making one part of the Christian message (*entry into* the Christian life) into the whole of it. Our point here is not that there is virtue in retaining the past for its own sake, but that the southern church's image of itself as the ultimate in orthodoxy lacks historical accuracy, and that its orthodoxy is in terms of *certain* easily datable norms, associated with a left-of-center variety of Christianity and early modern Protestant scholasticism-pietism, as these have been adapted to the American setting.

The perceptive student of theology will ask immediately how any branch of the Protestant family tree can be both scholastic and pietistic, since a rationalism which understands Christianity in propositional terms and the mellow interiorism of pietism would appear to belong to irreconcilably different orders. Apparently, the two can be held together only in one of three ways—by the deftest maneuvering of the psyche, by the powerful grip of a religious authority, or by the practical ignoring of one element. The southern church has chosen the first course. It has affirmed an essentially static theology replete with crisp propositions, easily stated, quickly exhausted, and unarguable. Few seem to have noticed that the propositions have little or no correlation of tone, or for that matter of substance, with religious experience of the revivalistic sort. In other words, the *dynamic* deity whom Southerners are urged to experience is described by *static* concepts.

In sum, the southern church's theology is outdated and has little relation to the dynamism which is the hallmark of southern religious experiences.

The Pivotal Problem

The myriad problems which beset the southern church today may be gathered up under one, which is, stated simply: The southern church is miscast for the part it is now called upon to play. This is not to suggest that it has no vital mission to accomplish. Rather, much more must be expected from the southern church than it can possibly produce under present circumstances. Given its institutional, ideological, and moral domination of the society, the responsibility for Christian ministry to everyone in the regional society clearly belongs to popular Protestantism. The fact is that whatever Christianity is expected to do to, within and for the regional society should belong chiefly to the Baptists and Methodists as their inescapable charge.

Unfortunately, the popular southern church is incapable of representing Christianity in its richness, fullness, depth, and comprehensiveness. Religious impulse is too exclusively given over to the emphases of a sect. The focus of southern Christianity does not really lie with efforts to move outside the church into the world for the sake of serving that world through comprehensive ministry to it in all its parts—the intellectual, the artistic, the political, the economic, and so on.

Difficult as the theoretical suggestion may be for southern churchmen to grasp, we submit that sect-type forms of Christianity *are meant to be minority movements,* both within the larger Christian realm and within human societies.[6] The tragedy in the South is not only that the sect-type groups which dominate there often regard themselves as essential Christianity, but also that they have been entrusted with the responsibility for rendering the whole Christian service. The crisis confronting them would be of far less consequence if their role were comparable to that of, say, the Pentecostal sects. As is well known, Pentecostals aspire to little else than the conversion of individuals and the creation of intensely devout communities of the faithful. The southern church's pretensions are susbtantially more. It means to represent Christianity. It generates large-scale programs with the purpose of bringing every individual into the fold. But again, it does not realize that society is more than the aggregate of individuals, that the individual life is more than "soul," and that truth is broader and deeper than their simplisms. Church-type responsibilities (which need not exclude sect-type responsibilities) ill become it, although the peculiar twists of southern social history have thrust those duties upon an instinctively sectarian people. As presently oriented, they cannot rise to the occasion.

The Baptist denomination is particularly unprepared, since nothing about Baptist life fits it to its southern role. What we referred to in Part III as the one-doctrine character of Baptist beginnings has, on the whole, persisted, having the predictable effect of rendering the denomination incapable of carrying a multifaceted load. Now Baptism has made a great and genuine impact on the whole church and on Western civilization, along several important lines. The negative judgments offered here are pertinent only in a context where the Baptists have become the bearers of Christianity. Their contribution in the English setting, to cite an example, has been significant, no doubt partly because they have not aspired to grandeur in a domain where a church-type Christian tradition prevails.

If Baptists in the South could enjoy the luxury of a semi-conventicle existence, or if they could live in an ecumenical framework where their contribution could stand alongside others, their future would be far more promising. In other words, the denomination would be more authentically itself if it were free to play its sectarian role. However, Baptists have been and are much too integral a part of the southern world to withdraw from major involvement in the new society now being developed.

The Southern Baptists have embraced their provincial world and identified themselves with it, but without developing any awareness that the kind of world in which they minister and with which they are so closely identified must determine how they will go about that ministry. They are in the early stages of experiencing the shock of finding themselves prepared by their history *for a radically different age and climate* than the one now unfolding all about them. Their decline from the place of prominence is almost certain to produce deep frustration within them and unrest in the regional religious sector at large.

Curiously, at the same time these developments are occurring in the American South, the world church is witnessing the birth of a new form of corporate Christian life which bears several analogues to the South's declining sect-type. A new manifestation of the sectarian spirit is being urged by church leaders, and here and there is making its appearance. This form is calculated to be to the increasingly secularized "post-Christian" world what the church-type institution was to Christendom when Establishment prevailed, and what the denomination has been to Christendom's pluralistic societies. It aims to draw together the essential ingredients of both classic types. On the "church" side, it assumes responsibility for the whole of society, seeking to relate itself redemptively to every level of the human venture. It endeavors to fit its ministry to the bidimensionality of man's life, that is, his relation to God and to his fellows in society. Moreover, this new church form is theologically astute. It cares greatly about the perpetuation of Christianity, hence gives high place to theology, sacraments, and liturgy, and accordingly magnifies worship. At the same time it displays sectarian impulses in self-consciously resisting identification as a culture-religion, at the level of ideology, commitment, and mission. The motto of this form of Christianity might well be "in, but not of, the world."

Chances appear good that some such "sectly church-type" will prevail as the most authentic vehicle for Christian ministry in the foreseeable future. This church form could stand as a kind of model for enabling the southern church to use its greatest asset, sectlikeness (the prophetic instinct), in tandem with a newly acquired churchlikeness, so that its ministry could again be relevant.

Ways Out of the Problem

The southern church's overarching problem, that of being thrust into a role it is not now capable of playing, is soluble—in principle, at any rate. For example, by displaying certain new attitudes and achievements, the southern church could rise to the occasion to which history has brought it. Concretely, the question of the hour is how the Baptists and Methodists of the South, practicing sectarians, can be liberated to a willingness to undertake full responsibility for relating the comprehensive Christian message to the whole social order.

To begin with, the development of a sense of history would produce several changes. An alertness to the inevitability of modification in the church's empirical nature and the specific character of its mission as social change occurs would result. Until now, the southern church has been naively optimistic that nothing could arrest the spectacular advances it has witnessed in recent years. The knowledge that social upheavals alter the church's role in society would be conducive to greater circumspectness and depth.

Again, a sense of history would reveal to the southern church how new on the stage of Christian history its variety of Protestantism really is. They would then be able to see that theirs is a partial, albeit genuine, version of the faith. Recognition that their version was significantly conditioned by concrete temporal conditions in early modern Europe could go far toward preventing their absolutization of it. Most important of all, the cultivation of a sense of history by the southern church would destroy its pretensions to being the restoration of "New Testament Christianity."

A second "way out" is theological objectification. The church, wherever found, no matter how genuine its striving for purity of doctrine and life, is a fallible human institution, susceptible to a thousand errors and deviations. Nor does an announced allegiance to the pure Word of God remove this danger. The church in history cannot hope even to approximate to its transcendent norms without acknowledging some basis for judgment or correction. Otherwise it surely lapses into becoming a mere cultural residue or a subsidiary institution of society. A strong theological or creedal heritage is a basic way to cope with this menace. In the case of an anticreedal tradition where the Bible is exalted as the only creed—itself an inherently perilous and ambiguous notion—a theologically informed leadership must be present to interact with the more pietistic masses, if understanding is to be broad and deep. Needless to say, theologians are liable to comparable errors. But they are more aware of the leverage which theological objectification provides, and more likely to capitalize on it.

As the last third of the twentieth century commences, and rival truth-systems present formidable challenge to the church's teachings, the southern church would do well to demonstrate a genuine respect for theological education; otherwise, there is little chance that it can catch a vision of the depth and breadth of the Christian message and of its own ministry.

Liturgical objectification offers a third avenue of escape from popular southern Protestantism's sectarian animus. A new and serious commitment to objective forms in worship would provide a greater opportunity for transcending provinciality of understanding. Awareness that the inner life of faith is not pure spontaneity would release the southern church to implement its avowed prophetic spirit by upholding objective beliefs and values.

The fourth potential "way out" of provinciality is a church structure which facilitates penetrating self-evaluation and requisite change. The vesting of authority with persons, offices, and agencies where there is circumspectness and reasonable liberty of action is necessary in all human institutions. In today's world especially, the church must respond to social change in much the same way as all other historical institutions. Accordingly, a denomination's structure must allow for, as well as give direction to, that change.

The southern church appears sluggish and immobilized by a polity in which leaders conceive their role to be one that represents popular consensus. It does not take seriously the notion that persons with expertise in the formulation of creeds and the treatment of substantive issues should be given primary responsibility to work in those areas. In them, as well as in business matters, popular opinions and prejudices have tended to dominate policy. Such an arrangement places obstacles in the path of substantive change. To take a concrete example, in the Mississippi Baptist Convention of November, 1964, after opposition had crystallized against the denomination's Christian Life Commission which had made repeated appeals to the churches to work for racial justice, a motion calling for the abolition of the Commission was defeated. Then the convention adopted a milder resolution criticizing the Commission for taking "liberal positions not in accord with the thinking of many Southern Baptists." Clearly, majority opinion was tendered greater authority than a denominational agency composed of knowledgeable persons entrusted with responsibility on ethical issues. When the power to govern is deployed in this way, there is little opportunity for self-criticism, and even less for putting into effect the changes implied in that criticism. Moreover, southern congregations possess the power to manage their ministers, virtually as hired men, and denominations do not structure a place for the prophet who would call the body to repentance.

The final "way out" of provinciality for a sectarian body which has been cast in a church-type role is ecumenical involvement. By means of thoroughgoing participation in the larger body of Christians, it could, in addition to flavoring the larger body with its contribution, realize a greater balance, depth, and richness in its own life. The southern church's most severe maladies could perhaps be cured better by ecumenical participation than by almost any other means. This is made more dramatically true by the fact that, historically, denominations have been inclined to continue to concern themselves with their original *raison d'être*, a fact which almost certainly narrows the range of vision. The Baptists' preoccupation with baptism and church-state separation, and the Methodists' with alcohol, to cite two examples, would be modified and healthfully broadened.

The overcoming of isolation and excessive self-estimation are other fruits of ecumenical participation. Early in 1965 a prominent Southern Baptist spokesman, in what was actually one of the more conciliatory and perceptive statements to come from that denomination in a long time, made it clear that the ecumenical movement would have to come around to Southern Baptist positions before the Convention could consider affiliation. Underlying such self-esteem is the fear that inexcusable compromise of the denomination's "distinctives" would follow from ecumenical affiliation. What is hidden from their vision is the knowledge that the so-called distinctives, left to themselves, represent a badly partialized Christianity, and that their spiritual ends can be best attained in a wider context.

What of the Future?

It remains now to consider possible resolutions of the southern church's overriding problem. By what means can it be liberated from a sectarian mentality so that it may more generously comprehend the mission history has delivered to its charge?

We have consistently maintained that the present and the immediate future form its decisive hour. Until recently, the geographical and historical situation has provided the church with a kind of "continuous frontier," an abundance of persons to be won and enlisted, and a plethora of organizational tasks to occupy its attention. Now in the 1960's, that frontier has been abruptly closed. Almost no one is "unchurched," at a time when the denominations are prepared, organizationally, to undertake any challenge.

In the face of an unprecedented delimitation of their vast energies, the religious bodies grow restless and seethe with frustration. Not that there is not plenty to capture the church's dynamism, for the regional society all about it groans under the anguish of upheaval. But the churches do not hear these cries for ministry. There are mountains to be moved on its terrain, but the southern church does not really see any vital connection between its commission and those difficult tasks. All the while, the church comes under sharper criticism from a growing segment of educated younger white Southerners—not to mention the world Negro community—for whom the church is a symbol of reaction and obscurantism.

The crisis is especially acute for the parochial Southern Baptists who, because they are so closely identified with regional traditions and values, can expect fewer significant accomplishments in the transformed society of the future. Already much of their opportunity for bringing about major modifications has passed by. Despite their many face-liftings in the realm of organization, relatively speaking the denomination is hardly more in touch with the accelerated movements of the modern world which are today pressing in so vigorously on the once isolated South. Conspicuously absent are any rationalizations of the "social implications" of the gospel, genuine respect for academic freedom and appreciation of ideological leadership, respect for prophetic voices, any keen sense of being part and parcel with historical and contemporary world Christianity.

Self-fixation can lead only to frustration, irrelevance, and disobedience. Whereas leaders of earlier generations can be acclaimed for their spirit of moderation,[7] that kind of leadership on the contemporary scene will force the denomination ever farther behind. Institutional adolescence must give way to maturity; that is, the body's vision must transcend its own accomplishments, its "distinctives," and its self-imputed preeminence. In adjusting to radical change the Southern Baptists will have to surrender crippling isolation and a tendency to narcissism.

Today there are some stirrings—a company of "young Turks" has emerged over the past half-dozen or so years and currently occupies rural pastorates and associate minister positions. The way of thinking about Christianity characteristic of these men, and others engaged in Ph.D. programs in religious studies throughout the country, is qualitatively different from the traditional Southern Baptist patterns. There is reason to hope that in time they may infiltrate the power structure and introduce change. The Christian Life Commission of the denomination is well staffed, progressive, and surprisingly influential. Some faculty members in all the denominational seminaries are abreast of world currents and in touch with reality. Several editors of state papers are both citizens of the world and courageous individuals who speak forthrightly.

Nevertheless, the picture of the Southern Baptist future is depressing. This is so in part because the sound impulses of so many leaders are stultified by tradition. Moreover, the stirrings of the "new breed" do not have an institutional structure which permits implementation, nor ready categories of thought inviting new interpretations. The tardiness of the Southern Baptist reformation would not be so serious if there were apparent agents of the denomination's redemption. The tragedy is that, so far as one can tell, not one of the five "ways out" is accessible to the Southern Baptist denomination. Its leadership and its people lack a sense of history. The Convention lacks theological and liturgical objectification of any rich and effective sort and a structure which enables circumspect leadership to come to power;

also, it is farther than ever from entering into ecumenical relationships. As an isolated sect, identified with outdated modes of thinking and immobilized by a severely abridged list of concerns, the Southern Baptists will continue nevertheless to perform a vital ministry—increasingly restricted to the lower middle classes and upper lower classes, almost certainly not effective with the strategically influential elites of the post-New South and with the society and culture at large.

Persons inside and outside the denomination must be warned against expecting more from the Southern Baptists than they are capable of producing. Without doubt, some important changes will be made, and the ranks of the devoutly concerned will expand. At least for as far into the future as the mind's eye can see, however, the Southern Baptists give promise of remaining a provincial body, persisting in taking many of its cues from the South's dying culture. Meantime, growing numbers of progressives will take their leave—into other denominations, and from the Christian church. The progressives who remain will inevitably learn to cultivate patience and to be satisfied to work against enormous pressures, not expecting miracles.

In terms of the recent past and the present, the Methodist picture is, if anything, less encouraging. For one thing, revivalism-fundamentalism is deeply embedded in Methodist life, dominating many congregations and providing the unconscious frame of reference for thousands in the more "liberal" churches; as everywhere, it produces the standard array of problems. On top of this, Methodism in the South, especially in higher-class, urban congregations, has shared with American Methodism at large a tendency to discard theological norms almost altogether, supplanting them with a thinly disguised secular humanism. To the extent that this situation obtains, Methodism "has no theology," as it is usually said, acknowledges no sturdy objectivism to serve as basis for judgment and renewal. From one angle of vision, this is a predictable eventuation of subjectively inclined Methodism's confrontation with the emotionalism of the American frontier culture. But whatever the cause, this brand of Methodism has had growing currency among the southern congregations in recent years. Its chief symptom is the substitution of a peace-of-mind ideology and moralistic value-structure for any serious call to commitment and service.

But there are signs of hope in the immediate present. It often happens that a Protestant body whose origins were conservative must pass through a liberal period before it can adjust to a vastly changed social order. Judging from the direction in which southern (and national) Methodist seminaries are moving, the end of the denomination's liberal phase, and even more certainly the end of fundamentalism, may be in sight. Obviously, major segments of national Methodism leadership are in touch with changes in the world church and in the American social order. Already some of this impact is being felt in the South, especially by the younger clergy. It does seem reasonable to infer from present developments that the thisworldly folk religion which dominates numbers of churches will in time yield to a more authentic form of Christianity.

Moreover, Methodism has available within its own heritage all five of the "ways out." The Wesleyan interpretation of Christianity upheld the basic themes of the classical heritage, and many of its stalwarts have perpetuated the substance of that interpretation. Both theological and liturgical objectification are structured into the heart of historic Methodism. Its polity at least allows for creative change. Finally, it participates actively in the ecumenical movement. Ironically, Methodism's problem may be its bewildering variety of dimensions and features. Perhaps no Protestant institution can house so much under one roof. But theoretical musings aside, although southern Methodism faces many problems at the present time, there are signs of significant change already under way, and the genuine prospect of many more.

In spite of our generally negative evaluation of the religious situation in the South, we are obliged to note that the church, whatever the quality of its performance, still occupies a place of high potential in a society where there is, especially now, so much to be done. It is still the spiritual home of a great company who look to it for solace, strength, guidance, and hope. There are millions to be ministered to, and undeniably the popular churches are best equipped to serve them. Moreover, in a considerable and increasing number of *local* situations, churches give evidence of deeper understanding and a more sensitive commitment to Christian service. (The really serious shortcomings appear at the level of large-scale institutional life, most flagrantly in the Baptist hierarchy where the very structure makes difficult any substantial innovations.)

Popular southern Protestantism is a chapter—perhaps only a footnote—in the history of Christianity. This is not to say that it will die out—nor do we mean to intimate that it should. But it cannot be the bearer of Christianity for very long in the context of a broad cultural environment.

In measure, this book is a call to the more mature Christian bodies in the South, which, to be sure, are beset by real problems themselves, to "take up slack" for the popular churches' incapacity or negligence to carry out the full Christian task.

It cannot be said too often that the southern society's well-being is at stake in the church's self understanding and reformation. We have constantly maintained that church and society took on a largely new appearance in the process of adjusting themselves in order to communicate to the masses. Now another reformation is required, both by the emergence of a new cultural condition in the South and by the world church's dramatic recognition that it stands under transcendent norms.

Notes

1 The Changing South and Regional Religion: An Overview

1 One author who does so argue is James McBride Dabbs. See *Who Speaks for the South?* (New York: Funk & Wagnalls, 1964), p. 52.

2 The literature on the changing South is enormous. Indicative of its general tone is the title of a recent contribution to the field: "Social Change, Social Movements and the Disappearing Sectional South," by Selz C. Mayo, *Social Forces*, XLIII (October, 1964), 1–10.

3 One major interpreter of the South goes so far as to judge that "the Federal-Aid Highway Act of 1956 promises to have the most enduring effect on the South politically and economically of any single piece of national legislation in American history." See Thomas D. Clark, "The South in Cultural Change," in Allan P. Sindler, ed., *Change in the Contemporary South* (Durham, N. C.: Duke University Press, 1964), p. 7.

4 This point is illustrated by the latest (at the time of this writing) book to appear: *The South in Continuity and Change,* John C. McKinney and Edgar T. Thompson, eds. (Durham, N. C.: Duke University Press, 1965).

5 In general the historians of the South have concurrently valued regionalism as preserving the rich variety of life in the United States, championed the reintegration of the South into the national culture, and attacked the South's biracial caste system. George B. Tindall's clear if cautious statement sums up this attitude: "It may be . . . that a South

moving into the mainstream need not reject out of hand and indiscriminately its history and traditions for some unified national culture pattern." See "The South: Into the Mainstream," *Current History*, XL (May, 1961), 290.

6 James McBride Dabbs, *op. cit.*, p. vii.

7 C. Vann Woodward, *The Burden of Southern History* (Baton Rouge: Louisiana State University Press, 1960), pp. 3–25.

8 Clement Eaton, *The Growth of Southern Civilization 1790–1860* (New York: Harper & Row, 1961), p. 298.

9 Two major publications of 1964 allude to this. Dabbs writes of the Southerner's poetic, imaginative mind as largely lacking in the analytic impulse or in an urgency to subject the world to sharp scrutiny (*op. cit.*, Chaps. 1 and 2). Another contrasts the South's former mode of searching for who the Southerner *is* with its new quest: "Our preoccupation today is with how Southerners *do* and *act*." See Leslie W. Dunbar, "The Changing Mind of the South: The Exposed Nerve," *Journal of Politics*, XXVI (February, 1964), 4. [Italics added.]

10 It should be noted that the practice of self-analysis and criticism gained currency in the 1920's and 1930's. Writing at the end of that era, historian Paul H. Buck could applaud the "vigor and intelligence of the critical minority in the South." See "The Genesis of the Nation's Problem in the South," *Journal of Southern History*, VI (November, 1940), 468–469.

11 Among the more important exceptions are: Kenneth K. Bailey, *Southern White Protestantism in the Twentieth Century* (New York: Harper & Row, 1964); Walter B. Posey's several books and articles on certain phases of southern religious history; various denominational histories; the insights of W. J. Cash in *The Mind of the South* (New York: Vintage Books, 1961); and Liston Pope, *Millhands and Preachers* (New Haven: Yale University Press, 1942). Edwin McNeill Poteat suggested some reasons for which religious Southerners are reluctant to submit religion to analytical treatment. See "Religion in the South" in W. T. Couch, ed., *Culture in the South* (Chapel Hill: University of North Carolina Press, 1935), pp. 248–269.

12 Edwin McNeill Poteat, *ibid.*, p. 253. Cf. also R. M. Weaver, "The Older Religiousness in the South," *Sewanee Review*, LI (April, 1943), 237.

13 Francis B. Simkins, *The Everlasting South* (Baton Rouge: Louisiana State University Press, 1963), p. 79.

14 The same point is made by L. C. Rudolph in his observation that "evangelical Protestantism had become the folk religion of the Appalachian South [with which subarea of the South he is exclusively concerned], and what proved to be but a transitional phase in the culture of the Northeast became deeply ingrained in the states south of the Ohio River and lasted a long, long time." See *Hoosier Zion* (New Haven: Yale University Press, 1963), p. 27. Had Rudolph been producing a study on southern religion, he might well have added "all the way into the 1960's."

15 Thomas D. Clark lists religion and politics as the two areas of southern life which have escaped basic change in the current period of transition (*op. cit.*, p. 3). John Samuel Ezell, describing the South of 1960, expands the list by one item: "Only in religion, politics, and certain areas of public opinion, such as attitudes of race, were there large gaps in

reconciliation between the South and the rest of the nation." See *The South Since 1865* (New York: Macmillan, 1963), p. 477.

2 The Southern Accent in Religion

1 Leslie W. Dunbar, writing in an article published early in 1964, concurs: "I premise that there has been such a thing as a southern folk, clearly if not definably more a single people than any other Americans" (*op. cit.,* p. 3).

2 Wilbur Zelinsky, "An Approach to the Religious Geography of the United States: Patterns of Church Membership in 1952," *Annals of the Association of American Geographers,* LI (June, 1961), 139–193. His findings were based on the elaborate statistics concerning religious affiliation compiled by the Bureau of Research and Survey of the National Council of Churches of Christ in the U.S.A., which were in turn based on reported church membership for the year 1952, or nearest practicable date.

3 *Ibid.,* p. 164. Even in the cities of the South, a "uniformly British and native Protestant character" is to be found, by contrast with the highly pluralistic character of American cities elsewhere. See Nathan Glazer and Daniel Patrick Moynihan, *Beyond the Melting Pot* (Cambridge: Massachusetts Institute of Technology Press, 1964), pp. 9–10. Only the presence of Negroes significantly intrudes upon the pattern of a white Protestant population whose ancestors came from the British Isles.

4 Minor variations appear in the Roman Catholic territories in west central Kentucky and the larger St. Louis area, and in the Disciples of Christ country of east north-central Kentucky. Significantly, each of these variations is exactly on the border between North and South.

5 Here an insight of Walter B. Posey's is worth recalling: "Each of the major dissenting groups in America was a copy of some church organization in England, but held no closer relation to the European groups than a fraternal feeling. Actually, all the Protestant churches in America by spirit and practice were closer to each other than to their counterparts in Europe." See *Religious Strife on the Southern Frontier* (Baton Rouge: Louisiana State University Press, 1965), p. xvii.

6 Francis B. Simkins, *A History of the South,* 3rd ed. (New York: Alfred A. Knopf, 1963), p. 425. Note also Edwin McNeill Poteat's description: "A study of the denominational press of the South and the doctrinal statements of the various denominations reveals a marked accord in the fundamental tenets they preach. In spite of considerable ecclesiastical differences the theology of the South is the same in its broad essentials among all the religious groups. . . . Scratch any sectarian skin and the same orthodox blood flows" (*op. cit.,* p. 236).

7 One scholar ventures caustic judgments on the southern church's use of the Bible: "The fundamentalist sees in the Bible exactly what he wants to see, an idealized projection of himself, his desires, his hopes, protected and rationalized as only man can protect his pride"; and further, "nothing can be accepted except what may be used to bolster up that which is already established." See Clyde L. Manschreck, "Religion in the South: Problem and Promise," in Francis B. Simkins, ed., *The South in Perspective* (Farmville, Virginia: Longwood College, 1959), p. 79.

8 See Rodney Stark and Charles Y. Glock, "The 'New Denominationalism,'" *Review of Religious Research*, VII (Fall, 1965), 8–17.

9 See Charles Y. Glock, "On the Study of Religious Commitment," *Religious Education*, Research Supplement, July–August, 1962, S98–S110.

10 Leslie W. Dunbar, *op. cit.*, p. 6.

11 As an example, take the statement of James C. Hinton, who long ago judged that "the leaders of the southern churches, having considered the matter [!], have been convinced that the religion existing among the whites of the South was of a purer form than that existing in the North." See "Educational Problems in the South," *Quarterly Review of the Methodist Episcopal Church, South*, V (October, 1883), 697, quoted in Kenneth K. Bailey, *Southern White Protestantism in the Twentieth Century*, p. 2n.

12 See Francis B. Simkins, "The South," in Merrill Jensen, ed., *Regionalism in America* (Madison: University of Wisconsin Press, 1954), p. 162.

13 Willie Snow Ethridge, "Liberalism Stirs Southern Churches," *The Christian Century*, XLIX (March 9, 1932), 317

14 The map inside the back cover of Edwin Scott Gaustad, *Historical Atlas of Religion in the United States* (New York: Harper & Row, 1961), is an indispensable tool for students of American religion (and American culture generally). Throughout this discussion, the work of Gaustad and Zelinsky (in the article already cited) will be relied on heavily.

15 Wilbur Zelinsky makes the same point, although confining himself to the Baptist denomination, in noting its (their) apparent adoption "as the creed most compatible with the genius of the region long after its personality had become clearly defined" (*op. cit.*, p. 166).

16 The statistics utilized are those produced by the National Council of Churches in the U.S.A., in 80 bulletins published in New York (1956–1958) under the heading, *Churches and Church Membership in the United States: An Enumeration and Analysis by Counties, States and Regions.*

17 Zelinsky's Figure 1 on p. 168, *op. cit.*, communicates this forcefully.

18 Wilbur Zelinsky, *op. cit.*, p. 150.

19 The South's percentage of over-all membership, nearly 75 per cent, is highest among the nation's four regions. This is especially true with reference to the juxtaposition of figures for the Northeast's dominating Roman Catholicism, 35 per cent, and the North Central States' dominating Protestantism, 29.9 per cent, as against the dominating Protestantism of the South, 50-plus per cent. Obviously the northeastern states' 63.3 over-all percentage is considerably higher when the comparative calculation is based on absolute members, without adjustments of the non-South figures. But this fact is misleading for purposes of measuring the non-South alongside the South, owing to the formidable strength of the "inclusive" churches, especially the Roman Catholic Church in the Northeast, whose membership is measured by the statisticians to run 30 per cent higher than that of "exclusive" churches. (Correspondingly, in the other non-South sections, the statistics require adjustment in virtue of Lutheran or Episcopal, as well as Roman Catholic, prowess.) Offsetting the southern lead, or at least diminishing its importance, however, is the analogous hold which Catholics and southern Protestants have on their children with respect to keeping them within the family's religious

tradition. The likelihood that the child born into a southern Baptist or Methodist home will fail to affiliate with the church when he comes of age is negligible. In practice, there would appear to be little difference between the results of the South's "voluntaristic" system and those of the Roman Catholic *modus vivendi,* in which baptism unfailingly follows birth.

20 This judgment, though true, is partly irrelevant. One scholar has judged that "it seems extremely unlikely that the Presbyterians could have attained . . . pre-eminence in numbers without sacrificing certain standards fundamental to Presbyterianism." See review by Lewis G. Vander Velde of *Religion on the American Frontier,* Vol. II: *The Presbyterians 1783–1849,* by William Warren Sweet, in *Mississippi Valley Historical Review,* XXIV (June, 1937), 74.

3 The Peculiarity of the Southern Religious Situation

1 Carl N. Degler, "The South in Southern History Textbooks," *Journal of Southern History,* XXX (February, 1964), 50.

2 The same phenomenon was discovered by Victor Obenhaus in his research into the religious beliefs and practices of a north central Illinois county. Noting that one of the many groups in his "Corn County" were Baptists who had moved there from Kentucky and Tennessee, he concluded that these "newcomers did not find the more modestly emotional life of the churches previously established congenial to their type of religious expression." As a consequence of their aggression, in less than half a century, the Baptist churches of the New England type reflected "an emphasis generally associated with Southern Baptist churches." See *The Church and Faith in Mid-America* (Philadelphia: Westminster Press, 1963), p. 38.

"Infiltration," with a correspondingly gradual alteration of tone and emphasis in the northern Baptist churches, seems to have been the usual product of northern and southern confrontation until the post-World War II era. Once that era had commenced, the softer approach that had been characteristic of Baptists from the South burgeoned into a swash-buckling institutional self-consciousness which advocated the establish-ment of "only hope" churches under the banner of the Southern Baptist Convention.

3 No mention has been made of the northern resettlement of many Methodists from the South because there is no "Southern Methodist Church" to be transplanted to northern climes. At least four factors help explain the differences between Baptists and Methodists in this respect. First, Methodists, with their greater devotion to subjectivist Christianity, seem less disposed to do battle in behalf of a highly particularistic theology. Second, because of the polity under which they live, they are less inclined toward divisive action, even in the name of truth, which might splinter existing congregations. For these reasons, Methodists infiltrate existing churches in preference to starting new ones, and it remains to be seen whether time will transform a considerable number of northern Methodist churches into congregations having a southern personality. Third, The Methodist Church flexibly allows for considerable

diversity within an acknowledged unity. Fourth, an ecumenical spirit generally prevails, rather than strident, self-conscious, and self-confident denominationalism.

4 Francis B. Simkins, *The Everlasting South*, p. xiii.
5 Perry Miller, *Errand Into the Wilderness* (Cambridge: Belknap Press, 1956), pp. 99–140.
6 James McBride Dabbs, *op. cit.*, Chaps. 2 and 3.

4 The Shaping Forces in the Southern Religious Heritage

1 Francis B. Simkins, *A History of the South*, p. 156.
2 George G. Smith, *The History of Methodism in Georgia and Florida, 1785–1865* (Macon, Georgia: John W. Burke, 1877), p. 27.
3 Hugh Talmage Lefler and Albert Ray Newsome, *North Carolina, The History of a Southern State*, rev. ed. (Chapel Hill: University of North Carolina Press, 1963), p. 122.
4 Franklin H. Littell, *From State Church to Pluralism* (Garden City, N. Y.: Anchor Books, 1962), p. 17.
5 William Wilson Manross, *A History of the American Episcopal Church*, 3rd ed. (New York: Morehouse-Barlow, 1959), p. 92.
6 Thomas Jefferson Wertenbaker, *The Old South* (New York: Charles Scribner's Sons, 1942), p. 155.
7 Hugh T. Lefler and Albert Ray Newsome, *op. cit.*, p. 123.
8 Francis B. Simkins, *A History of the South*, p. 155.
9 See James McBride Dabbs, *op. cit.*, ch. 2, for a discussion of the ways in which the South weighed the utility of particular traditions, discarding some, retaining others, and nearly always modifying.
10 Thomas Jefferson Wertenbaker, *op. cit.*, p. 155.
11 Quoted in William Warren Sweet, *Virginia Methodism* (Richmond: Whittet and Shepperson, 1955), p. 12.
12 Philip Vickers Fithian, *Journals and Letters, 1773–1774* (Williamsburg, 1943), p. 220.
13 A revealing, and not singular, symbol of the Baptist-Methodist "takeover" from the Church of England is the Lower Methodist Church in Middlesex County, Virginia. The present building, which dates from 1717, was, like the original edifice, constructed as an Anglican place of worship. After 1792 the church was used only by Baptists or Methodists. In 1857 it was purchased by Robert Healey, who gave it to the Methodists. It continues to serve The Methodist Church as part of its Piankatank Parish.
14 As history clearly reveals, the conversion of the masses of Southerners did not occur overnight. During the last quarter of the eighteenth century the winning of a war, the establishment of a government, and the creation of a new economy diverted Americans generally from spiritual concerns. The decade 1800–1810, which spawned the Second Awakening, gave the religionizing impulse new life. But, as we shall see, although the contest for men's spiritual allegiance had been won by this time by revivalistic Protestantism, the task of winning the majority remained until the post-Civil War period.

15 In his definitive history, *Presbyterians in the South* (Richmond: John Knox Press, 1963), Ernest Trice Thompson writes: "The Presbyterian Church was the first church in eastern Virginia to appeal to the people neglected by the Establishment, and which, by means of its favored position, should have become the leading church in the colony, was passed rapidly by the Baptists and the Methodists, who represented later but more vigorous waves of the Great Awakening." See Vol. I, p. 61.

16 In all fairness it must be noted here that the Presbyterian Church in the South has exerted an influence on the region which is out of all proportion to its numerical strength, no doubt largely because so many leaders in southern society have come from its ranks. For the beginnings of its considerable contributions to education, see Ernest Trice Thompson, *op. cit.*, pp. 80–83.

17 Quoted in C. C. Goen, *Revivalism and Separatism in New England, 1740–1800* (New Haven: Yale University Press, 1962), p. 297.

18 Winthrop S. Hudson, *American Protestantism* (Chicago: University of Chicago Press, 1963), p. 30.

19 In treating New England revivalism, Goen avers that three parties formed within Protestantism in response to its appearance. The opponents, the Old Lights, were countered by two pro-revival parties, the conservative New Lights and the extreme New Lights (*op. cit.*, pp. 34–35). The conservative ranks included the major figures, Edwards and Whitefield, and the segment of Protestantism which would be the central tradition of the region. The extreme New Lights dimmed with the passage of a few years in both the Baptist and Congregationalist denominations—except for the small band of Separate Baptists who, having ventured onto the unchurched southern frontier, flourished richly.

20 Quoted in Robert B. Semple, *A History of the Rise and Progress of the Baptists in Virginia* (Richmond, 1810), p. 2.

21 Despite the greater influence of the Separates in the West and the Regulars in the upper East, mutual interpenetration has always existed. The Separate influence is real, in some places dominating, on the Atlantic side of the mountains. A fascinating instance of east to west currents may be found in the character of the Southern Baptist Theological Seminary, founded in 1859. Its tone continues to reflect the eastern influence of its origin in Greenville, South Carolina, appreciably more than the conservative climate of the Louisville, Kentucky, habitat to which it was moved in 1877.

22 H. Richard Niebuhr, *Social Sources of Denominationalism* (New York: Holt, Rinehart and Winston, 1929), p. 167. He cites as an example of his point the way in which Baptist churches on the western frontier (e.g., New York State) "seemed to become the frontier branch of Congregationalism" (p. 168).

23 C. C. Goen, *op. cit.*, p. 285.

24 *Ibid.*

25 "Historic," or "classical," Baptism is not a univocal term. H. Richard Niebuhr, in a classification of American Protestant denominations based on the times of their origins, lists "some Baptist societies" under "the churches of the eighteenth-century Awakening and Enlightenment." See "The Protestant Movement and Democracy in the United States," *The*

Shaping of American Religion, James Ward Smith and A. Leland Jamison, eds. (Princeton: Princeton University Press, 1961), pp. 25–26. See also the discussion of the "three strands in American Baptist life" in Winthrop S. Hudson, ed., *Baptist Concepts of the Church* (Philadelphia: Judson Press, 1959), pp. 21–29.

26 It is significant that even after the Great Revival on the frontier, Baptists were slow to become as enthusiastic about revivalism as Methodists. For a long time, Baptist services were more emotionally restrained than Methodist. Finally, seeing the obvious fruits being gleaned by their Methodist "rivals," they capitulated to the propriety of the technique. See Walter B. Posey, *The Baptist Church in the Lower Mississippi Valley, 1776–1845* (Lexington: University of Kentucky Press, 1957), p. 155.

27 Long ago in his now classic treatment of the sociology of religion, Emile Durkheim called attention to this function of effervescent religion among the Australian tribes. American historians continually point to the way in which farmers here have lived isolated, apart from the larger society, as one of the basic distinctive features of the society.

28 See William Warren Sweet, *Virginia Methodism*, p. 45.

29 Winthrop S. Hudson, *American Protestantism*, p. 97.

30 Ross Phares, *Bible in Pocket, Gun in Hand* (Garden City, N. Y.: Doubleday, 1964), p. 2.

31 Francis B. Simkins, "The South," *loc. cit.*, p. 151.

32 David C. Shipley has portrayed sensitively the early American Methodist character: "The Methodists in America cherished from the beginning the actuality and memory of Methodism in Britain, but from this actuality and memory they selected, as occasion demanded, exactly those vital developments which were particularly useful to their own awareness of vocation and mission." See "The European Heritage," in Emory S. Bucke, ed., *The History of American Methodism* (New York: Abingdon Press, 1964), I, 11.

33 Clement Eaton, *op. cit.*, p. 314.

34 Clement Eaton, "The Ebb of the Great Revival," *North Carolina Historical Review*, XXIII (January, 1946), 12.

35 John Samuel Ezell, *op. cit.*, p. 355.

36 *Ibid.*

37 Francis B. Simkins, *A History of the South*, p. 411.

38 See Stewart A. Newman, *W. T. Conner, Theologian of the Southwest* (Nashville: Broadman Press, 1964), p. 83.

39 Gerhard Lenski, "Religious Pluralism in Theoretical Perspective," in *Religious Pluralism and Social Structure* (International Yearbook for the Sociology of Religion; Köln und Opladen, 1965).

40 Howard Becker, "Sacred and Secular Societies," *Social Forces*, XXVIII (May, 1950), 361–376.

41 *Ibid.*, p. 363.

42 *Ibid.*, p. 364.

43 These features of the southern religious mentality go far toward accounting for southern Methodists' minor and sometimes dissident role in larger Methodist and ecumenical operations, and for southern Baptists' adamant and often hostile refusal to participate in world Christianity. An insight of Karl Mannheim's is astonishingly accurate here: "As long . . . as the

traditions of one's national and local group remain unbroken, one remains
so attached to its customary ways of thinking that the ways of thinking
which are perceived in other groups are regarded as curiosities, errors,
ambiguities, or heresies. At this stage one does not doubt either the
correctness of one's own traditions of thought or the unity and uniformity
of thought in general." See Karl Mannheim, *Ideology and Utopia* (New
York: Harcourt, Brace, & World, 1952), p. 6.

5   The Central Theme

1   See Philip Schaff in Perry Miller, ed., *America* (Cambridge: Harvard
University Press, 1961), p. 98. Schaff describes American religion as he
found it in the 1850's, but his description has remarkable pertinence to
the contemporary South.

2   Thomas F. Pettigrew and Ernest Q. Campbell have also suggested that
the "peculiarly rugged, forceful brand of religion in the South stems
in part from the frontier need for a strong God." See *Christians in Racial
Crisis* (Washington: Public Affairs Press, 1959), p. 4. In a parallel interpretation, Hudson argues that Calvinism was well suited to the needs of
men struggling to tame the American wilderness. See Winthrop S.
Hudson, *American Protestantism*, p. 23. Concerning the latter interpretation, however, allowances need to be made for the disparity between
mainstream American Protestantism's keener corporate sense and the
South's individualizing and atomizing of the responsibility to Christian-
ize.

3   A mainstream Protestant theologian who taught for a time in a southern
seminary has described this phenomenon exceedingly well: "Some groups,
notably in our day the Southern Baptists, have made evangelism the
central core of the church, and their experience reveals the problem
involved. For then ministers tend to be taught, not how to care for their
flock by preaching, counseling, and worship, but how to evangelize—i.e.,
how to persuade other people to join the flock. And when these new
members ask, 'Now that I have joined, what am I to do?' the answer is
apt to be 'Go out among your neighbors and bring in some more'—who,
presumably, will in turn themselves merely seek new additions among
their neighbors. Being a Christian thus becomes merely the operation of
expanding itself. And with this the religious reality of Christianity, both
as a personal relation to God through the hearing of His Word and the
worship of His glory, and the incarnating of that Word in acts of love
and reconciliation, is in danger of being lost." See Langdon Gilkey, *How
the Church Can Minister to the World Without Losing Itself* (New York:
Harper & Row, 1963), p. 64n.

4   It must be emphasized that Calvin denied the reality of *any* cause-effect
relation between anything that man does or is and the divine election.
These criteria give a man purchase for testing his salvation, but they are
not proofs in any wise.

5   It has often been observed that Southerners detest abstraction, and this
doctrine must seem an abstraction to them. Robert Penn Warren has
written of their "fear of abstraction . . . the instinctive fear . . . that the
massiveness of experience, the concreteness of life, will be violated." See

Segregation: The Inner Conflict of the South (New York: Random House, 1956), p. 15. According to this habit of thought, only a consciousness-grounded assurance is concrete.

6 W. J. Cash, *op. cit.*, p. 58.

7 C. C. Goen, *op. cit.*, p. 44.

8 *Ibid.*, p. 48.

9 Baptists and Methodists are quite familiar with the dissimilarity between their respective concepts of assurance. In southern jargon, the Baptists are alleged to believe in "once saved, always saved," whereas the Methodists are reputed to affirm the possibility of "'falling from grace." Stated tersely, the views differ, in that the Baptist position is a bit harder and more vertically oriented, less given to emotional extravagances than the Methodist. The Baptists, while insisting that assurance is "felt," depend more on the rationalized theological assertion that "if . . . , then . . ." The corruption of this position is a *doctrine* of assurance, a scholasticization unrelated to experience. Methodists depend on the experience itself as affording direct testimony. Consequently its potential corruption is the view that assurance may be divorced from any objective rootage. Incidentally, Wesley refused to maintain that there is no valid justifying faith without assurance, but he did urge that normally they ought to concur and reinforce each other. See Albert C. Outler, ed., *John Wesley* (New York: Oxford University Press, 1964), p. 209.

10 David C. Shipley, *op. cit.*, p. 31.

11 Leland Scott, "The Message of Early American Methodism," in Emory S. Bucke, ed., *op. cit.*, I, 300.

12 Colin W. Williams, *John Wesley's Theology Today* (New York: Abingdon Press, 1960), p. 122.

6 Theological Fruits of the Central Theme

1 Victor Obenhaus, *op. cit.*, p. 89.

2 See Charles G. Finney in William G. McLoughlin, ed., *Lectures on Revivals of Religion* (1835) (Cambridge: Harvard University Press, 1960), Ch. 14.

3 See James F. White, *Protestant Worship and Church Architecture* (New York: Oxford University Press, 1964), Ch. 1.

4 See Liston Pope, *op. cit.*, p. 86.

5 See Archie Robertson, *That Old-Time Religion* (Boston: Houghton Mifflin, 1950), p. 15.

6 Langdon Gilkey has effectively described the differences between the objective and subjective orientations (*op. cit.*, pp. 6, 10). For objectivist groups, scripture, apostolic clergy, sacraments, canon law, dogma, and the like are the "separated elements" which are the "locus of the 'holy.'" The subjectivist groups make transcendent the inner experience of the human spirit, the mind reading the Bible, and communal consensus. Gilkey's stated polarity is church-sect, not objective-subjective. Nevertheless, there is correspondence between church-sect typology on the sociological level and objective-subjective orientation on the theological level.

7 As is well known, the conviction that painting, sculpture, and literature

may illustrate theology, or the more radical notion that artistic forms may *be* the bearer of divine reality, has been largely foreign to the Protestant tradition. On the whole, Protestant sensibilities have stressed *hearing* God, usually overlooking the possibility that communication might come through other senses as well.

8   Albert Henry Newman, *A History of the Baptist Churches in the United States* (New York: Charles Scribner's Sons, 1915), p. 519.

9   In his penetrating book about Southern Baptist life, *W. T. Conner, Theologian of the Southwest,* Stewart A. Newman outlines the changing criteria for faculty selection during the youthful decades of another of the seminaries, Southwestern, at Fort Worth, Texas. "The conservative mind of the region gradually affected the academic policies of the institution. Perhaps this is no more conspicuously in evidence than in its policy of faculty 'inbreeding' . . . its first faculty was Baptist, but its members had been recruited from remote regions. In time these were replaced by a generation, all of whom were Southern Baptists. The third group was chosen almost entirely from the ranks of the school's own graduates" (p. 80).

10 Some of these same deficiencies are reputed to characterize another institutionally oriented branch of Christianity, the Roman Catholic Church. See Daniel Callahan, "The Schools," *Commonweal,* LXXXI (January 8, 1965), 473–476.

7   Practical Fruits of the Central Theme

1   Albert C. Outler has remarked that "this insistent correlation between the genesis of faith and its fulness marks off Wesley's most original contribution to Protestant theology" (*op. cit.,* p. 251).

2   C. C. Goen, *op. cit.,* p. 159.

3   This story is recounted in a very important book on southern Protestant life: Findley B. Edge, *A Quest for Vitality in Religion* (Nashville: Broadman Press, 1963).

4   This is an important point, for in classical Methodism justification is not regarded as forensic; it was only when scholasticism invaded its life that justification and sanctification ceased having dynamic continuity. Methodism's more common heresy has been the obscuring of justification by emphasizing sanctification. On the other hand, the Baptist inclination to scholasticism has often led to a dissociation of the two realities, easily leading to the "heresy" of a theoretical antinomianism, augmented by superimposed legalisms. In the southern experience, revivalism and fundamentalism have seduced classical Methodism into divorcing Wesley's two basic components.

5   Howard Moody, "Toward a New Definition of Obscenity," *Christianity and Crisis,* XXIV (January 25, 1965), 284–288.

6   W. J. Cash, *op. cit.,* p. 136.

7   Clement Eaton, *The Growth of Southern Civilization, 1790–1860,* p. 315.

8   Liston Pope, *op. cit.,* pp. 28–29.

9   At the same time, they continued to support the basic institutions and values of their society, resisting cultural practices only on matters which lay within a narrow code of personal morality presumed to incorporate

the salient biblical teachings. See Rufus B. Spain, "Attitudes and Reactions of Southern Baptists to Certain Problems of Society." Unpublished
Ph.D. dissertation, Vanderbilt University, 1961.

10 Thomas F. Pettigrew and Ernest Q. Campbell, *op. cit.*, p. 130.

11 H. Richard Niebuhr, *The Kingdom of God in America* (New York:
Harper & Row, 1959), p. 162.

12 Clement Eaton has written that, as a matter of fact, southern Evangelicalism "tended to become anti-liberal in its social effects." See "The Ebb
of the Great Revival," *loc. cit.*, p. 11.

13 Sidney E. Mead, "The Rise of the Evangelical Conception of the Ministry
in America: 1607–1850," *The Ministry in Historical Perspectives*, H.
Richard Niebuhr and Daniel D. Williams, eds. (New York: Harper &
Row, 1956), p. 228.

14 Timothy L. Smith, *Revivalism and Social Reform* (New York and Nashville: Abingdon Press, 1957), esp. Ch. X.

15 R. M. Weaver, *op. cit.*, p. 244.

16 William G. McLoughlin, *Modern Revivalism* (New York: Ronald Press,
1959), p. 526.

17 *Ibid.*, pp. 504–505.

8 Southern Religion in Relation to Historical Christianity

1 As historians such as Kenneth Scott Latourette and Sidney E. Mead have
felt constrained to point out, the American church has been typified by
its historylessness. This trait in American Christianity serves as incentive
for the present chapter and the substance of Chaps. 11 and 12. See
Sidney E. Mead, *The Lively Experiment* (New York: Harper & Row,
1963), pp. 108–113.

2 Robert N. Bellah, "Religious Evolution," *American Sociological Review*,
XXIX (June, 1964), 366.

3 Several features of the Lutheran interpretation of Christianity make this
true: (1) the believer is to have an entirely trustful attitude toward God,
resulting in a great quietude of soul; (2) justification is an end in itself
in the sense that the soul has a present sense of satiety; (3) single-edged
predestination is affirmed, making hell something less of a problem for
men, with the consequence that heaven is less a conscious concern; and
(4) this special way of correlating justification and vocation shifts the
accent to serving God in the daily life, and tends to make service, not
status, the central objective.

4 We are calling Geneva-originated Calvinism a segment of British
Protestantism on the grounds that American Puritan Calvinism came
mainly by way and through the cultural mediation of Englishmen and
Scotsmen who were Calvinists, not the Swiss or German or Dutch.

5 This quality within Calvinism was perceived by Schaff when he called
attention to the correlation between the rigor with which Calvinist
groups avow the doctrine of predestination, and the meaning of the
Eucharist in the common life of the church. Where predestination is
taught rigidly, the Eucharist is symbolic. (In Protestant bodies theological
logic and sacramental mystery coexist fitfully.) Where the teaching
concerning predestination is more relaxed, Calvinist congregations

celebrate the Presence with a high sense of mystery. See Philip Schaff, *op. cit.*, p. 108.

6 For Luther, of course, the recovery of New Testament forms was an irrelevant concern. What was relevant in the New Testament was its gospel. Scripture had not defined the forms to be used, but had left these matters open and permitted the church to adapt them to the changing conditions and needs of man. See Jaroslav Pelikan, *Obedient Rebels* (London: SCM Press, 1964), Chaps. I and V.

7 One submovement coming out of nineteenth century southern Baptist life, the Landmark movement, gives urgent attention to the era from 100 to 1600 by (erroneously) turning up alleged bearers of the Baptist witness across those centuries.

8 See Hans J. Hillerbrand, "Anabaptism and the Reformation: Another Look," *Church History*, XXIX (December, 1960), 416–418.

9 George Huntston Williams, *The Radical Reformation* (Philadelphia: Westminster Press, 1962), p. 863.

10 *Ibid.*, p. 861.

11 Hans J. Hillerbrand, *op. cit.*, p. 412. Robert Friedmann refutes the antitrinitarian charge directed against them, contending that they accepted orthodoxy, but describing Anabaptism as "primarily a pragmatic movement, . . . not much concerned with dogmatic issues." See "Conception of the Anabaptists," *Church History*, IX (December, 1940), 345.

12 This is reminiscent of David C. Shipley's insight that Wesley's theology was "never a set of required beliefs in themselves but rather was intended always to be, everywhere and by all, an attempt to think clearly concerning how to live the Christian life" (*op. cit.*, p. 11).

13 Robert Friedmann, *op. cit.*, p. 358.

14 See Friedmann's heuristic device of characterizing different Christian groups by the New Testament literature they emphasize (*ibid.*, pp. 361–363). The Anabaptists stress the Synoptic gospels; the southern church, the Pauline epistles.

15 See Dale W. Brown, "The Problem of Subjectivism in Pietism: A Redefinition with Special Reference to the Theology of Philipp Jakob Spener and August Hermann Francke." Unpublished Ph.D. dissertation, Northwestern University, 1962.

16 Generally speaking, in Baptist life a strong streak of "hard" verticalism lives alongside the "soft" pietistic element, owing to the residual old Calvinist theology which poses life before God in terms of contractual status more than dynamic inwardness.

17 H. Richard Niebuhr, *The Social Sources of Denominationalism*, pp. 67, 69.

18 Philip Schaff, *op. cit.*, p. 142.

19 See William G. Pollard, *Chance and Providence* (New York: Charles Scribner's Sons, 1955), pp. 135–137, for an excellent discussion of the Christian paradox of sovereignty and freedom.

20 See George Croft Cell, *The Rediscovery of John Wesley* (New York: Holt, Rinehart and Winston, 1935), p. 25.

9 *Church-Type, Sect-Type*

1 This is W. Seward Salisbury's summary of Troeltsch's description. See

Religion in American Culture (Homewood, Illinois: Dorsey Press, 1964), p. 96. Troeltsch's argument is found in *The Social Teaching of the Christian Churches*, trans. Olive Wyon (London: George Allen and Unwin, 1931), I, 331.

2 W. Seward Salisbury, *ibid.*, paraphrasing Ernst Troeltsch, *ibid.*

3 See *What Baptists Stand For* (London: Kingsgate Press, 1947), p. 13.

4 See *A History of British Baptists* (London: Charles Griffin, 1923), p. 4.

5 Robert Friedmann has observed that in general English Christianity of the sixteenth and seventeenth centuries was preoccupied with questions having to do with church polity. See "Conception of the Anabaptists," *loc. cit.*, p. 364.

6 Troeltsch asserted that with the passage of time the Baptists deserved to be called Baptist "Free Churches" rather than Baptist "sects" in view of the fact that the Baptists had made their peace with the world (Vol. 1, p. 708). We are willing to go farther to say that this was a natural development for the Baptists, given their one aim and their rootage in Calvinism. On the English scene, the Quakers, not the Baptists, were the counterpart of the sect-type Anabaptists. See H. Richard Niebuhr, *The Social Sources of Denominationalism*, pp. 39 ff.

7 An illuminating discussion of the character of original (and recent) British Methodism appears in John H. Chamberlayne, "From Sect to Church in British Methodism," *British Journal of Sociology*, XV (June, 1964), 139–149.

8 *Ibid.*, p. 144.

9 In fact, a great deal about Methodism's history is explained by the strong middle-class orientation of its founders. Its original leadership was strong. See H. Richard Niebuhr, *The Social Sources of Denominationalism*, pp. 59–66.

10 Albert C. Outler, *op. cit.*, p. 350.

11 *Ibid.*, p. viii.

12 *Ibid.*, p. 33.

13 J. Milton Yinger, *Religion, Society, and the Individual* (New York: Macmillan, 1957), pp. 142–155.

14 Earl D. C. Brewer, "Sect and Church in Methodism," *Social Forces*, XXX (May, 1952), 400–408. Theodore L. Agnew makes a similar point in his value-laden observation that in its early career in America, Methodism as a whole "suffered an almost irreparable loss in the rupture of the meaningful contact with Wesley's balanced churchly-plus sectarian formulation of Christian truth" (p. 544).

15 Earl C. Brewer, *op. cit.*, p. 404.

16 *Ibid.*

17 *Ibid.*, p. 405.

18 *Ibid.*, p. 402.

19 See Bryan R. Wilson, "An Analysis of Sect Development," *American Sociological Review*, XXIV (February, 1959), 3–15.

20 *Ibid.*, p. 11.

21 Wilson's conclusion is that the conversionist type is "most likely to fulfill the conditions which transform sects into denominations and are least likely to enjoy the circumstances preventing this process" (*ibid.*, p. 14) .

22 J. Milton Yinger, *op. cit.*
23 Manford H. Kuhn and Thomas S. McPartland, "An Empirical Investigation of Self-Attitudes," *American Sociological Review*, XIX (February, 1954), 68–75.
24 Ernst Troeltsch, *op. cit.*, p. 337.
25 Earl D. C. Brewer, *op. cit.*, p. 405.
26 *Ibid.*, p. 406.
27 See Paul M. Harrison, "Weber's Categories of Authority and Voluntary Associations," *American Sociological Review*, XXV (April, 1960), 232–237.
28 Howard W. Odum, *Understanding Society* (New York: Macmillan, 1947), pp. 707–708. This classification is another variation on Tönnies' classical distinction between *Gemeinschaft* (community) and *Gesellschaft* (society).
29 In David O. Moberg's words, "When the sect does not have a powerful ecclesiastical organization against which to protest, its distinctive sectarian characteristics often are dissipated, and it tends to become much more inclusive in its membership than the typical sects of the sixteenth and seventeenth centuries." See "Potential Uses of the Church-Sect Typology in Comparative Religious Research," *International Journal of Comparative Sociology*, II (March, 1961), 53.

10   The Uses of Religion in the South

1 Quoted in C. Vann Woodward, *Origins of the New South* (Baton Rouge: Louisiana State University Press, 1951), p. 169.
2 Several good treatments of the functionality and dysfunctionality of religious faith, with particular reference to the American scene, have appeared lately. Among them are: Paul M. Harrison, "Functional Theory and Christian Doctrine," *Theology Today*, XIX (April, 1962), 59–70; David O. Moberg, *The Church as a Social Institution* (Englewood Cliffs, N. J.: Prentice-Hall, 1962), pp. 162–164, 175–177; W. Seward Salisbury, *op. cit.*, pp. 477–478; and J. Milton Yinger, *op. cit.*, pp. 78–80, 209.
3 Liston Pope, *op. cit.*, p. 90.
4 Charles Y. Glock, "The Role of Deprivation in the Origin and Evolution of Religious Groups," *Religion and Social Conflict*, Robert Lee and Martin E. Marty, eds. (New York: Oxford University Press, 1964), pp. 24–36.
5 James McBride Dabbs has described this attitude incisively. See *op. cit.*, pp. 32–33.
6 John Samuel Ezell, *op. cit.*, p. 346.
7 Quoted in Walter B. Posey, *The Baptist Church in the Lower Mississippi Valley, 1776–1845*, p. 36.
8 Frederick Lee Olmsted, *A Journey in the Seaboard Slave States* (New York: G. P. Putnam's Sons, 1904), I, 451–452. A survival of this phenomenon is constantly before the public eye today, inasmuch as the southern civil rights activities are almost invariably planned in and launched from church buildings.
9 Liston Pope, *op. cit.*, p. 73.
10 Edwin McNeill Poteat, *op. cit.*, p. 257.
11 Quoted in Edwin S. Gaustad, *op. cit.*, p. 41.

12 Richard C. Marius, "Ruleville: Reminiscence, Reflection," *The Christian Century*, LXXXI (September 23, 1964), 1171.
13 Liston Pope, *op. cit.*, pp. 28–30.

11 The Threat of Rejection

1 Victor Obenhaus, *op. cit.*, p. 17. [Italics added.]
2 For a broadly pertinent allusion to the "clash of civilizations" elsewhere in Christendom, see Fernand Boulard, *An Introduction to Religious Sociology*, trans. M. F. Jackson (London: Darton, Longman, and Todd, 1960), Ch. 2.
3 Gerhard Lenski, *The Religious Factor* (Garden City: N. Y.: Anchor Books, 1963), p. 9.
4 See Louis Wirth, "Urbanism As a Way of Life," *American Journal of Sociology*, XLIV (July, 1938), 1–24.
5 Wilford E. Smith, "The Urban Threat to Mormon Norms," *Rural Sociology*, XXIV (December, 1959), 355. [Italics added.]
6 *Ibid.*, p. 361, with a reference to Pauline V. Young, *The Pilgrims of a Russian Town* (Chicago: University of Chicago Press, 1932).
7 I am indebted to David O. Moberg's terse statement of this truth in his article, "Potential Uses of the Church-Sect Typology in Comparative Religious Research," *loc. cit.*, especially p. 48.
8 Howard W. Odum, *The Way of the South* (New York: Macmillan, 1947), pp. 23–24.
9 Carl N. Degler, *op. cit.*, p. 81.
10 Francis B. Simkins, *A History of the South*, pp. 597–599.
11 Harold A. Bosley, "Editorial," *Religion in Life*, XXXIII (Summer, 1964).
12 The term and its definition are borrowed from Thomas F. O'Dea. It is striking how appropriate O'Dea's description of the stresses in the American Catholic situation is to the contemporary South. See *American Catholic Dilemma* (New York: Sheed & Ward, 1958), p. 88.
13 Kenneth K. Bailey, *op. cit.*, p. 7.
14 Winthrop S. Hudson, *American Protestantism*, p. 61.
15 Rodney Stark, "Class, Radicalism, and Religious Involvement in Great Britain," *American Sociological Review*, XXIX (October, 1964), 701. Stark's research is based on a theory developed by Glock, Yoshio Fukuyama, and Jay Demerath.
16 Charles Y. Glock, "On the Study of Religious Commitment," *loc. cit.*, p. 28.
17 R. Segundo, "The Future of Christianity in Latin America," *Cross Currents*, XIII (Summer, 1963), 274.
18 One of the best means for understanding popular southern Protestantism in the context of rapid social change is to compare its situation with the impact of similar social forces upon the Roman Catholic Church in countries or cultures where it is the Established Church. The two situations are rendered comparable by the effective establishment of popular religion in the South and by the remarkable similarity in tone between Roman Catholicism, where it has been dogmatic, authoritarian, and exclusivistic, and revivalistic fundamentalism. Particularly striking is the close kinship between the Catholic Church and the Baptist institu-

tion in the South. At least four similarities appear: (1) Both have been
highly self-conscious institutions, devoted to spreading their own institutional brand of Christianity; (2) Both have been concerned to conserve
dogma, and more important, old forms of old dogmas; (3) Both have been
isolated from the wider Christian community, hence are ingrown; (4) Both
have dominated their respective landscapes and consequently have had
little incentive to be self-critical and reformist. The Roman Church is
moving rapidly into its new day. So far, the Southern Baptists have
retained their old ways, making changes only at superficial levels.

19 See Rodney Stark's findings for working-class participation in church life
in England (op. cit., p. 704).

20 See Benton Johnson, "On Church and Sect," American Sociological
Review, XXVIII (August, 1963), 539–549, for a fuller statement of this
contention. Also, see Leslie Dewart, "The Church in Cuba: A Universal
Dilemma," Commonweal, LXXIX (October 11, 1963), 67–69, for a concrete
illustration of this problem.

12 The Danger of Irresponsibility

1 Clyde L. Manschreck, op. cit., p. 81.

2 Martin E. Marty, "Protestantism-in-Pluralism," Commonweal, LXXVIII
(July 12, 1963), 418.

3 H. Richard Niebuhr, The Social Sources of Denominationalism, p. 67.

4 This understanding of the church is well represented by the following
words: "By drawing a cordon sanitaire between the gospel and society
the churchman abandons the world and dooms the gospel. The churches
were not called into being to rule the world but to serve it, not to reject
the world but to embrace it with a redeeming love, not to withdraw from
the world but to penetrate it with a healing and maturing spirit. When
churchmen deny their churches this role they are in fact denying their
Lord's sovereignty over the whole man." See Kyle Haselden, "The
Churches and the World," What's Ahead for the Churches?, Kyle Haselden
and Martin E. Marty, eds. (New York: Sheed & Ward, 1964), p. 200.

5 At this point we may note an interesting comparison between what Victor
Obenhaus found in his midwestern county and circumstances in popular
southern Protestantism. In Corn County the rank and file of church
members were not much aware of the distinctive meaning or claims of
Christianity. Whereas Obenhaus was led to conclude "that the essence
or content of the Christian faith is not a pressing and dynamic concern
of Corn Countians" (op. cit., p. 89), no such statement could be made
about the faithful within popular southern Protestantism. However, in
other respects the similarities are striking: The Corn Countian is "not
under compulsion to justify his faith alongside some other" (p. 88), since
he is "not in a religiously competitive situation. . . ." (p. 87); "he has
not been confronted with the necessity of choosing between well-defined
rival systems" (p. 88).

6 A number of students of Christianity and society have gone much further
to suggest that Christianity in any form could best be itself only when
it is a minority. Recently John O. Mellin has registered this sentiment:
"More harm has been done to the church and the gospel by a majority

approach to life than anything else. We are a minority, a mustard seed, a leaven, a saltiness which flavors the whole—not because we take over the city but because it takes over us." See "No Abiding City," *Religion in Life,* XXXIII (Spring, 1964), 211–212. Southern churchmen have few if any categories for perceiving the integrity of such a judgment.

7 Sydney E. Ahlstrom, "Theology in America: A Historical Survey," James Ward Smith and A. Leland Jamison, eds., *op. cit.,* I, 306.

Index